THE ART OF

# ONE WEEK LOAN

3 0 OCT 2000

27 SEP 2002

2 6 JAN 2004

# The Art of The State

CULTURE, RHETORIC,
AND PUBLIC MANAGEMENT

CHRISTOPHER HOOD

CLARENDON PRESS · OXFORD

# OXFORD

### UNIVERSITY PRESS

Great Clarendon Street, Oxford OX2 6DP

Oxford University Press is a department of the University of Oxford.
It furthers the University's objective of excellence in research, scholarship,
and education by publishing worldwide in

Oxford New York

Athens Auckland Bangkok Bogotá Buenos Aires Calcutta
Cape Town Chennai Dar es Salaam Delhi Florence Hong Kong Istanbul
Karachi Kuala Lumpur Madrid Melbourne Mexico City Mumbai
Nairobi Paris São Paulo Singapore Taipei Tokyo Toronto Warsaw

and associated companies in Berlin Ibadan

Oxford is a registered trade mark of Oxford University Press
in the UK and certain other countries

Published in the United States
by Oxford University Press Inc., New York

British Library Cataloguing in Publication Data

Data available

Library of Congress Cataloging in Publication Data

Hood, Christopher, 1947–
The art of the state : culture, rhetoric, and public management /
Christopher Hood.
Includes bibliographical references.
1. Public administration. I. Title.
JF1351.H66 1998 351—dc21 98–6177

ISBN 0–19–828040–8
ISBN 0–19–829765-3 (Pbk.)

Printed in Great Britain
on acid-free paper by
Bookcraft (Bath) Ltd.
Midsomer Norton, Somerset

# PREFACE

Nowadays we hear much about the 'state of the art' in this or that field. But this book is about the art of the state—or at least that part of it which belongs to the realm of public management. Public management has attracted a flood of discussion in recent years (not to mention jargon and hype), and there has been much talk of 'paradigm change' across the world. But there is no generally agreed 'ABC' for analysing public management. This book aims to explore what grid/group cultural theory, combined with a historical perspective, can do for the subject.

The book builds on my earlier work in public administration and management, but puts it in a different analytic perspective. The ideas about the often-overlooked use of randomness in the regulation of public administration which appear in Chapters 3 and 7 go back to my book *The Limits of Administration* published twenty years earlier. The ideas about the contested and essentially rhetorical nature of arguments in public management build on themes introduced in my book *Administrative Argument* (written jointly with Michael Jackson in 1991). The main development, however, is an attempt to improve the architecture of the argument by linking it to a cultural-theory frame which was lacking in my earlier work.

By teaching themes in public management to a cosmopolitan group of students at LSE and elsewhere over a number of years, I have learned three lessons the hard way. One is that the case-study approach to studying management is only effective if it can be related to a larger conceptual scheme. A second is that the apparent 'relevance' of looking only at currently fashionable doctrines in public management can severely limit perspective. The third is that the culture of management discourse itself—loquacious, competitive, fad-prone, guru-ridden—is too often ignored in the analysis of public management. These lessons have led me to think a critical approach which mixes contemporary with historical experience and places emphasis on how arguments are presented and packaged is needed for students trying to make sense of current managerial debate. This book aims to provide the outlines of such an approach.

I have many debts to acknowledge. My debt to Mary Douglas is obvious. I have learned much from Michael Barzelay with whom I have discussed many themes within 'New Public Management', and who has properly urged me to concentrate more on the organization of argument about management. Brendan O'Leary has sharpened my understanding of egalitarian organization, and particularly the phenomenon of 'hypera-countability'. I am grateful to Torben Beck Jørgensen, who helped me to develop the applied control-theory framework in this book during a visit I made to Copenhagen in the spring of 1995. Clare Hall, my colleague at LSE, introduced me to 'Trobriand cricket'. I am grateful to graduate students at LSE who have helped me to develop my ideas by offering criticism and encouragement. I am indebted to Anne Rahming who helped with the bibliography and getting the manuscript into shape, to my wife for her work on final preparation of the manuscript and the index, and above all I am grateful to Andrew Dunsire and Desmond King who took the trouble to go through the first draft of the book and offered valuable advice and comments. Any errors that remain are mine alone, but there would have been many more without their assistance.

Some of the chapters originated in work first published elsewhere. In particular, parts of the analysis in Chapters 3 and 10 build on an article on 'Control over Bureaucracy' which originally appeared in the *Journal of Public Policy* in 1996. Chapter 8 develops the argument of papers which originally appeared in *Public Policy and Administration* in 1995 and the *International Journal of Public Administration* in 1996. Papers reflecting the ideas of the book have been presented at a number of conferences and seminars, including a conference at Hong Kong City University (1995), the PAC conference in Sunningdale (1995), the PSA conference in Glasgow (1996), the APSA conference in San Francisco (1996), the EGPA conference in Leuven (1997), and the staff seminar at the University of Copenhagen (1995). I have benefited greatly from the reactions and comments offered on all those occasions.

This book has benefited from research support from a number of sources over the last few years which has helped me to develop my ideas on this book, at the same time that I was engaged in other projects. They include a Simon Senior Research Fellowship at the University of Manchester in the autumn term of 1994, which gave me the opportunity to start thinking about this project in the stimulating context of Manchester's Government Department. I also benefited from a Lever-hulme Senior Research Fellowship spent at Humboldt University in Berlin in the spring of 1995 and a D. N. Chester Senior Research Fellowship at Nuffield College in the summer term of 1995, during which I had a chance to think further about the role of randomness in organizational design. Over 1995–7, I have had support from the ESRC's Whitehall Programme which has enabled me to provide some empirical underpinning for some of the ideas developed here, and I gratefully acknowledge all those sources of support. However, most of the book was written on a part-time basis during a time when I was trying to practise public management myself in a modest and part-time way (wrestling with the problems of heading a talented but diverse group of 60-odd staff) as well as teaching and writing about it. Whether that experience has boosted or sapped my intellectual judgement I must leave for readers to decide.

Christopher Hood

*Department of Government*
*London School of Economics*
*October 1997*

---

# PREFACE TO THE
# PAPERBACK EDITION

---

The great legal scholar Lon Fuller, in the fifth chapter of the revised (1969) edition of his classic *The Morality of Law*, wisely notes that 'authors generally serve themselves badly when they attempt to defend their books against critical reviews'. He adds, 'Any reply to critical reviews is apt to become a muddled thing, mixing charges of misinterpretation with rearticulation of what the author claims he meant to say, intermingling awkwardly defense and counteroffensive, and ending with dark intimations that only limitations of space prevent him from demonstrating with devastating finality how completely mistaken his critics are . . .' (Fuller 1969: 187–8). (That observation did not, of course, prevent Fuller himself from going on to attempt a detailed refutation of his critics' claims.)

Since one of the main observations about this book to date is that it needs a paperback edition to make it more accessible to students, I trust one criticism at least can be answered with finality by the production of such an edition. Other criticisms are not, of course, so easily dealt with, but at least three deserve to be mentioned.

First, I have been represented as having written an 'anti-New Public Management' tract, but I do not myself see that as the central thrust of this book. Both the so-called New Public Management (or perhaps the variety of 'New Public Managements' that now seem to exist) and the various types of old public management involve elements of more than one way of life in cultural-theory terms. A cultural theory approach gives us a way of understanding that variety and thus probing beyond first-approximations accounts of those doctrines.

Second, I have been taxed with conflating social and administrative systems. I would agree that administrative systems and the some of the social systems with which they interact often embody different cultures and ideas, for example in the case of classical China, as noted in this book. But ultimately—and perhaps even proximately—the 'social' and the 'administrative' are not separable, administrative or managerial systems are themselves social systems, and even within a single country or state it is often possible to observe a striking variety of administrative cultures. The value of a cultural theory approach is precisely that it gives us a way of analyzing administrative systems as social systems and tracking their variety.

Third, in discussing continuing cultural and rhetorical variety I have been accused of flying in the face of an evident popular or professional consensus behind the well-known 'creating public value' framework expounded by Mark Moore (1995) of the Kennedy School. In fact I have the highest respect for Moore's craftsmanship, and mention him in the book as one of the leading contemporary exponents of public management doctrine. I would only suggest that the rhetorical appeal of the 'creating public value' framework lies precisely in the fact that it does not specify who sees what as public value. Again, a cultural-theory framework offers the prospect of tracing different conceptions of public value in public management in a way that culturally monochrome approaches cannot do.

I hope that the publication of the paperback edition of this book enables it to reach a wider audience and consequently brings many more such issues into fuller debate. Even for those who share Ernest Nagel's view that there is '. . . little intellectual nourishment to be found in rebuttals to rejoinders to replies' (quoted in Fuller 1969: 188), a wider dissemination of alternative views can only enhance the international 'conversation' over public management (as my colleague Michael Barzelay calls it). I would like to record my thanks to Dominic Byatt and Amanda Watkins of Oxford University Press for their support and help, and also to those who read the previous hardback edition of the book and encouraged the production of a paperback edition.

Christopher Hood

September 1999

REFERENCE

Fuller, L (1969) *The Morality of Law*, revised edition, New Haven, Yale University Press.

# CONTENTS

## PART II: CLASSIC AND RECURRING IDEAS IN PUBLIC MANAGEMENT

## PART III: RHETORIC, MODERNITY, AND SCIENCE IN PUBLIC MANAGEMENT

# LIST OF FIGURES

# LIST OF TABLES

# PART I

## INTRODUCTORY

This part of the book introduces its main themes and applies the analytic framework to two central problems of public management, namely the analysis of failure and collapse and the analysis of control and regulation.

# 1

## Public Management: Seven Propositions

> Whilst it is to be repudiated as one of the most disastrous
> fallacies . . . that public administration . . . needs neither
> special aptitude or study . . . , it should by all means be kept
> free from . . . sham science and mere craft . . .
>
> (Chadwick 1854: 177)

### 1. Public Management: Three Conventional Assumptions

Public management—'the art of the state'—can loosely be defined
as the problem of how to design and operate public services and the
detailed work of executive government. It is hardly a forgotten
topic. As a label and a subject, public management has been in high
fashion for well over a decade in the English-speaking countries.
Indeed, much of what used to be called 'public administration' has
been renamed 'public management' in the title of numerous college
courses, university chairs, papers, books, journals and conferences
(see Chandler 1991).

Why this shift in linguistic usage? There is no simple answer. But
public management is a term (like feminism) that denotes a
movement as well as an area of study. It matched a mood for
reform in state bureaucracies, making government more 'business-
like' and laying greater stress on the role of managers. And, like
most successful slogans, 'public management' is ambiguous, able
to convey mixed and multiple messages. Put the stress on 'public',
and the term appeals to those who think there is something
quite distinctive about government and public services, needing
its own special knowledge and practice. Put the stress on

'management', on the other hand, and the term appeals to those who think government and public services are just one more sphere for applying management methodologies from the business-school repertoire, focusing on the 'production-engineering' aspects of public service provision rather than the complexities of politics and accountability with which academic Public Administration is often obsessed.

Dwight Waldo (1968: 2) once jestingly referred to public administration as 'a subject-matter in search of a discipline', and that jibe could be applied equally well to the diverse literature on public management. Most of that literature consists of practico-descriptive accounts of specific reform themes and techniques like outsourcing, delayering, or performance pay. Some comprise attempts at broader-sweep generalization, assessing the extent to which a coherent new model of organization and service delivery has replaced the outmoded methods of the past. Some is evaluative, attempting to discover what has and has not 'worked' or to assess recipes for organizational design. Some is 'positive', seeking to predict (or 'retrodict') developments in public service reform.

However diverse, much of this burgeoning literature is built, implicitly or explicitly, on three closely related assumptions. The first, and commonest, is that public management is in the throes of a millenial transformation to a new style. Societies worldwide are seen to be moving down a one-way street from outmoded tradition to managerial 'modernity' in public services. And modernity is often held to bring convergence, through the logic of a globalized economy and the inexorable force of information technology in reshaping 'industrial-era bureaucracies' for 'the information age' (in the words of the 1993 US National Performance Review (Gore 1993: 3)). More or less explicit assumptions of convergence and modernity provide the *raison d'être* of a range of professional reformers, including management consultants, central agencies, and international organizations like the World Bank, IMF, and OECD. The mission of these professional reformers is to encourage 'laggard' countries or institutions to catch up with the most up-to-date 'best practice' of the vanguard.

Second, it is assumed that today's 'new' public management ideas differ sharply from those of earlier eras. Indeed, it is often suggested that serious thinking about public management only really began in the 1980s.[1] The outmoded 'traditional model' of public administration is often portrayed as fairly homogenous. The conventional story is that a fairly uniform old-fashioned style— typically characterized as rule-bound and process-driven—is being replaced by results-driven, managerially orientated approaches to public service provision with a particular stress on efficient least-cost provision (which for some reason traditional public administration is assumed not to have been much concerned with, even though it originally developed in societies far poorer than those of the wealthy democracies of today). Even traditionalist critics of 'modern' public management ideas often share this assumption of a radical break with all past ideas. The difference between the traditionalists and the modernizers, however, is that the former use rose-tinted spectacles to view the past and grey-tinted glasses to look at the present, while for the latter the lens tints are reversed.

Third, the favoured doctrines of contemporary public management tend to be question-beggingly dubbed as 'economic rationalism'—by definition enhancing rather than reducing efficiency, by techniques like Total Quality Management (TQM) derived from private business practice. Metaphors from engineering often reinforce this impression of technical progress, as in the familiar jargon of 'business process re-engineering' (to mean reorganization) and of 'benchmarking' (the idea of establishing best practice from whatever countries or organizations are at the leading edge of modernity and measuring the rest against that standard). Management in government, such powerful metaphors imply, is a form of engineering. Some may rail at the cult of efficiency and plead for the incorporation of other 'humanist' values into public service organization (in the conventional idea that efficiency has to be traded off against equity and other considerations), but it tends to be assumed that efficiency itself is a technical issue, such that economists and management experts can more or less agree on what it is and what produces it.

[1] See, for instance Wanna, O'Faircheallaigh, and Weller 1992; Hughes 1994; Walsh 1995. There is an analogy with the way many orthodox American-inspired public administration texts locate the origin of that subject with the onset of the Progressive movement in the 1880s.

## 2. What This Book Argues

Each of these conventional assumptions embraces a widely held perception. But they all merit closer attention than they usually receive, because they cut to the basics of what the world of public management is like and what sort of knowledge is needed to understand it. This book looks at public management from a rather different perspective. It argues that variation in ideas about how to organize public services is a central and recurring theme in public management, and that such variation is unlikely to disappear, in spite of the engineering metaphors and the prophets foreseeing convergence on a new stable form of 'modernity'. It argues that, far from being new-minted in the 1980s, most of the basic ideas about how to manage in government have a history. And it aims to use grid/group cultural theory to get an analytic purchase on a number of themes in public management, including the exploration of underlying patterns of control and regulation, the disaggregation of forms of persuasive argument about management, and the discussion of types of failure in public management. Reduced to seven related propositions, the book's argument is:

- grid/group cultural theory captures much of the variety in both current and historical debates about how to organize in government and public services, because it offers a broad framework for analysis which is capable of incorporating much of what is already known about organizational variety;
- application of a cultural-theory framework can illuminate many of the central analytic questions of public management, including the analysis of collapse and failure in public services, the analysis of control and regulation, and the analysis of how public management ideas become persuasive;
- if we look across time and space, we can identify ideas about how to organize government and public services that correspond to each of the four polar categories contained in cultural theory;
- no one of those recipes for good organization has a clear claim to be considered more 'modern' than any of the others and each has in-built weaknesses leading to negative side and reverse effects;
- variation in ideas about how to organize in government is not

likely to disappear, and hence there are sharp limits to the extent to which public management worldwide can be expected to converge on a single stable approach;

- the dimensions identified by cultural theory enable analysis of organizational variety to be pursued at a range of levels, to explore variants and hybrids as well as broad-gauge polar forms;

- the understanding of cultural and organizational variety, within a historical perspective, merits a central place in the study of public management. Without such a perspective, there is no way to grasp the range of differences about what 'good management' means, what is the available range of viable models of organization, and what are the typical ways in which each model tends to collapse or self-destruct.

These seven propositions overlap, and some of them are given more space than others in the book. This chapter concentrates mainly on the first proposition, and aims to introduce grid/group cultural theory in the context of public management. But the other six propositions are also discussed more briefly, as a way of setting the scene for the remainder of the book.

## 3. Grid/Group Cultural Theory and Public Management

Grid-group cultural theory is a form of analysis originating in the work of the world-famous anthropologist Mary Douglas (1982) but now increasingly applied in institutional analysis across the social sciences. It aims to capture the diversity of human preferences about 'ways of life' and relate those preferences to different possible styles of organization, each of which has its advantages and disadvantages but is in some sense 'viable' (cf. Thompson, Ellis, and Wildavsky 1990). For cultural theorists, the plurality of possible ways of managing or regulating is rooted in two fundamental dimensions of human organization. Variation on those dimensions links to irreducibly different attitudes and beliefs about social justice, blame and guilt, the link between human beings and the natural environment, and the nature of good government more generally.

Those two organizational dimensions are 'grid' and 'group'.

'Grid' denotes the degree to which our lives are circumscribed by conventions or rules, reducing the area of life that is open to individual negotiation. For instance, if parents name their children at will after their favourite pop star or sports idol, they are in low-grid mode. The more they are constrained by rules—for instance if choice is limited to a fixed set of names by religion or family convention, as in the Chinese practice of having a preset name shared by all siblings of each generation—the more 'high-grid' is their position. 'Group', by contrast, denotes the extent to which individual choice is constrained by group choice, by binding the individual into a collective body. For example, if we live in a community which involves common pooling of resources and is differentiated from the world outside—as in a monastic community, a hippy commune, or even some types of exclusive 'clubland' environment—we are operating in high-group mode. If we live a more isolated, atomized, or promiscuous existence, we are in low-group mode.

'Grid' and 'group' are fundamental to public management. After all, much of the debate over good government over the past 2,000 years or so has concerned the extent to which it is feasible or desirable to work by 'rule and rote' or 'a government of laws and not of men', as against enlightened discretion or case-by-case bargaining. 'Grid' is central to such debates, currently represented by the tension between constraining public organizations and those who run them by strict regulatory rules, versus the contradictory doctrine that managers should be 'free to manage' and be judged on results rather than processes. Similarly, a perennial issue in public management concerns who should do it. How far should basic public services or government functions like policing or defence be provided by dedicated professionals segregated from society at large? To what extent should they be provided by private business or even by citizens at large, following the principle of citizen militias or community policing? 'Group' is at the core of such debates about how to organize, as reflected today in debates between communitarians, advocates of for-profit privatization of public services, and defenders of professional public service.

Put the 'grid' and the 'group' dimensions together, and they take us to the heart of much contemporary and historical discussion about how to do public management. When the two dimensions are combined into a simple matrix, as shown in Table 1.1, we identify a

TABLE 1.1. *Four styles of public-management organization: Cultural theory applied*

| 'Grid'[a] | 'Group'[b] | |
|---|---|---|
| | Low | High |
| High | *The Fatalist Way* Low-co-operation, rule-bound approaches to organization. *Example*: Atomized societies sunk in rigid routines (Banfield 1958). | *The Hierarchist Way* Socially cohesive, rule-bound approaches to organization. *Example*: Stereotype military structures (Dixon 1976). |
| Low | *The Individualist Way* Atomized approaches to organization stressing negotiation and bargaining. *Example*: Chicago-school doctrines of 'government by the market' (Self 1993) and their antecedents. | *The Egalitarian Way* High-participation structures in which every decision is 'up for grabs'. *Example*: 'Dark green' doctrines of alternatives to conventional bureaucracy (Goodin 1992). |

[a] Extent to which public management is conducted according to well-understood general rules.
[b] Extent to which public management involves coherent collectivities, institutionally differentiated from other spheres of society.

*Source*: Adapted from Douglas 1982; and Thompson, Ellis, and Wildavsky 1990.

range of basic organizational types, now familiar in cultural theory. Ways of life which are high in both 'group' and 'grid' are conventionally termed 'hierarchist'. The corresponding labels for the other major types are 'fatalist' (high 'grid', low 'group'); 'egalitarian' (high 'group', low 'grid'); and 'individualist' (low 'group', low 'grid'). A 'fatalist' approach to public management will arise in conditions where co-operation is rejected, distrust widespread, and apathy reigns—a state of affairs which will be far from unfamiliar to many readers. A 'hierarchist' approach will be reflected in a structure of organizations which are socially coherent and operate according to well-understood rules of procedure. 'Egalitarian' forms of organization are socially distinct from the world outside but the rules of the game are constantly 'in play', giving rise to continuous debate about how individual cases or issues are to be handled. An 'individualist' approach to public management, on the other hand, involves antipathy to collectivism and a preference for handling every transaction by trading or negotiation rather than by preset rules.

Cultural theorists would expect each of these polar types to provide the basis of a more-or-less viable way to do public management, and each will be examined in the four chapters of Part 2. To be 'viable' (that is, capable of cohering, attracting loyalty, and surviving over time), a way of life must consist of a mutually supportive relationship between a structure of organization and a set of values and beliefs (Thompson, Ellis, and Wildavsky 1990: 1–2). So each of the polar types can be seen as 'structure with attitude', so to speak, and indeed the two elements of structure and attitude need to be combined to produce robust forms of organization.

For example, egalitarian forms of organization (to be explored in Chapter 6), which involve relatively weak formal leadership and rely heavily on communal 'participative' decision-making involving most or all of the members, are chronically vulnerable to collapse if opportunistic members either exit or seek to 'free ride' on the contributions of a few naïve public-spirited members, who will eventually themselves be discouraged (see Hirschman 1970; Olson 1971). Given that such dangers are far from imaginary, egalitarian organizations (currently in high fashion with the re-emergence of the communitarian approach to grass-roots public service provision and the fashion for team working and front-line employee 'empowerment' within management structures) can only continue to exist if the people they contain share beliefs and values that make the structure work. To some extent the structure may help to generate the beliefs and values (see Douglas 1987: 38–40). And the same goes for other forms of organization. Only when the structure matches the appropriate values and beliefs can an organization or way of life be 'viable'.

Moreover, cultural theorists argue the number of viable ways of organizational life is limited. There is not an infinity of possibilities. The possibilities are limited because the only viable ways of life tend to be those which cluster in the corners of the conceptual space created by the two dimensions of 'grid' and 'group' as illustrated in Table 1.1. But why exactly do the ways of life go out into the corners? Wouldn't it be more logical to expect them to converge in the middle, to get the best of all worlds? The argument is that the ways of life tend to go out into the corners because each way of life constitutes a reaction against the disliked alternatives (Thompson, Ellis, and Wildavsky 1990: 4). So if egalitarians did not exist, hierarchists would need to invent them, to provide an awful warning of what organizational life is like when there is no effective chain of command or stable rules of the game. Without fatalists, there would be little to support an egalitarian mission to 'empower' the apathetic against the heartless atomism of individualist market-worship or the inherent folly and moral failures of hierarchist approaches to social steering. Without the threat posed to their way of life by egalitarians, some of the moral fervour of individualists for market solutions against ill-conceived collectivist meddling would also be likely to subside. In other words, cultural dynamics work by mutual antagonism among opposites seeking to blame adherents of alternative ways of life for the social ills they are held to create. Cultural theorists are not the first to have noticed that in matters of organization and management, we tend to formulate ideas about reform through a process of reaction against what we see as an unsatisfactory status quo, rather than beginning the process of institutional design from a genuinely 'zero base'. But that observation is central to their ideas about what sustains organizational variety.

Grid/group cultural theorists are by no means the first or only school to offer a frame for categorizing different fundamental forms of organization. Typologies of organizational variety can be traced back at least as far as Aristotle, and in the twentieth century, many different typologies of organization have been created. Early in the century, Max Weber (Gerth and Mills 1948) identified a range of types of authority (charismatic, traditional and rational-legal) lying behind methods of rule, and since the 1950s it has become commonplace to distinguish segmented rule-bound structures, with a high differentiation of rank and specialism, from more 'organic' structures in which flexible team working is emphasized above a rigid division of functions (cf. Burns and Stalker 1966; McGregor 1966). Much writing in this vein works through dichotomies, but there are exceptions. To take a few leading examples, the Canadian management guru Henry Mintzberg (1993) has made a well-known and much-used distinction between five types of organizational structure, which he calls 'simple structures', 'machine bureaucracies', 'professionalized bureaucracies', 'divisionalized

forms', and 'adhocracies'. The political scientist James Q. Wilson
(1989: 159 ff) has likewise distinguished between 'craft', 'coping',
'procedural', and 'production' organizations in public management. And the political economist Susan Rose-Ackerman (1978),
in a landmark analysis of bureaucratic corruption, distinguished
four types of bureaucracies in a typology which comes fairly close
to that of the cultural theory. She termed the four types 'disorganized' (meaning that procedures are obscure and unpredictable),
'fragmented' (meaning that the parts work quite independently of
one another), 'sequential' (the organization is divided, but cases
have to go through it in a fixed sequence), and 'hierarchical' (there
is a vertical chain of command, in which those at the top exercise
oversight over those at the bottom and appeals can be passed up
the hierarchy).

To use a cultural-theory framework is not to deny the insights
contained in such typologies. On the contrary, all of the three
multi-part typologies mentioned above overlap with many of the
categories of the cultural-theory approach. So the cultural-theory
categories are not unique in going beyond the 'the deeply-
ingrained worship of tidy-looking dichotomies' (Austin 1962: 3)
that dominates so much categorization of organization. Nor can it
be claimed that the types of organization and world-view identified
by cultural theory have never previously been discovered by students of organization and management. Rather, what cultural
theory provides is an overall framework or architectonic, and that
is why it is used here as the point of departure, rather than any of
those alternative approaches. The framework is grounded on
something more than *ad hoc* listing of different types of organization, and consequently it generates a typology which is demonstra-
bly complete in the sense that it is derived from two fundamental
underlying dimensions of human organization and infinitely scal-
able in the sense that it can be applied at varying levels of detail.

## 4. Putting Cultural Theory to Work in
## Analysing Public Management

The second of the seven propositions noted earlier is that grid-
group cultural theory can be put to work to illuminate some of the
central analytic questions of public management. In the next

chapter it is applied to the problem of failure and collapse in public management, to explore what are the characteristic 'Achilles' Heels' of different forms of organization, and what constitutes 'failure' from different world-views. Catalogues of blunders and dysfunctions in public management are often cited, but what cultural theory can do is help to clarify who sees what as crippling failures and what kinds of organizations are predisposed to what kinds of failure. In the following chapter, the cultural-theory framework is applied to explore another central and often-discussed issue, namely how to characterize the basic forms of control or regulation available in public management. Cultural theory suggests a way of ordering 'first order' alternatives which gives a distinct perspective on the control and regulation problem, while encompassing much of what is known from other forms of analysis.

In Part 3 cultural theory is applied to the analysis of globalization and rhetoric. It is now commonly recognized that the 'science' of public management—indeed management generally—is heavily rhetorical, in that persuasive what-to-do argument typically does not rest on the orthodox methods of experimental science—crucial experiments, 'before' and 'after' comparisons in carefully controlled conditions, processes of rigorous logical reasoning in formal language, systematic and replicable analysis of a population of cases (see Mackenzie 1975: 8; Hood and Jackson 1991; Huczynski 1993). Most what-to-do arguments in public management rely on circumstantial evidence and rhetorical power. Controlled experimentation is rare, careful evaluation almost unknown. Deliberative argument about management and administration is dominated by 'doctrines' (Dunsire 1973*b*: 39) or 'industry recipes' (Spender 1989: 60–7)—that is, bodies of ideas that fall well short of the requirements of a scientific theory or formula, but contain assumptions about cause and effect which purport to guide action. In spite of commonly used engineering metaphors about 'best practice' production engineering in service delivery and the equally pervasive—and beguiling—language of 'economic rationalism' in public management, the history of ideas in the field suggests there is no idea about how to organize that is not contestable, no doctrine that cannot be countered by a contradictory doctrine (Simon 1946). Even lessons taken from disaster are seldom unambiguous. Such features are shared with political and (according to 'critical' legal theorists at least) legal argument (cf. Unger 1986: 17, and 1996: 65, 77).

What cultural theory can add to the small but growing literature on management rhetoric is a way of identifying *multiple* forms of rhetoric about how to organize public services. The argument offered in Chapter 8 is that cultural variety tends to be missing from the analysis of management rhetoric, notably in Andrez Huczynski's (1993) leading work on management gurus, and that the 'guru ideas' Huczynski discusses can be better framed by using cultural-theory categories than the *ad hoc* classification of management ideas he himself offers. Linking cultural theory with rhetorical analysis is a way of getting away from simply listing forms of argument (the conventional 'stamp collecting' approach of rhetorical study) to identify different 'families' of rhetorics about management and the organizational stories, metaphors, and paradoxes that link to each of cultural theory's major world-views.

### 5. Combining Cultural and Historical Perspectives

The third proposition advanced earlier was that we can identify what-to-do ideas about public management which correspond to each of the four polar categories if we take a comparative and historical perspective. Accordingly, cultural theory is used as a loose organizing frame for an account of recurring streams of ideas about public management in the four chapters of Part 2. It is said that most contemporary novelists are working with one out of perhaps half-a-dozen basic plots for a story which have recurred throughout literary history (Kennedy 1993: p. ix). In the same way, debates about how best to do public management tend to throw up the same fundamental ideas in different times and places. A cultural-theory approach helps to order those patterns and fit them into an overall frame.

Contrariwise, a historical perspective is a natural complement to cultural theory in the analysis of variety in organizational forms and doctrines. If cultural theory is correct, it should be possible to observe similar organizational ideas emerging at different points in history, and that prompts us to look for patterns of recurrence beneath apparent novelty. For example, when this book was first being drafted (1996), 'hot desking'[2] and removal of offices was in high managerial fashion in parts of the business world. Some companies (like Rank Xerox) also removed individual offices for more senior staff, so their executives had to work at a common table (these arrangements were claimed to produce faster decisions, better communications, and more accessibility of senior staff (*Sunday Times* 30 June 1996)). What in one sense looks like the latest corporate fad—crazy or liberating, according to your point of view—is in another sense rather an old idea. In fact, nearly two centuries ago Jeremy Bentham prescribed a form of public organization in which all official business had to be done in a 'common room', for similar reasons to those given by Rank Xerox today (though Bentham was also concerned to avoid corruption through the ability to make secret deals in private (see Bahmueller 1981)). And, as we will see in Part 2, the idea of collegiate decision-making has frequently been advanced as a design principle of public organization in the past.

The same applies to other doctrinal debates in public management. An example is the frequent advocacy since the 1980s of a stricter approach to framing 'contracts' within public management (the major theme of the reconstruction of public-service organization in New Zealand in the 1980s (cf. Boston *et al.* 1996), a model much discussed and influential elsewhere). The underlying claim of the 'contract' school is that the more the obligations and entitlements of the various parties involved in public management (producers and providers, consumers and producers, 'principals' and 'agents') can be specified in formal documents, the less will be the scope for shirking and distortion by public managers and workers. The particular vocabulary in which we debate this issue today is certainly new, using a developed metaphor of 'principal' and 'agent' and a new literature on the role of 'trust' in institutions and societies (cf. Fukuyama 1995). But the fundamental debate is something that has run and re-run in public management. As long ago as 330 BC Chinese 'legalists', notably Shen Pu-Hai from the state of Han in northeast China, argued that government should be conducted according to fixed and transparent rules, against those

[2] 'Hot desking' meant not assigning permanent desks to staff, so they had to lead a nomad-like existence within the organization.

who argued for 'Confucian' principles of public service, using what we would today call high trust and limitedly specified contracts (Kamenka 1989: 38). At that time, the Confucian side of the argument became the dominant one. But in a parallel debate in early nineteenth-century Germany, the argument went the other way, when the jurists achieved supremacy over the cameralists. Today, both models can be found among the richest industrial countries, and no sooner has the low-trust 'contract' model of public-service provision achieved a following than the advantages of the contrary pattern of high-trust contracts and organization have been strongly pressed (cf. Sako 1992).

We could add other cases, such as contemporary debates about the desirability of public management imitating business management—a recurring theme in US public administration since the advent of the 'city manager' movement over a century ago (see Downs and Larkey 1986) and a key idea of Sir Edwin Chadwick, quoted in the epigraph to this chapter, in the 1850s. The point is that taking a historical perspective on today's apparently new-minted management ideas can add an extra dimension to the analytic framework of cultural theory, in two ways. First, historical experience gives us additional cases to assess the strengths and weaknesses of contemporary ideas. For instance, if outsourcing public services is as advantageous as some contemporary advocates of contracting-out claim, why should it ever have been abandoned in the past, as in the cases of tax-farming or mercenary armies? If other currently fashionable recipes for better public management, like pay for performance or quasi-markets in health care, are keys to better performance, what led them to be scrapped in the past? (For instance, the UK abandoned quasi-markets in health care in the 1940s after more than thirty years, and pay for performance was abandoned for schoolteachers in England and Wales in 1902.)

Second, and relatedly, combining a historical perspective with the analytic framework of cultural theory increases our awareness of alternative possible states of the world. By 'enabling us to see beyond the political and administrative fads and fashions of the day' (Raadschelders 1994: 123), it makes us less likely to take any given status quo or current orthodoxy as the only imaginable way to do public management. Limiting discussion to the very recent past and neglecting the major historical traditions of thought in public management can narrow debate and criticism, by implying there is 'no alternative' to whatever modernity is held to mean. At worst it can have the stultifying effect of making us slaves to the current fashion (Boulding 1970: 156). Historical knowledge is a good antidote to naïve acceptance of novelty claims, and history in this sense is potentially subversive. That is why authoritarian regimes—within organizations just as much as at state level—often try to suppress or rewrite it, and why we are sometimes encouraged to think that public management is too 'modern' to have any history. History, unlike distance, does not always lend enchantment to the view; but it does help to sharpen perspective. Embracing a historical perspective does not mean we need to be ancestor-worshippers, as sociologists are often accused of being. But we do need to know where ideas come from historically, to become aware of the recurring nature of public management doctrines and of the range of different doctrines which have fought for supremacy across space and time.

## 6. Modernity and Convergence in Cultural and Historical Perspective

The fourth and fifth propositions advanced earlier concern 'modernity' and 'convergence'. The fourth claim is that no single one of the polar recipes for good organization that cultural theory encompasses has any overriding claim to be considered inherently more 'modern' than any of the others. As soon as we move from 'hard' technology to human organization—and certainly at the interface between technology and organization—'modernity' becomes a highly problematic idea. Information technology is often said to be a central force in transforming contemporary society, with potentially more revolutionary results than the changes stemming from railroads and telegraphs in the nineteenth century. Indeed, that idea is one of the commonest clichés of the age. But, as will be discussed later, that technology is capable of supporting different and even contradictory social developments—for example in buttressing hierarchies by increased surveillance and monitoring, buttressing markets by reducing the transaction costs of complex bidding processes that would be much more laborious in a pre-electronic age (as in the case of markets for electricity (Foster

1992: 73))), buttressing social solidarity and community through networking, or making the world more random by increasing serendipity, chance encounters, and inexplicable failures in the 'internet society'. Should we conclude that the 'modernity' that information technology is set to bring to the world of government is hierarchist, individualist, egalitarian, or fatalist? Part 2 of the book suggests that each of the polar types of organization identified in cultural theory not only has a track record of historical recurrence but is capable of sustaining a plausible vision of organizational 'modernity'.

An additional problem with the notion of any single organizational way of life becoming permanently entrenched as the route to managerial modernity is that each polar approach will tend to have built-in failings. This problem is discussed in Chapter 2, and Chapter 8 returns to it. One of the recurring themes across the social sciences is the analysis of unintended consequences—the propensity for organizational and policy recipes designed to solve particular problems either to produce unanticipated side-effects or even to achieve the opposite of the intended goal. Chapter 8 argues that the more reliance is placed on any one polar form of organization, the more likely it is that such an effect will occur. That is because problems associated with resistance from those who espouse alternative preferences about how to organize are likely to increase as any one form of organization becomes dominant, or because 'blind spots' built-in to any one approach to organization are likely to become more severe the more entrenched it is. If such effects serve to limit the effectiveness of any one organizational recipe, the course of modernity—like true love—is not likely to run smooth.

The fifth and closely related proposition concerns the prospects for global convergence. As noted earlier, many contemporary voices claim 'modernity' is inevitably ushering in an era of global convergence around a single 'best practice' model of public management. By far the most famous of those voices are those of David Osborne and Ted Gaebler (1992), guru authors of the American best-seller *Reinventing Government*. They see a public-management future involving entrepreneurial or visionary leadership somehow mixed with 'empowered' front-line staff and clients. The common belief in a millennial once-for-all transformation of public management is apparently underpinned by the emergence of a common vocabulary of 'managementspeak' in government, like 'TQM', 'business process re-engineering', 'empowerment'. But contrary to such received ideas about global convergence, Chapter 8 argues that different and sharply conflicting ideas about how to do public management are likely to continue to exist. That does not mean that particular buzzwords are not spreading worldwide, as has often happened in previous eras, only that there are reasons to think no universally agreed recipe for success in how to *organize* (in the broadest sense) is ever likely to emerge.[3] And that in turn means the subject will continue to be interesting, and not turn into the kind of skills (like shorthand or typing) you can learn through computer programs or hypnosis.

The expectation of continuing variety rather than a homogenous 'modernity' in public management rests on two arguments. First, earlier prophecies about convergent modernization have turned out to be wrong or at least short-lived. Early twentieth-century ideas that a single global model of 'modern' public or private sector organization would develop proved to be unfounded (see Silberman 1993). Mid-twentieth century ideas that the future for public management in rich and poor countries alike meant a steady expansion of state activity and independent public enterprise (see, for instance, Robson 1948) met a similar fate. Not all states followed that path and even for those that did, an alternative vision of 'modernity' as meaning privatization and slimming down the state developed within a generation to challenge the earlier view. There is no reason to suppose that today's supposedly global recipes for public and private management 'excellence' will be markedly more durable or universal.

Historical precedents are of course only circumstantial evidence. Conceivably things could be different *this time*, if the fundamental causal processes at work were really different, as today's prophets

---

[3] *Trobriand Cricket*, a famous ethnographic film, documents the way the game of cricket has come to take on a different form and significance since it was introduced by Methodist missionaries into the Trobriand Islands in the early twentieth century, for example with war magicians functioning as umpires and no limit on the numbers in each of the rival teams. To assume that a game must have the same function and characteristics in the Trobriand Islands as it does at the home of the Marylebone Cricket Club simply because both are called 'cricket' is an elementary institutional fallacy, and just the same may apply to the trappings of contemporary management vocabulary. Look beneath the ubiquitous catchwords, and convergence may be more problematic than it may at first appear (cf. Hood 1996).

of convergence through globalization assert. But there is another reason for supposing variety rather than convergence may continue to be central to public management. Cultural theory suggests that beyond a certain point convergence on a single management model is not simply implausible but likely to be impossible. Against the pervasive notion of 'modernity' as having only a single 'leading edge', it suggests there are multiple approaches that are capable of working in organizing public services. Each of the available options has its strengths and weaknesses, but none will serve 'for all seasons' for the simple reason that incompatible administrative values cannot be pursued simultaneously (Hood 1991*a*) and none can ever win over its competitors by a knock-out.

## 7. The Stretchability and Centrality of the Cultural-Theory Frame

The sixth and seventh propositions advanced earlier concern the 'stretchability' of cultural theory as an analytic frame and its possible role in the science of public management. The sixth proposition claims that the analytic resources of cultural theory are not exhausted by a simple four-part typology. Each of the major 'families' of ideas about public management associated with each of the four polar types come in a number of variants, some of which are explored in the chapters of Part 2. Critics of cultural theory often argue the categories are too broad for fine-grained analysis, but the dimensional approach that cultural theory embodies can be applied at a variety of different levels of detail. Using an optometric analogy, Gerald Mars (1982: 38) suggests, 'It is always possible . . . to slip a more powerful . . . lens into any quadrant by . . . dividing it into a further $2 \times 2$ matrix and to continue to do so until the analysis applies at the level of the individual . . .' This approach is followed at various points in this book, for example to distinguish different subtypes of control and regulation in Chapter 3 and to categorize varieties of 'management guru' ideas in Chapter 8.

The seventh and most general proposition, which stems from the previous six, is that analysis of cultural variety, within a historical perspective, deserves to be central to the study of public management. If the three assumptions bound up with much contemporary discussion of 'public management' are more contestable than they appear at first sight, we need an alternative way of framing the subject—a different ABC or set of basic propositions. As implied by Sir Edwin Chadwick in the epigraph to this chapter, public management is too important to be left to 'sham science' making casual assertions about waves of the future or international 'best practice'. An approach to public management which is anything other than a redescription of current trends or a glorification of the role of Armani-suited accountants or MBA graduates in provision of public services needs to be tuned to pick up the maximum amount of possible variation in organizational styles in space and time.

## 8. The Plan of the Book

The structure of this book aims to bring out the seven propositions discussed above. In the next two chapters, the cultural-theory framework is used to explore two central problems of public management—the analysis of the characteristic ways in which different forms of organization can collapse and fail, and the analysis of the range of forms of control and regulation (in the broadest sense) available in public management. In both cases, an examination through the lens of cultural theory can add an extra dimension or an alternative perspective to the analysis.

In the four chapters of Part II, public management ideas that loosely correspond to each of the four polar 'world-views' identified by cultural-theory are discussed. Here the cultural theory framework is mixed with an historical perspective to survey recurring approaches to public management that can be loosely characterized as 'hierarchist', 'individualist', 'egalitarian', and 'fatalist'. The first three categories are more familiar than the last, but a cultural-theory framework enables us to 'place' and notice approaches to interpretation and even doctrine that lay heavy stress on randomness and unpredictability.

The third part of the book returns to the general question of what sort of 'science' public management is or can be and how cultural theory can contribute to that science. If public management is (as suggested earlier) dominated by rhetorical forms of argument, cultural theory can help us take one step further than conventional analyses of rhetoric by differentiating rhetorical 'families', and that theme is explored in Chapter 8. Chapter 9 critically discusses the pervasive ideas of 'modernization' and 'global convergence' in a cultural-theory framework, suggesting there are more forces for divergence and less common ground on what 'modernity' means in matters of organization than is commonly recognized. Chapter 10 concludes the book by taking stock of the cultural-theory approach as a framework for analysing public management, surveying its strengths and weaknesses. It does not claim there are no problems with the approach. On the contrary, there are major gaps and ambiguities and some of the underlying logic needs attention. But in spite of such weaknesses, the claim is that a cultural-theory framework has much to contribute to a way of thinking about 'the art of the state' which is neither 'sham science' nor 'mere craft'.

# 2

# Calamity, Conspiracy, and Chaos
# in Public Management

> Their entire navy, consisting of two vessels—the aircraft-
> carrier *Melbourne* and the destroyer *Voyager*—had contrived,
> despite several thousand miles of empty coastal waters, to
> crash into itself.
>
> (Jacobson 1987: 169)

Mark Moore (1995), one of the leading contemporary writers on
public management, has stressed the role of public managers and
their organizations as 'creating public value', in the sense of producing services or outcomes that 'add value' to society. This chapter starts from the opposite end, looking at the ways in which public
managers and management can *detract* from public value. It examines the problem of failure and collapse in public management and
identifies a number of ways in which 'negative public value' can
be created, with selected examples. As noted in the last chapter,
the aim of this analysis is to show how a cultural-theory perspective can be used to analyse one of the central problems of public
management—how organizations fail.

Focusing on calamity rather than the positive side of managerial
achievement and value-creation may seem an excessively down-
beat and pessimistic approach to the subject. But there are at least
three things to be said for such a perspective. First, sharp thinking
about how to do public management is typically prompted by
responses to disaster rather than reasoning about how to 'create
value' on a blank page. Prescriptions about how to organize,
as noted in the last chapter, tend to stem from reactions against

failures (or perceived failures) of current institutions. Recipes for organizational success often amount to turning round what is seen as a recipe for disaster.

Second, the disasters that prompt such prescriptions are rarely far to seek. Even in what pass for the best-regulated states, malodorous stories about public services are common enough. Tales of monumental blunders, blatant self-interest and corruption, self-destructive organizational civil wars and feuds, astonishing failures to look ahead or take any initiative in the face of the most pressing problems are far from unusual in most societies, even if the incidence of such stories (and the extent to which they are aired in the media) varies. Any account of public management that ignores or downplays such phenomena is a case of *Hamlet* without the Prince of Denmark.

Third, there is currently no generally accepted theory of collapse and failure in public management. Though many different lists of the ways that government institutions can fail have been drawn up since classical Chinese times (see, for example, Hood 1976: 17–29), those lists tend to be *ad hoc*, in the vein of travellers' tales. What is lacking is an overall frame for the discussion.

This chapter aims to show how a cultural-theory perspective can assist the analysis of public management failure and collapse in two ways. First, such a perspective can help to bring out some of the varying and contradictory attitudes towards scandal or catastrophe in public management, in the sense of who to blame or how to put matters right. Second, the four basic organizational ways of life that cultural theory identifies (as introduced in the last chapter) can each be expected to have its own characteristic pattern of inbuilt failure.

## 1. Responses to Public-Management Disasters

It was suggested above that public management is like the drains, in the sense that it normally only grabs attention when there is a nasty smell of some kind. But a cultural-theory perspective suggests that what counts as a bad smell is not likely to be the same for everyone. What to one person is an intolerable stink may be scarcely noticeable to another. Views will often diverge sharply on who or what is at fault and what should be done to fix the problem. There is no universal agreement on what counts as 'problem' and what as 'solution', or when the point is reached where the 'solution' becomes worse than the 'problem'. Law enforcement, the heart of public management, typically attracts such disagreement (Marenin 1985: 103). What some may see as vigorous promotion of order and public safety (for instance through 'zero tolerance' of street crime) may be viewed by others as a needless provocation of petty offenders or even an all-out war on the disadvantaged, only a short step away from the sort of rapacity conducted by fascist and authoritarian states against marginal or dissident members of society (cf. Nicholson 1986).

Indeed, responses to scandal or catastrophe in public management—such as police brutality, major safety lapses or dramatic financial misappropriation—are likely to be a key test of cultural bias. Table 2.1 summarizes four patterns of blame and proposed remedies following disasters that align with the major organizational world-views of cultural theory.

One of the commonest responses to disaster ('hierarchist' in cultural-theory terms) is that the problem (whatever it was) could have been averted if only there had been more co-ordination, better procedures, more planning and foresight, clearer assignment of authority, more general 'grip' on the part of experts, professionals, or managers. The people to blame are those who were not following prescribed procedures or best practice, and the solution (recommended by countless post-disaster inquries) is to tighten up the rules and the authority structures to prevent a recurrence.

A contrary (egalitarian) approach, however, may take authority and expertise as the *reason* why catastrophes happen, the problem rather than the solution. Pinning blame on some hapless individual operative or manager who failed to follow rules may obscure the real villain of the piece—the overall system in which public servants or contractors are obliged to work, which so often turns out to involve contradictory rules or rules which are tacitly expected to be broken if people are to get their jobs done at all (cf. Hennestad 1990). Such practices may buttress the ability of those in powerful institutional positions to 'blame the victim' and walk away from responsibility when disaster strikes. The egalitarian solution accordingly involves more 'democracy' and 'empowerment' of people at the bottom to challenge authority and professional self-interest, 'blowing the whistle' over matters of public concern.

TABLE 2.1. *Four responses to public-management disasters in a cultural-theory frame*

| Fatalist response | Hierarchist response |
|---|---|
| *Stress on*: unpredictability and unintended effects | *Stress on*: expertise, forecasting, and management |
| *Blame*: the 'fickle finger of fate' (or 'chaos theory' interpretation of how organization works) | *Blame*: poor compliance with established procedures, lack of professional expertise |
| *Remedy*: minimal anticipation, at most *ad hoc* response after the event | *Remedy*: more expertise, tighter procedures, greater managerial 'grip' |
| *Watchword*: 'resilience' | *Watchword*: 'steering' |
| **Individualist response** | **Egalitarian response** |
| *Stress on*: individuals as self-interested rational choosers | *Stress on*: group and power structures |
| *Blame*: faulty incentive structures through over-collectivization and lack of price signals | *Blame*: abuse of power by top-level government/corporate leaders, system corruption |
| *Remedy*: market-like mechanisms, competitions and leagues, information to support choice (e.g. rating systems) | *Remedy*: participation, communitarianism, whistle-blowing |
| *Watchword*: 'enlightened self-interest' | *Watchword*: 'community participation' |

The individualist perspective brings in a different approach to diagnosis and prescription. From this perspective, many of the typical failings of public management stem from *too much* collectivism and organization, not too little. It is the misplaced faith in running societies or organizations by planning, authority, and rules rather than price systems, tort law, 'internal markets', or other incentive structures, which so often leads to disaster through poorly designed incentive systems. Whistleblowers' charters or stress on collective empowerment will either lead to a minority of cranks and zealots running institutions or lead to the common situation of 'what is everybody's business is nobody's business'. For individualists, the only way to make public management work is by working with the grain of personal ambition and self-interest. That means more stress on competition among individuals within and between organizations and the use of markets or mechanisms that resemble markets as closely as possible.

Finally, the fatalist response may see the failing in question (whatever it was) as a unique one-off event. Tragic or embarrassing as they may be, many disasters are only ever truly foreseeable in hindsight, and even—perhaps especially—the most complex and intensively planned systems are subject to unpredictable and indeterminate 'X-factors' that can confound expectations about how they will behave. To pin blame on any individual or system for such outcomes can only be arbitrary if results arise from compound causes (cf. Hardin 1996). Any simple confident all-purpose remedy is as likely to worsen as to improve the problem.

The analysis in Table 2.1 suggests two things. First, 'disasters' in public management are not always objectively identifiable and universally recognized. Who believes what to be a 'disaster' can be a litmus test for attitudes towards justice and blame. What is seen as vice and what as virtue in public management is not likely to be distributed randomly around the population, but will tend to correspond with entrenched world-views. Second, even for those events that everyone recognizes as disasters (and they are far from uncommon), recipes for what to do to improve matters or prevent a recurrence will also tend to vary according to different world-views, and will tend to emerge as the sort of organizational prescriptions we explore more fully in Part 2.

## 2. Four Types of Failure and Collapse

A cultural-theory perspective suggests that different sorts of failure are not likely to be randomly distributed around the world of organizations either. Each major organizational way of life is likely to have its own inbuilt Achilles' Heel or characteristic path to collapse. Accordingly, the major types of failure in public management could be expected to consist of these Achilles' Heels. Individualist failures are likely to consist of cases where private self-interest is put before public or collective interest, for example in turning justice or law-enforcement into private-market

TABLE 2.2. *Built-in weaknesses of major organizational types: Four Achilles' Heels*

| Type of organizational bias | Achilles' Heel | Makes it vulnerable to: |
|---|---|---|
| Hierarchist | Misplaced trust in authority and expertise coupled with high mobilization capacity | Dramatic collapse of ambitious 'think big' plans or projects |
| Egalitarian | Unwillingness to accept higher authority to break deadlocks | Failures stemming from unresolved feuds or collegiality degenerating into coexistence |
| Individualist | Tendency to put individual before collective benefit | Failures stemming from lack of co-operation or individual corruption |
| Fatalist | Unwillingness to plan ahead or take drastic measures in extreme circumstances | Failures stemming from excessive inertia and passivity |

transactions. Hierarchist failures are likely to consist of cases where authority or expertise is insufficiently questioned, such that a large edifice comes to be built on shaky foundations, leading to dramatic collapse. Egalitarian failures are likely to consist of cases where debate cannot be closed, feuding and factionalism goes unchecked, and the organization collapses amid a welter of mutual recrimination. Fatalist failures, on the other hand, are more likely to consist of inaction or inability to change course even in extreme and pressing circumstances calling for a decisive response outside normal routine. Table 2.2 summarizes these characteristic types of failure and the next four sections discuss and illustrate each of them.

## 3. Private Gain from Public Office

In the Confucian tradition (on which we touch briefly in Chapter 4), those who rule are expected to put the interests of others ahead of their own. They must behave like selfless trustees, putting the welfare of their beneficiaries before any personal interest. But real-life public management often falls far short of this lofty ideal. One of the commonest types of failure or collapse comes when those managing or producing a service put their own interests first and the interests of their clients or customers second—or nowhere.

There is now a vast literature examining the problem of how legislatures or the public at large, conceived as 'principals', are to control their 'agents', that is, executives and bureaucrats. If the latter seek to 'look after Number One'—the watchword of individualism in cultural theory—the sort of failures that are likely to arise will come about through disdain for any collective restraint on the ability of individuals to shape their jobs as they choose, turn public affairs into private-market transactions, and public organizations into personal property. Three of the commonest failings of this type are bribery and extortion, front-line abandonment, and the use of public organizations for personal ego-trips.

## Misappropriation, Extortion, and Bribery

'Local officials in Mexico City announced this week that a new community centre would open soon on the city's outskirts. The centre will occupy a mansion built by Arturo Durazo, who used to be the city's police chief, but, as so often happens with police chiefs everywhere, is now facing criminal charges. The mansion cost $US 6.6 million to build in the mid 1970s and includes stables (where Mr. Durazo kept 20 thoroughbreds), an exhibit hall for his 23 motor cars, a greenhouse and a gamesroom. At the time the mansion was built, the police chief's official salary was $US 65 a week. He must have been very good at budgeting his money' (*Sydney Morning Herald*, 5 Nov. 1986).

Misappropriation, extortion, and bribery are among the commonest failings in public management. What they have in common is the use of public office to make illicit private gains in some form: for example, by private appropriation of public property, by accepting money from willing hands (bribery) or extracting it from unwilling ones (extortion) for performance, non-performance or prompt performance of their duties (cf. Bentham 1983: 309). Transforming public assets into private property can range from petty pilfering to massive illegal privatization operations (like the reported illegal sale of weapon systems belonging to the former Soviet Union) or even outright sale of public office, as in parts of India (or according to Voslensky (1984: 191), the Transcaucasian republics in the dying days of the Soviet Union).

In Western countries, bribery and extortion are often most blatant in big city police forces, particularly in domains where police monopolize enforcement (meaning they have no rivals to whom frustrated victims can turn) and where the violations involved are 'victimless' so there is little scope for private-actor enforcement (as in the familiar cases of illegal drugs, betting, and prostitution).[1] Where that happens, public service organizations have become part of the crime problem rather than the solution. And it is particularly likely to occur in law enforcement because (as Wilson (1968: 7) points out) police are an unusual kind of public organization in which discretion tends to increase as you go down the hierarchy, so decisions can be sold by those at the bottom just as (if not more) easily than by those at the top. The same can apply to other kinds of law-enforcers too, as in the official admission that Ukranian troops serving as part of the UN forces in Sarajevo in 1992–3 had sold cigarettes and food on the black market and disputed allegations that UN peacekeeping troops had also dealt illegally in heroin, fuel, and weapons (*Independent*, 27 Aug. 1993, p. 6). Indeed, international organizations are often said to be especially vulnerable to scandal and graft, because of their remoteness from public opinion and the tendency for their top-level leaders to be appointed wholly on the basis of patronage and political connections rather than of any demonstrated managerial talent (cf. Perri 6 and Sheridan 1994).

Misappropriation, extortion, and bribery have been considered a central 'problem' of management (public and private) since the earliest writings on the subject. But (as with brutality and rapacity), what counts as outright corruption for one person may be seen as perfectly acceptable behaviour by another. Indeed, using a cultural-theory perspective, Gerald Mars (1982) has shown how different occupations tend to generate different characteristic

---

[1] One of the most graphic cases in recent years came to light in the Northern Australian state of Queensland in the 1980s (see *Report of a Commission of Inquiry Pursuant to Orders in Council*. Brisbane: Government Printer, (i) 26 May 1987; (ii) 24 June 1987; (iii) 25 Aug. 1988; (iv) 29 June 1989.)

'fiddles' and different views about where the line is to be drawn between 'honest graft' and unacceptable cheating. Moreover, for some the cure to the corruption problem may be deemed worse than the disease. For example, Frank Anechiarico and James Jacobs (1996: 193), writing about corruption control in New York (and the USA more generally), argue that the ever-expanding ambit of what counts as 'corruption' and the growth of anti-corruption bureaucracy contributes heavily to a paralysis of public management 'while having no significant impact on the corruption rate. We now have a corruption-control problem as well as a corruption problem.'

## Front-line Abandonment

Paul Hockenos (1993: 23–7) describes an ugly racial attack in Hoyerswerda in September 1991, a year after German unification. Once a village, Hoyerswerda was expanded into an industrial barracks of 70,000 people in high-rise tower blocks by East German planners in the 1960s and 1970s. In the 1980s, workers from other communist countries—Mozambique, Angola, and Vietnam—were sent there as an extra source of labour. By 1990 there were some 400 of them. Housed in special dormitories, the foreign workers were disliked by many of the locals, but the fraternal 'solidarity' imposed by the East German state authorities had limited racial discrimination to a relatively petty, albeit wounding, level. But local resentment against the foreigners grew as the town's unemployment rose from nil to 7 per cent in a single year after the collapse of the DDR. Those feelings were intensified as the new German federal government sent Hoyerswerda 230 applicants for political asylum from Romania, Cameroon, Turkey, Yugoslavia, Senegal, and Ghana.

Attacks against Hoyerswerda's foreign inhabitants started with local skinheads attacking Vietnamese street traders and schoolchildren breaking windows in the Vietnamese and African workers' dormitory. Shortly afterwards '. . . a crowd no longer confined to teenagers gathered outside the foreign workers' apartment block on Albert Schweitzer Street. The adults egged the youth on as they pelted the tower with rocks and empty bottles. About fifty local Skinheads and neo-Nazi types appeared on the scene, contributing their expertise to the action. The police were nowhere to be seen' (ibid. 26). Social workers warned the foreign workers to expect more of the same the following day ('They're coming to get you'), and in fact fifty-odd thugs began to attack the apartment block with stones, fireworks, and Molotov cocktails, while the terrified and unguarded inhabitants crouched in their bathrooms. In spite of the social workers' accurate intelligence, the police had not been on the scene when the attack began, and in fact took several hours to cordon off the building. The next day, the foreign workers were evacuated from Hoyerswerda. But in spite—or more likely, because—of this retreat, over 120 Nazis now descended on the political refugees' quarters. Again, there were no police on guard when the Nazis arrived, although the police turned up later and a pitched battle began. Two days after the battle (which left no glass in the windows of the refugees' building below the fifth story and produced twenty-nine wounded and four badly injured), the refugees were in turn evacuated amid insults from assembled locals. 'The final rocks thudded against the buses as they lumbered off to an unspecified location. Hoyerswerda, the fascists rejoiced, was finally an *ausländerfreie Stadt* . . . The state had capitulated to the mob' (ibid. 27).

The problem highlighted by this story is very different from outright theft or blatant misappropriation of public property. If Hockenos' account is accurate, it shows the 'private interest' of public-service providers being pursued in a subtler way, by avoiding unpleasant or dangerous front-line work, putting producers' comfort or safety first and being 'nowhere to be seen' when ugly events occur. An ever-present problem for public management is that those who provide public services—private contractors just as much as public bureaucracies—too often opt for the easy and congenial work rather than more stressful and 'nitty-gritty' operations, even where it is the latter that are most valued by society at large. Working with high-status colleagues, in pleasant surroundings, during regular hours, with plenty of opportunity for 'on-the-job leisure' (seminars, conferences, study tours) and freedom to shape the way work is done are commonly preferred to work with the opposite characteristics (grinding routine, close attention to detail, acrimonious confrontation with 'difficult' people from different backgrounds). If such tendencies are not checked the effect is seriously to skew public management in welfare-reducing directions (see Dunleavy 1991).

Closely related to the Hoyerswerda problem, perhaps the best-known example of front-line abandonment is urban solo-beat patrol by police, involving as it does the need to deal disproportionately with the intractable problems posed by low-status people who are mentally disturbed, under the influence of drink or drugs, foul-smelling, visibly affected by all the ills of poverty. Nor is this kind of work much rewarded in career terms as a rule, leading to well-known problems of 'patrol avoidance' (Wilson 1968: 52). Jones (1980) shows how in an English police force in the 1970s, 61 per cent of police officers were in the uniform branch, but only about 6 per cent of the total staff were actually on patrol at any one time. He attributes this behaviour, strongly at odds with the 'beat ideology' (the idea that beat patrol is the most important part of police work) ritually intoned by politicians and police chiefs, to factors like better career prospects for officers not engaged in patrol duties and the use of uniform patrol as a punishment for officers from the non-patrol section (ibid. 156 ff).

Police patrol is not the only example of the problem. 'Teaching avoidance' is commonplace in universities and 'management avoidance' in public-service organizations generally. Tax and regulatory officials often prefer to concentrate on easy work that will not stir up powerful opposition forces at the expense of work that is less straightforward or has greater downside risks (Cranston 1979; Grabosky and Braithwaite 1986). Indeed, Murray Horn (1995: 58) sees concentration on small 'winnable' cases by regulatory agencies as a product of a career structure in which regulators' subsequent employment prospects in the private sector are related to their reputation for regulatory expertise and performance.

Of course, behaviour that some people might pejoratively label as 'front-line abandonment' can be classed by others as giving proper attention to planning and strategy, avoiding the perils of over-concentration on routine operations and what is often claimed to be the besetting sin of public bureaucracies—preoccupation with low-level routine, often at the expense of the substantive purposes of the organization. To critics, on the other hand, such defences evoke an image of World War I generals, ensconced in comfortable quarters and pleasant surroundings far from the carnage and chaos of the 'front line'. Such critics see 'bureau-shaping' activities by top bureaucrats as likely to result in over-outsourcing and corporatization of activities that would be better provided as part of core

government operations if least-cost and transaction-cost considerations were as important to organizational design as reorganization
rhetoric tends to imply.

## *Grandeur, Self-Indulgence, and Ego-Tripping*

A related problem arises when public servants appear to behave
like France's pre-revolutionary aristocrats, cocooning themselves
in luxury or shaping their organizations to their own personal
whims instead of submitting to uniform public-service styles or the
penny-watching restraint so often associated with public organization. Such an issue lay behind the resignation in 1993 of Jacques
Attali as President of the European Bank for Reconstruction and
Development (EBRD), a development institution set up by the EU
in 1991 to assist the transition to free-market economies in Eastern
Europe and the ex-Soviet Union. Attali, a former confidant of
President Mitterand of France, resigned in the aftermath of a
highly critical report by the EBRD's audit committee and its
external advisers (the accountancy firm Coopers and Lybrand).

Much of Coopers and Lybrand's criticism focused on what was
portrayed as the extravagantly self-indulgent luxury of EBRD's
expensive headquarters building in the City of London—which the
auditors claimed to cost between two-and-a-half and four times as
much per square metre as similar projects undertaken for international financial organizations in North America and Europe. The
sum of nearly US$100m spent on refitting the building attracted
great attention, particularly the replacement of the marble cladding
in the building (at a cost of well over $1m) which drew unfavour-
able comparisons between the bank's expenditure on its own building and the amount it was spending on its notional clients in the
former USSR and Eastern Europe.

In addition to the bank's 'marble halls', criticism was directed at
the jet-setting corporate lifestyle of M. Attali and his entourage—
including allegedly extravagant use of chartered aircraft by M.
Attali, more than twenty costly supersonic flights on Concorde in
a single year by the bank's top directorate (in contravention
of the organization's own staff travel policies), and lavish use of
rental cars by M. Attali in 1991, creating 'an impression of
extravagance . . . inappropriate for the head of a development
institution' (*Independent*, 17 July 1993, p. 17).

Behaviour of the type alleged in this case will attract immediate condemnation from those whose nostrils are hypersensitive to any scent of autocracy or self-indulgence at the top at the expense of clients or subordinates. But what some may see as unacceptable personal 'ego-tripping', treating public organization as a private fief, may be interpreted by others as a legitimate 'read-across' of corporate business styles to public management. Hence the activity of high-profile public entrepreneurs like M. Attali, who put a distinctive stamp on the bureaucracies they lead and brush aside the pettifogging clerical mentality and colourless, often self-defeating, parsimony of orthodox 'public service', typically attracts strongly conflicting interpretations. Does the emphasis on the importance of managers that lies at the heart of many contemporary public-service reforms across much of the OECD world simply reflect a public-spirited search for greater economy and effectiveness? Or does it reflect the pursuit of power by 'macho managers', diverting resources that could be spent on clients, students, or patients into the pursuit of ever-more management for its own sake? If the cultural theorists are correct, there will never be any agreement on which interpretation is correct, but it can also be expected that stories of private gain from public office will continue to be one of the most-commonly discussed failings of public management.

## 4. Fiascos Resulting from Excessive Trust in Authority and Expertise

If the characteristic failing that individualism produces in public management is unchecked private gain at private expense, the corresponding hierarchist failing is organizational collapse brought about through unfounded trust in expertise and authority. This failing is reflected in the frequent stories about expensive fiascos produced by 'groupthink', erroneous over-confidence in 'think big' solutions, excessive trust in top-level leadership, in the authority of science (natural or social) or professional wisdom, combined with an apparent inability to learn from the experience when sooner or later the inevitable disasters occur. The result is a recognizable syndrome of recurring major errors which has been identified in different ways by many analysts of organization and public policy, and in the growing literature on 'policy fiascos' (Dunleavy 1995; Bovens and 't Hart 1996).

On the face of it, the most dramatic recent example of this syndrome is the world's worst nuclear accident—the 1986 fire at the No 4 reactor of the Chernobyl nuclear-power plant in the Ukraine, which smashed the top of the reactor core after the explosion of a hydrogen pocket, releasing large quantities of radioactive debris into the atmosphere, with serious long-term effects across much of Europe (see Hawkes *et al.* 1986). The accident, linked by Piers Paul Read (1993: 455) to the subsequent 'meltdown' of the Soviet state itself, was produced by an experiment. The experiment, designed to reduce the risks of nuclear meltdown, ironically produced the very catastrophe it was intended to avoid (Haynes and Bojcun 1988: 1). The Chernobyl plant had standby diesel generators to power the cooling pumps if there was a loss of electric power from any reactor, but there was a 40/50 second gap between a total loss of reactor power and the start-up of the diesel generators. The aim of the experiment was to discover whether a special magnetic field regulator on the No. 8 turbine generator connected to the No. 4 reactor could help to cover the gap, by powering the cooling pumps in the event of reactor failure 'for a few tens of seconds as the turbine rotor spun to a halt' (ibid. 6).

During the experiment, which was conducted while the reactor was decommisioned for maintenance, the operators broke many of the plant's most important safety rules.

- They switched off the reactor's emergency core cooling system (Mould 1988: 9).
- They failed to reset the automatic control rods to hold the power above the 700 MW level needed to prevent the reactor from becoming unstable through low power.
- Then, to raise the power of the reactor, they withdrew control rods from the reactor core, leaving less than the minimum number of rods needed to keep the reactor from having an uncontrollable burst of power.
- They disengaged the emergency protection controls attached to the turbine's steam drums; and blocked the trip which would shut down the reactor when the No. 8 turbine generator was switched off for the experiment.

Each of these steps, taken in an attempt to stabilize the reactor so the experiment could be carried out, paved the way for the eventual disaster. The sudden decrease in water in the reactor caused by the shutdown of the turbine generator caused steam pressure to rise and with it a power surge in the unstable reactor, taking it within seconds from 200 MW to over 140,000 MW, 440 times full power (Haynes and Bojcun 1988: 9). The operators tried to shut down the reactor by dropping all the control rods into the core, but there was a momentary snag and by then it was too late to prevent the exploding materials of the reactor core from breaking through the floor, the walls, and the roof (ibid).

Though there was an elaborate organizational apparatus of controllers and overseers, not just within the plant, but also at a higher bureaucratic level, none of this machinery in practice checked what Grigor Medvedev (1991: 61) calls 'offhand, criminally negligent attitudes'. Though in retrospect numerous experts have shown the plan for the Chernobyl experiment was fatally flawed, no reply had in fact come from the superior 'expert' authorities (the Gidroproyekt Institute and the Nuclear Safety Committee) to whom the plan had been submitted three months before the accident (ibid. 36). The lack of any effective system of reporting nuclear accidents and mishaps in the USSR for thirty-five years meant nuclear-power plant operators could not learn from others' mistakes and might develop an unrealistic sense of over-confidence. Within the Chernobyl plant, the human ingredients of the tragedy came in the form of a fatal mixture of an ailing but ambitious chief engineer determined to make his mark, a pliant director, and a senior reactor control engineer on the shift who was susceptible to pressure from his superiors (if the experiment had been called off because of the instability of the reactor, it would have been another year before it could be conducted again).

Hawkes *et al.* (1986: 110) note that after the disaster, 'nuclear authorities across the world acted . . . to distance themselves from the Chernobyl accident. "It couldn't happen here. We design much better plants and we take greater care about safety," was the continual response of utility and reactor programme chiefs speaking on television and radio and to newspaper reporters . . .'. Ironically, that had been exactly the reaction of the Chernobyl engineers and managers to a near-meltdown at a US nuclear plant (Three Mile

Island) in 1978. It seems to have been assumed that unlike the inevitably corner-cutting safety culture of nuclear industry under capitalism, Chernobyl was different because it had double containment facilities and state-of-the-art safety systems. The plant's chief engineer, Nikolai Fomin, had declared: 'Even if the incredible should happen, the automatic control and safety systems would shut down the reactor in a matter of seconds . . .' (ibid. 6–7).

Excessive faith and trust in organizational competence have been identified by David Collingridge (1992) as lying at the heart of what he calls 'inflexible technologies' like nuclear power and large-scale transport projects. The paradox of such technologies resembles the well-known problem of 'groupthink' screening out critical judgement in top-level policy or management groups (Janis 1972). A high degree of trust has to develop among the key participants (contractors, public bureaucracies, professional experts) for such projects to be developed at all; but that high-trust relationship tends to make the whole process impervious to what may be only too well-founded doubts and questions coming from outside the charmed circle. The result of unchallenged faith in particular 'technological fixes' include the fiascos stemming from post-World War II beliefs that nuclear energy could produce clean and cheap power (Williams 1980) or the beguiling but often disappointed hope that expensive new computer systems can save money, improve accuracy, and increase efficiency (Margetts 1991).

In a similar vein, many writers have identified the chronic tendency of military planning to produce blunders of astonishing dimensions. Studies like Barbara Tuchman's *March of Folly* (1984), chronicling the conduct of the Vietnam war by the USA, underline the false assumptions and massive errors of judgement which led to the defeat of the world's greatest superpower by a guerilla army on bicycles. Nor was this military fiasco, epoch-making as it was, an isolated episode. The syndrome keeps recurring, with no evidence of learning from experience. Norman Dixon (1976: 45), citing a long historical catalogue of military errors involving astonishing lapses of common sense in the face of the clearest possible warnings, sees orthodox military organization as particularly prone to produce recurrent massive mistakes. Patrick Dunleavy (1995), in a review of recent UK policy fiascos, makes a similar point and relates what he claims to be the exceptional incidence of such fiascos in the UK to a range of institutional features including over-centralization, weak external scrutiny, and over-confidence in official expertise (contrast Gray 1996).

*Why* the recurring failure to learn from experience in this type of organization? Dixon claims the learning problem comes from the social psychology lying behind the conventional military structure. He argues, 'It is a sad feature of authoritarian organizations that their nature inevitably militates against the possibility of learning from experience through the apportioning of blame. The reason is not hard to find. Since authoritarianism is itself the product of psychological defences, authoritarian organizations are past masters at deflecting blame. They do so by denial, by rationalization, by making scapegoats, or by some mixture of the three ... However it is achieved, the net result is that no real admission of failure or incompetence is ever made by those who are really responsible; hence nothing can be done about preventing a recurrence.'

A different perspective is offered by Charles Perrow (1984: 179). In his well-known book *Normal Accidents*, Perrow discusses 'error-inducing' organization—an interaction of technology, incentives, and structure that produces recurring fiascos. His example is that of marine accidents, paradoxically rising in spite of the dramatic potential for increased marine safety through technological developments over the last half-century. The industry is an 'error-inducing organization', according to Perrow, because of a cocktail of financial pressures (often working against safety considerations), chronic communication difficulties (created by recruitment of crews with no common language and high staff turnover), and lack of incentives to maintain or even learn about failure-prone technology (created by crew turnover, resulting in faulty and dangerous equipment). Barry Turner (1978) also identifies a critical 'incubation process' of multiplicative effects from individually trivial malfunctions that lie at the heart of organizationally created disasters. Such processes are commonly observable in public management, given its typically multiple objectives, the incentives to strip out necessary 'redundancy' in naïve pursuit of efficiency (cf. Hood and Jackson 1991*b*; Landau 1969) and the tendency to conceal potentially embarrassing evidence of failure or danger to avoid giving ammunition to political enemies.

Even so, what exactly produces large-scale errors is not generally agreed, and here again cultural variety is likely to produce different

diagnoses. Was the Chernobyl disaster produced by an organizational culture excessively steeped in 'hierarchism'—or by an
organization that was not hierarchist *enough*, in that it blatantly
failed to follow its own rules? Was the US Vietnam débâcle caused
by a mentality of blinkered militarist authoritarianism—or by a
failure to be authoritarian enough? We will see in Chapter 7 that
there is no scientific agreement on the organizational factors that
produce high reliability or major accidents. Indeed, in some cases
even what is to count as an error or fiasco is itself debatable. What
looks like an unambiguous fiasco from one perspective may seem
like a 'blessing in disguise' from another (cf. Dunleavy 1995: 52–
3)—defeats that prompt dramatic fight-backs, catastrophes that
lead to adaptation. Even disasters like the Chernobyl tragedy might
be seen as contributing to 'resilience' by those who see coping in
the face of continual challenges, rather than 'anticipationism', as
central to social survival (Wildavsky 1988). There may be 'loser's
blessings' to match what economists call 'winner's curse'. To some
extent, fiascos, like beauty, can be in the eye of the beholder.

## 5. Unresolved Conflict and Internecine Strife

A third class of commonly observed failings in public management—and the one most likely to be associated with the egalitarian
approach to organization—is a lack of ability to resolve disputes or
exert effective authority. Organizations without such capacity can
experience unresolved civil wars and internecine feuds sometimes
extending over decades, and may be partially paralysed because of
lack of any central authority against strong-willed individuals or
powerful barons. That syndrome is classically associated with the
pre-1791 constitution of Poland, which gave the nobility immunity
against the law coupled with the right of open rebellion against the
king and the *liberum veto* decision rule allowing any one of the 460
deputies to veto a measure in the parliament (a practice which
produced deadlock and civil wars involving foreign troops and
eventually led to the disappearance of Poland as a state until after
World War I). Authority deficits of a similar, if typically less
extreme, kind are far from uncommon in those areas of contemporary public management, notably health and education, where
'professional authority' and 'management' are in tension, and
where norms of professionalism involve both collegiality and a

respect for the professional judgement of individual practitioners (expressed as notions of clinical or academic freedom).

Outright disobedience of lawful authority by public officials is far from unknown in public management. For example, Neville ('Nifty') Wran, Labor premier of the Australian state of New South Wales (NSW) between 1976 and 1986, said that one of the major tribulations he had to endure during his premiership was the 'calculated disobedience' of the NSW police force to his government in the late 1970s (Wran 1986: 10–11). The ultimate form of disobedience comes in the form of *coups d'état* or mass demonstrations by police or military forces, as in the case of the attempted takeover of the Spanish Parliament by the head of the *Guardia Civil* in 1981 or of the 3,000 Paris police who marched on and laid siege to the French Parliament in March 1958, thereby contributing to the collapse of the Fourth French Republic (see Roach 1985: 112). Even governments disposed to favour a measure of egalitarian organization in other policy domains will falter when security forces refuse to obey their orders.

As noted above, problems stemming from lack of authority to 'close a case' or resolve a dispute also often arise when institutions that are nominally controlled by a 'collegial' process in which the individual is answerable to a group, in fact degenerate into 'coexistence', with a tendency for each of the colleagues in the group to avoid asking awkward questions about the behaviour of colleagues. A graphic example of such a problem is the 1993 Birmingham cancer affair, in which an independent public inquiry into the Royal Orthopaedic Hospital in Birmingham, England, found evidence of persistently inaccurate diagnoses of suspected bone tumours, meaning at least forty-two patients were either treated for cancers which they did not have, or wrongly told their tumours were benign. Shocking as they may seem, these findings were not surprising to insiders in the case. Surgeons from the hospital had been dissatisfied for years with the work of the laboratory run by one of the hospital's consultant pathologists, to the point where they had begun asking for second opinions from another specialist 300 miles away in Scotland. But top management took no action, claiming that formal complaints by the surgeons concerned only *delays* in diagnosis, not errors. The public inquiry's report blamed an ill-defined management structure at the hospital, and found the pathology service was hampered by infighting and poor communication between senior health service managers and consultant surgeons. It seemed clinical staff did not know the procedures for complaining about clinical incompetence by medical colleagues (*Independent*, 1 Sept. 1993).

Perhaps the classic example of spiralling conflict and internecine strife in public management since World War II is the orthodox account of what happened to the 'community action' strategy for combating poverty, crime, and delinquency in the famous 'war on poverty' declared by US President Lyndon Johnson in 1964. The title of Daniel Moynihan's famous (1969) book *Maximum Feasible Misunderstanding* is a play on the words 'maximum feasible participation of the residents of the areas and the members of the groups' involved in local anti-poverty community action programmes, a clause that appeared in Title II of the Economic Opportunity Act of 1964. Moynihan (ibid. 87) claims the élite Washington lawyers and economists who drafted the bill inserted the phrase 'maximum feasible participation' simply to ensure that unorganized poor Southern blacks were not excluded from the programmes by the white supremacists who controlled the Southern states at that time. Almost completely ignored in the Congressional debates on the bill, the phrase came to legitimate a 'radicalization' of the CAP in directions quite unintended and unanticipated by the measure's original framers, most of whom seem to have conceived CAP as 'nothing more than an effort to give grown-ups in the neighbourhood roles that would encourage them to teach their kids to behave' (ibid. 107).

But instead of remaining an apolitical means for helping the poor to solve their private difficulties, the community action programmes rapidly came to develop as a frontal challenge to the legitimacy of city government and the American power structure generally. The CAP was used as a vehicle for organized rent strikes, school boycotts, mass demonstrations, and confrontations with elected politicians—events which rapidly led to its demise as an aghast US Congress moved quickly to cut the programme's funds and rein in its administrative powers. What had developed was a structure in which the 'community organizations' fostered by CAP presented themselves as more representative and legitimate than the Congress or City Hall and in which there was no agreement on where ultimate authority rested or even what 'community action' meant (ibid. 168).

Moynihan sees the 'Frankenstein monster' unintentionally produced by the original architects of CAP as a product of an unrecognized clash of cultures—between a 'top-down' and 'bottom-up' mentality, between 'Washington' and 'New York' attitudes, between lawyers and economists concerned with orderly and efficient social engineering and reforming radicals intent on confrontation. He also speculates whether the attractions for many social scientists of that time of the basic theory underlying the CAP (that community action offers a cure for deviance and delinquency) lay in the way it chimed with their social and even religious biases, rather than because of the weight of evidence in support of the theory (ibid. 175)—indeed, he claims, 'The community action ideology became in many ways more, not less, extreme in the face of evident failures' (ibid. 182).

But—perhaps even more than the other two forms of collapse discussed earlier—what counts as failure or disaster in such cases is likely to be disputed. Observers like Moynihan see such challenges to public authority as undermining democracy and effective government. (Moynihan sees the mayhem created by the CAP as caused by a small group of activists whose views were not shared by most of the communities they claimed to represent and who put back the cause of effective social justice programmes in the USA for a generation by effectively waging a civil war against the established institutions of democratic and constitutional government.) But others, approaching public management from a different cultural bias, may well see willingness to challenge the mind-set and misguided or corrupt instructions coming from 'above' as a virtue, not a vice, in public management. Indeed, many have argued that public officials have a moral duty to *disobey* their lawful masters if the orders they are given conflict with some higher moral code (cf. Hood and Jackson 1991: 103). The 'duty to disobey' is often proclaimed by 'whistle-blowers' and other public servants resisting what they consider to be 'unconscionable' orders or a morally intolerable regime.

## 6. Apathy and Inertia: Lack of Planning, Initiative, and Foresight

A fourth common class of failing in public management is loosely associated with the 'fatalist' world-view. It consists of a cocktail of lack of enthusiasm, lack of disposition to take responsibility or to plan for apparently predictable events. Such attitudes may be common in what Marshall Meyer and Lynne Zucker (1989) term 'permanently failing organizations'. Such organizations are entities which continue to exist yet fail to achieve their avowed objectives over long periods of time, thus defying the conventional economic or evolutionary assumption that failure leads to extinction or disappearance. Meyer and Zucker's main examples are taken from the private sector, but they argue permanent failure is likely to be equally common, if not more so, in public-sector organizations (ibid. 135–40). We will look more closely at the 'fatalist syndrome' in public management in Chapter 7.

What Meyer and Zucker do not discuss at any length is the effect within organizations of a widespread *perception* that survival is not linked to performance; but such a perception poses fundamental challenges to any sort of management. Indeed, it was exactly such problems (and the associated disasters of the Crimean War) that led to the famous 1854 Northcote–Trevelyan Report heralding a merit system of appointment and promotion in the British civil service. At that time, most senior jobs in the bureaucracy were filled by 'lateral entry', not career progression, and the key requirement for gaining a plum position was family and political connections. Such a system created no incentive for junior public servants to work hard or effectively, since there was no reliable link between performance and preferment in the organization. Hence there developed a corrosive culture of apathy and incompetence, of a kind very familiar in those contemporary contexts where the same practices apply—for example, the many international organizations whose heads are appointed by political power-broking, horse-trading, and patronage and those countries where top public servants gain their positions by political connections rather than by any track record of managerial competence.

A somewhat related problem can arise when public management appears to be sunk in inappropriate routines and incapable of responding to extreme events. It is an old theme of organization theory that 'organizational process defeats . . . the purposes for which organizations were created in the first place' (Meyer and Zucker 1989: 146). Stories about the handling of disasters often reveal such behaviour. A case in point is the earthquake that occurred in the Japanese city of Kobe in January 1995 and killed more than 5,000 people. In the wake of the disaster, many journalists commented on the unreadiness, the lack of planning, and lack of effective steering of the rescue efforts by the public authorities. One of them, Peter Popham (1995: 23) comments: 'There were appalling stories: the four-hour delay before the government of the prefecture despatched the necessary written request to the Self-Defence Forces (Japan's army) to take part in the rescue; the 36-hour wait before accepting the Swiss offer of sniffer dogs (it's surprising that they didn't slap them in quarantine at the airport). A British medical team was belatedly admitted, but was unable to get down to work because they did not possess Japanese medical qualifications. An operative at the gas authority, meanwhile, neglected to switch off gas supplies to the area struck by the quake—13 hours elapsed before this finally happened, by which time fires caused by broken gas-pipes were raging out of control across the city.' The underlying problem in such cases is passivity and unwillingness to abandon normal routines on the part of public organizations, even in manifestly extreme circumstances demanding decisive action and leadership.

Lack of initiative, planning, or foresight will always count as a cardinal sin for those who see 'proactivity' as the watchword for good management and organizational effectiveness. Indeed, inaction and failure to co-operate or change course in the face of pressing demands for strategic action are often seen as the antithesis of management. But, as with the other three general types of public management failing discussed in this chapter, relative passivity or going with the flow may be seen by some as a virtue rather than a vice in some circumstances. After all, if there is, as Meyer and Zucker claim, no necessary link between organizational success and survival and no clear way of foreseeing the consequences of any management action, apathy may make sense and 'proactivity' may be as likely to lead to disaster as to success. That perspective will be explored further in Chapter 7.

## 7. Accounting for Failure in Public Management

One of the central tasks for an adequate theory of public management is to give an account of collapse and failure—currently a void at the heart of the subject. As this chapter has suggested, cultural theory has something to offer to such an analysis, by its plural account, not only of perceptions of what counts as 'failure' and what should be done about it, but also of the kind of Achilles' Heels which are built into the DNA of different organizational types. Each type of failure discussed above represents a recognizable and frequently encountered family of shortcomings, regularly appears in different guises and contexts, and serves to trigger-off ideas about how to organize to correct or avoid such failings. Indeed, if grid-group cultural theory successfully captures much of the fundamental variety of organizational 'ways of life', the sorts of problems discussed in the previous four sections ought to constitute the most-commonly encountered shortcomings in public management.

A cultural-theory perspective, as summarized in Table 2.2 above, suggests that the failures discussed above will tend to link to the four polar ways of organizing. The sort of organization that remains passive, sunk in inappropriate routines, and unable to plan or take initiative even in the face of palpable disaster is not likely (at the same time, at least) to be the same sort of organization that makes large-scale mistakes resulting from over-confidence in 'big ideas' in policy or technology that fail to take account of the whole range of human behaviour (as in the Chernobyl case, where the possibility of the plant's safety engineers turning off the automatic safety systems was not included on the 'fault tree' in the formal risk assessment). Similarly, the sort of organization that cannot settle its internal civil wars or agree on a stable authority structure may find it difficult to accumulate a large enough concentration of resources or trust to produce 'big project' disasters brought about by excessive faith in technological 'fixes'. What it is more likely to produce is socially created disasters, for instance in failures of 'caring services' where an ideology of collegiality can in some conditions prevent decisive action against errant individuals such as paedophiles in education or social-work services. Disasters brought about by excesses of zeal for some (albeit misguided) view of the common good are unlikely to be associated with the sort of organization in which everyone is out for 'Number One'. Such organizations are not likely to maintain the kind of common front needed for the creation of such disasters. The sort of collapse that sort of organization engenders is more likely to be an erosion of, or failure to support, the collective or non-market elements needed to ensure that markets and individual competition can function effectively.

The ultimate metric of organizational failure is a 'body count' and each of the four types of failure indicated in Table 2.2 and the preceding discussion can produce its toll of human life. Avoidable deaths can be caused just as much by failure to act (as in the Kobe earthquake case) as by spectacular system failures created by misplaced faith in large-scale complex project plans (as in Chernobyl-type disasters). Corruption or other ways in which individual interests are placed before overall safety can often contribute dramatically to disaster. To take a common example, lives are often unnecessarily lost from cyclones or hurricanes as a result of flying debris from collapsing buildings, which would not come apart if they were constructed according to building regulations shaped by experience of previous cyclones. Such an outcome can readily come about when construction contracts are awarded to the lowest bidder in a fiercely competitive process, creating incentives for building contractors to cut corners to avoid or stave off bankruptcy. So we can expect each form of built-in weakness built into different forms of organization to be capable of taking a dramatic toll of human life and 'public value'.

This analysis suggests that no basic form of organization is proof against collapse or failure, and that the central design problem in public management is how to organize governmental and public-service structures in a way that simultaneously avoids all of the major types of failings that human organization is heir to. That is not a new revelation for those who see 'dilemmas' or 'polylemmas' as lying at the heart of public administration and management (cf. Hood 1976; Dunsire 1978). But it does provide a distinctive way of framing those dilemmas. And it offers an antidote to the claim, discussed in the last chapter and to be examined further in Chapter 9, that the world is currently witnessing the emergence of a new paradigm for public management which can be expected to be failure- and collapse-proof.

The four-part analysis of types of failure, summarized in Table 2.2 and explored in the previous four sections, is a first step towards an account of failure and collapse in public management. Pure forms of the four polar ways of organizing may be expected to have their own inbuilt forms of collapse along the lines discussed above. But failure and collapse may also be triggered by a mixing of organizational ways of life which prevents the matching of attitudes and organizational structure needed to sustain each of the four polar types. An ostensibly hierarchist structure which in practice fails to check technically unsound plans by ambitious plant engineers (as in the Chernobyl case) can be a dangerous hybrid. So can an ostensibly egalitarian structure in which the power of the collegial group to call erring members to account degenerates into an uneasy coexistence among individuals (as in the Birmingham cancer case). Hybridity may itself be a cause of collapse. As we will see in Chapter 9, an unrecognized clash of cultures or mixture of different organizational biases seems to be one of the major triggers for several well-known mechanisms which produce 'reverse effects' in policy and organization.

# 3

## Control and Regulation
## in Public Management

'What a wonderful place the world would be,' cry the devotees
of each way of life, 'if only everyone were like us.' We can now
see the fallacy in this frequently expressed lament: it is only
the presence in the world of people who are different from
them that enables adherents of each way of life to be the way
they are.

(Thompson, Ellis, and Wildavsky 1990: 96)

The first chapter sketched out the outlines of the cultural-theory
approach and the second chapter applied it to the analysis of types
of failure and collapse in public management. This chapter aims to
explore how cultural theory can be applied to another central
problem of public management, namely control and accountability.
Specifically it aims to illuminate some of the organizational 'DNA'
from which different approaches to control and accountability can
be built.

Chapter 1 suggested each of the four polar forms of organization
is capable of supporting a broader philosophy of public management—that is, an overall perspective on how to design and operate
organization for providing public services. If each of those polar
types, summarized in Table 1.1 in Chapter 1, is associated by cultural theorists with a distinctive view of nature (both physical and
human), a view of who or what to blame when things go wrong,
how to align needs and resources and how to organize more generally, they ought to convey distinct approaches to regulation and
control also.

It is not claimed cultural theory is the only fruitful analytical base for illuminating the range of basic control systems in public management. Other generic forms of analysis, notably cybernetic theory (cf. Beer 1966; Dunsire 1978, 1990) and institutional economics (cf. Horn 1995), have major insights to contribute on this central issue too. Cybernetics, the science of general control systems, helps us to distinguish control in the sense of deliberate top-down oversight from control in the sense of any process which keeps a system in check in some way, not necessarily involving self-conscious 'controllers', and to understand the sharp limits of top-down oversight as a means of steering complex institutions (cf. Hood 1986). Institutional economics likewise directs our attention to the important difference between command-based approaches to control and controls based on market or other incentive systems,

TABLE 3.1. *Four generic types of control in public management*

Contrived Randomness
  (a) *Internal*: Organization as gaming-machine. Example: traditional tax bureaucracy
  (b) *External*: Semi-randomized state. Example: US Grand Juries
  (c) *Related doctrine*: 'Chancism'
Competition
  (a) *Internal*: Organization as arena. Example: role-antonyms like prosecution/defence, buyer/seller
  (b) *External*: Competitive provision of public services. Example: regulatory competition in EU
  (c) *Related doctrine*: 'Choicism'
Oversight
  (a) *Internal*: Ladder-of authority organization. Example: military chain of command
  (b) *External*: 'dedicated' outside review. Example: Chinese Imperial Censorate
  (c) *Related doctrine*: 'Bossism'
Mutuality
  (a) *Internal*: Collegial organization. Example: team structures like police patrol in pairs
  (b) *External*: Co-production or community organization. Example: citizen armies
  (c) *Related doctrine*: 'Groupism'

and also highlights the limitations of command-based controls. Different in their analytic axioms, what those approaches have in common is an emphasis on the importance of 'inspector free' forms of control (in the words of Beck Jørgensen and Larsen 1987: 279) and on the idea that control systems will only be effective if they can work 'with the grain' of human motivation and immanent social processes. Indeed, many of the ideas of modern management doctrine are related more or less self-consciously to these fundamental propositions.

This chapter aims to build on those important insights, by putting them together in a single framework which identifies a set of basic forms of regulation or control linked to a view of what makes different groups cohere. Four generic types of control and regulation in public management are discussed below, each of which is loosely linked to one of the polar ways of life identified by cultural theory. The four approaches are 'bossism', which is linked to control by *oversight*; 'choicism', which is linked to control by *competition*; 'groupism', which is linked to control by *mutuality*; and 'chancism', which is linked to control by *contrived randomness*. Each of these approaches to control and regulation can operate at several different levels of organization. That is, they can be applied to the ways organizations control their clients, to the way control relationships operate inside organizations, and to the way organizations are themselves controlled by external forces. Each is also capable of being linked to a broader view of good government and accountability. Table 3.1 summarizes the four types, which will be discussed below and to which we will return in Parts 2 and 3 of the book.

## 1. 'Bossism': Oversight and Review as an Approach to Control

*Oversight* is the approach to control which aligns most naturally to a 'hierarchist' world-view on public management. Control from this perspective implies a ladder of authority, conscious oversight and inspection, formal power to approve or reject, to pronounce on disputes or complaints, to forbid, command, permit, and punish. After all, the linkage of authority to scrutinize with the ability to command action or require correction is what most people mean by 'control' in ordinary English.[1] Control in that sense has to mean one person or organization lording it over another in some visible way, like the referee in a game of football or the conductor of an orchestra.

Many control processes by, within, and over, public management do indeed take just such a form. After all, much of public management consists precisely of wielding authority over citizens, from the direction of traffic by police to the more draconian exercise of state power, such as compulsory removal of children from the care of parents the state declares to be unfit to care for them. (The fact that public organizations are distinctive in exercising such powers is often said to be a reason why it can be misleading to 'read across' from market-oriented business practices to conduct of the government's business.) Whenever plans need to be checked, premises or machinery inspected, approvals obtained or judgement pronounced, government is using some form of oversight to steer society.

Frequently, too, analogous processes operate inside organizations. The stereotype of control within firms or bureaucracies is the activity of the supervisor, quality checker, or internal auditor, and control is often equated with the extent to which those who occupy such roles have a tight grip on the organization. The general approach is formalized in Susan Rose-Ackerman's (1978) hierarchic model of bureaucracy, which incorporates procedures for approval and appeal up the line to some source of higher authority and expertise. In an analysis of corruption, she argues (ibid. 182–3) that hierarchical bureaucracy outperforms both stand-alone and sequential types if the least corrupt official is placed at the top of the hierarchy, and outperforms sequential bureaucracy even if not.

Similarly, when it comes to control *over* public management, the stock image is of a battery of oversight committees, auditors, inspectors, and central agencies (for example for resource allocation and efficiency allocation, but also a range of other purposes like safety,

---

[1] As distinct from the use of the word 'control' (or 'comptrol') in Continental European administrative usage, to mean formal checking, monitoring, inspecting, or auditing without necessarily implying the existence of a workable 'effector' to bring about change if the system swings off limits. The latter is normally implicit in the English usage of 'control'.

probity, equal opportunities). At this level, the 'controllers' are legislatures, constitutional/administrative courts and tribunals, independent auditors and inspectors, higher levels of government exercising *tutelle* or *aufsicht*, international bodies like the IMF or the World Bank. Perhaps the most famous historical example of that sort of control was the Chinese Imperial Censorate, an institution which helped to keep the Chinese imperial bureaucracy in check for over a thousand years. The Censorate (which was recruited from fresh graduates who had not succumbed to the process of 'mandarinization' and excluded close relatives of high officials of the third rank, to avoid conflicts of interest (Hsieh 1925: 98)) had draconian powers of impeachment, oversight, inspection for efficiency and integrity, and investigating and criticizing the policy of the topmost officials and sometimes even the Emperor. Contemporary government is exposed to many controllers and regulators concerned with honesty, efficiency, legality, or general legislative scrutiny.

What can be called 'bossism' is a general cast of mind which links 'accountability' with a ladder of authority and responsibility, and sees control by some form of oversight as the stock answer to the many problems and failures which continually appear in public management (as discussed in the last chapter). From a 'bossist' point of view, public management cannot be said to be accountable unless there are clearly identifiable officeholders with powers to make authoritative pronouncements, approve plans and proposals, resolve disputes, inspect, investigate, audit, certify, impeach, prosecute, and punish. So whenever public management goes wrong, the answer for those of a 'bossist' persuasion will normally lie in clarifying lines of authority and increasing the scope for courts, inspectorates, commissioners or committees of the great and the good to police the boundaries of appropriateness or acceptable conduct, often with increased penalties to apply to deviants who step out of line. Without a strong emphasis on the role of formal overseers, 'bossists' expect public management to degenerate into slackness, shirking, or chaos. They will have only limited faith in relying on competition or group self-policing for purposes of control: without firm regulation, they will expect such processes to produce a descent into mutually destructive behaviour, 'races to the bottom' (for example in welfare or safety regulation among states competing for business investment), or paradoxes of self-defeating 'exit' syndromes such as those identified by Albert Hirschman (1970). The persuasiveness of 'bossism' is reflected in the pervasiveness of oversight.

Oversight and review, however, is a very general category, embracing a variety of specific types of control and regulation. One way of bringing out some of that variety (as mentioned in Chapter 1) is to slip another grid/group lens into the analysis. When we do that we can notice that one important variable element in oversight is the extent to which those subject to control are being overseen by outsiders or 'people like them' in an organizational or professional sense (or by a mix of the two). The insider/outsider element represents the 'group' dimension of organizational variety in another guise. Likewise a second key variation is the extent to which oversight works through highly specified rules of procedure that can be known in advance, or by more *ad hoc*, 'play-it-by-ear' processes. For instance, if we take an incident such as the alleged shortcomings of the UN peacekeeping force in Bosnia in the early 1990s as noted in the last chapter, there is a variety of ways in which oversight procedures could conceivably come into play, ranging from an *ad hoc* internal inquiry to international court procedures for war crimes, as illustrated in Table 3.2. The formula-based/*ad hoc* element represents the 'grid' dimension of organizational variety in another form; and when the two dimensions are combined, it is possible to capture a substantial amount of variety in oversight approaches and to track changes across the quadrants of Table 3.2

TABLE 3.2. *Reviewing military conduct: Four possible oversight systems*

| Rules of the game | Composition of overseeing group (group differentiation) | |
|---|---|---|
| | 'Insiders' (low group differentiation) | 'Outsiders' (high group differentiation) |
| Highly specified procedure (high grid) | Court martial (by military officers) | Civilian court hearing (e.g. international war crimes tribunal) |
| Ad hoc procedure (low grid) | Internal *ad hoc* inspection or review | Legislative inquiry |

as climates of received opinion alter (for example in Britain in the early 1990s the introduction of a 'lay' element in the inspection of professional services like education and police was in high favour, whereas a parallel debate in France was more concerned to achieve greater professionalism in the *inspections génèrales*). Nor is it any surprise that the most hotly debated issues about the effective use of oversight in public management tend to concern what is the best mix of 'insiders' or 'outsiders' to act as gamekeepers and what is the best mix of formality and informality.

## 2. 'Choicism': Control by Competition

Distinct from 'bossism' as a basic approach to control is what can be called 'choicism'. Choicism sees *competition* or *rivalry* as the essence of all effective control. Choicism and its emphasis on rivalry links most naturally to the individualist world-view in cultural theory. Those who believe markets will always outperform command systems in checking waste and inefficiency are obvious exponents of this familiar approach to control. From this viewpoint, effective 'accountability' in public services means making producers responsive to customers in market-like relationships, just as business firms sometimes claim to be accountable to their customers.

Like oversight and review, competition and rivalry are pervasive processes in public management which have been around long before the contemporary economics-oriented 'New Right', and are often used for purposes quite different from the stock 'New Public Management' goals of containing cost and waste and pushing up service quality. For instance, competition is a standard recipe for avoiding corruption and abuse of office derived from overconcentration of power, notably in security services (it is a common maxim that having several security intelligence forces vying for favour and attention can help to limit the risk of government becoming a captive of its praetorian guard). Both traditional and contemporary 'potentates' (like bureau chiefs or university principals) often try to keep their hold on power within their organizations by working through a 'court' in which rival courtiers need to compete for the royal ear and approval. A generation ago, Charles Sisson (1976: 252) used exactly that metaphor to describe the workings of the senior British civil service, and it is commonly observable in private business empires too.

Like bossism, competition and rivalry can also be found in public management control processes at every level. Control over clients is often achieved by making them compete with one another for grants, official ratings, and all the other things that citizens or organizations value from government. Instead (or at least in addition to) the standard business stereotype of firms competing to supply customers, public services often involve the management of competition among clients for recognition and allocation of time or facilities (as every schoolteacher knows). Indeed, competition for positions within the public service itself is often a key feature of public management, in some circumstances allowing government to mould the wider educational system of the society as well as public organizations more narrowly. Again classical China provides the leading example in the form of the world-famous 'examination hell' for civil service recruitment, originating in the Han dynasties of 206 BC–AD 220. Using competition in that way, which in the Chinese system involved extraordinary rigour in examining the literary skills of a mass of hopefuls for public office (Creel 1964: 156–7; Kamenka 1989: 32; Miyasaki 1976), came to be a standard feature of recruitment to the public services in modern times, for example in the EU today. As we will see in Chapter 5, that approach was carried to its logical extreme in Jeremy Bentham's famous proposal (in his *Constitutional Code*, begun in 1820) for a two-stage competition for public service, in which the first stage was an examination to eliminate the technically or otherwise unfit. At the second stage, those who were still in the competition would be obliged to bid against one another for how little they were prepared to accept in salaries, or how much they were prepared to pay to secure public office, or a mixture of both (Bentham 1983: 337–8). This system has been approximated for purposes such as the allocation of TV broadcasting franchises, but has never formally been put into effect for high public office as Bentham intended, in spite of the supposed vogue in recent years for competitive answers to public management problems.

Inside organizations, competition is equally pervasive as a method of control. One of the standard ways of making members of an organization loyal, eager, and hard-working is to promote systematic rivalry among individuals and work units for selection, votes, promotion, salaries, bonuses, prestige, prizes, space, equipment, resources. Murray Horn (1995: 111) puts competition among officials for promotion in the upper reaches of public bureaucracies as a much more effective way to ensure responsiveness to the needs of governments or legislatures than the sanction of dismissal, because it lays the burden of proof on the best-informed party, that is the employees, to provide evidence that they have taken every opportunity to promote the interests of their superiors (ibid. 121–2). How far such a mechanism chimes with corresponding attitudes and beliefs of an organization's members may vary according to circumstances: those recruited to the higher organizational levels in public bureaucracies (who are likely to have succeeded in competition for high grades and academic honours at school and college) may well be more predisposed to fit with such a control system than those at the bottom of the scale.

Competition is also a way of establishing control *over* public organizations, if service providers or even governments and regulators can be made to compete for custom. Competition among governments is the core of Charles Tiebout's (1956) famous theorem, one of the landmarks of the modern public-choice literature, in which the ability of taxpayer-customers for public services to switch between one jurisdiction and another can act as a check on governments, offsetting what might otherwise be a tendency for majorities to exploit minorities and for citizens systematically to misrepresent both their demand and willingness to pay for public services. The adoption of 'parent-choice' regimes in several countries in the 1980s, in which schools are made to compete for pupil enrolments, is an attempt to move closer to the Tiebout notion of competition; and the same goes for the idea of regulatory competition, for example under the 'mutual recognition' regime in the EU adopted after 1979. If customers cannot pay for public services through user charges, a choicist approach will prompt a search for producing rivalry through a voucher system rather than direct assignment of customers to a single provider.

As the examples given above indicate, competition is no more confined to the private sector than monopoly is to the public sector, contrary to what 'New Right' rhetoric sometimes implies. Nor is competition as a technique of control in public management necessarily the same as *laissez-faire*. On the contrary, active state intervention may be the only way to promote effective rivalry in service provision in some circumstances. For example, if markets for public services are dominated by organized crime syndicates operating outside the normal framework of contract law, the only way to avoid cartels and monopoly may be a highly active process of public prosecution, blacklisting of mafia contractors (cf. Jacobs and Anechiarico 1992), or even the establishment of public enterprise to compete with dominant private-market players and keep them honest, as in the Australian tradition of 'metaphytic competition' (Corbett 1965).

Like bossism, 'choicism' is a cast of mind which sees rivalry and the discipline of competition as the solution to every public-management problem, and an inclination to see all such problems as rooted in monopoly, lack of adversarial challenge, and unmerited privilege. If bureaucrats are greedy or complacent, this approach suggests, let them compete for their own jobs in restructuring or market-testing exercises. If professionals are unresponsive to their clients, ratchet up the competition for funding. If regulators are inflexible or corrupt, encourage rivalry among regulators. If privileged enterprises are complacent or rapacious, open up their markets to wider competition or at least promote comparative rating exercises so that they start to pay attention to their 'league table' position. Much of the development of 'new public management' across different OECD states in the 1980s drew in part on this sort of logic, though it was selective and combined with a heavy dose of 'bossism' too.

Sometimes, the logic of control through competition points to the creation of role-antonyms, that is, inherently adversarial institutional relationships, like prosecution and defence attorneys in criminal justice and their analogies in other fields (like landlord and tenant, producer and consumer, employer and employee). The organization of 'adversary bureaucracies' to promote rival values or challenge entrenched positions is a long-established method of bureaucratic control. Indeed, a decade or so ago the reforming 'econocrats' of the New Zealand Treasury (1987: 78–9) went so far as to propose that Cabinet portfolios be divided according to value rather than by function, with rival desiderata used as the basic organizing principle. They argued that for government to make decisions in a way that most closely reflected the preferences of the electorate as a whole required:

... the elucidation of conflict between broadly-defined *values*—those fundamental goals of any society which must be traded off; that is, the goals to which it is the Government's responsibility to assign weights reflecting the preference of the electorate. Under this schema, for example, one could postulate a policy advisory agency concerned with the goal of maximising the wealth of the economy, analysing policy from the perspective of its impact on growth; another ministry could be given responsibility for looking at policy from the perspective of equity—how is any given level of income to be shared amongst participants in the economy and how will particular policies impact on the distribution of income? Advice provided on such a basis would make explicit, at a very fundamental level, the trade-offs the Government must make ...

Like bossism, there is no single form of competition and again the grid-group lens can be used to establish some first-order distinctions. That is, we can distinguish intra-group competition from competition at large and competition following ordered procedures from competition of a more *ad hoc* nature. For example, if competition were to be used in an attempt to deal with the problem of police, as discussed in the last chapter, the rivalry involved might be within the force (for instance with large rewards to encourage individual police officers to break with the solidarist police culture and inform on corrupt colleagues) or from outside it (for instance with lateral entry competition for higher positions in the police force), and likewise the competition might be *ad hoc* or more ordered. Table 3.3 illustrates a first-order array of possibilities, and each cell could be further differentiated by looking at a second-order quartet of possible types within each quadrant.

The problem for 'choicism' as a strategy of control over public management is that competition in one dimension may not be readily compatible with choice in another. It is not always easy to combine high levels of competition inside organizations with competition among them (an issue which has been debated in the business-management literature for at least sixty years (see Huczynski 1993: 18 and *passim*)). For example, there are obvious limits to the scope for rivalry within a rowing 'eight' competing against rival boats without damaging the synchronization and co-ordination essential for a crew to achieve victory. How commonly those conditions apply in organizations providing public services is debatable, though 'choicists' will naturally minimize the extent to

TABLE 3.3. *Limiting police corruption: Four types of competition*

| Rules of the game (Grid dimension) | Locus of competition (Group dimension) | |
| --- | --- | --- |
| | Internal | External |
| Ordered | Intensify regular rivalry for competition inside the force (e.g. by making senior positions fixed-term renewable rather than permanent/indefinite) | Throw senior positions open to all comers through regular 'lateral entry' contests to cut through police 'canteen culture' |
| *Ad hoc* | Stage periodic 'Prisoner's dilemma' exercises to encourage police to inform on corrupt colleagues (e.g. to gain promotion or obtain immunity from prosecution) | Stage periodic battles between police and anti-corruption investigatory agencies (or turf wars among rival security forces) |

which competition for clients or customers among rival governments or public-service providers precludes competition at other levels.

## 3. 'Groupism': Control by Mutuality

*Mutuality* is an overall recipe for keeping public management under control which is loosely aligned to an egalitarian world-view and to an overall logic of 'groupism' in government. 'Groupists' will be inclined to reject the choicist prescription of competition and rivalry as the sovereign remedy for all public-management ills. For groupists, organizations designed exclusively along such lines will have no social cohesion, and will consequently lack the capacity to broker social compromises or even to survive when they are pitted against rival organizations in extreme circumstances. After all, stockbrokers are rarely prepared to die for the stock exchange (Farrell 1979: 333): institutions built mainly on individual exchange relations are likely to get support only for what they can 'deliver', and for so long as they do. Accordingly, the mutuality approach to keeping public management under control places heavy stress on using a group process to check individuals, for example in appraising performance or arriving at policy positions. Even—and perhaps especially—organizations at the 'sharp end' of public management, like armed forces, emergency services, or police, often rely on internal processes of mutuality as much as competition for glory or promotion. The sort of 'accountability' that such an approach will tend to emphasize is 'peer-group accountability'—that is, mutual answerability among a group of equals rather than accountability to superiors or to customers—which is a recurring theme in the literature on institutional control (cf. Hague, Mackenzie, and Barker 1975).

Like competition and oversight, mutuality in various forms is a method of controlling public management which has a long history and potentially applies at every level of organization. At the point where organizations seek to control their clients, it is common to find groups being held to account for the acts of an individual. Traditional tax collection often worked by threatening penalties against all of the inhabitants of a village for revenue deficits. In extreme circumstances law enforcement works in a similar way and threats of group punishment for individual misdeeds often figure in school discipline. The US community action programmes of the 1960s, discussed in the last chapter, were an ill-fated attempt to ratchet up collective responsibility in American urban life.

Within organizations, similar processes are also commonly observable. A classic example is the famous Chinese law of mutual responsibility requiring one official to be answerable for the actions of another, which was introduced in 1650 under the Tsing dynasty. (The idea seems to have been to prevent officials from irresponsibly recommending friends or *protégés* for state service (see Hsieh 1925: 129).) Decision-making by teams or boards, too, is a longstanding approach to administration and management, from medieval church organization in Europe to the ubiquitous boards and teams of contemporary corporate life. The contemporary Japanese *ringisei* system, a process requiring all officials involved in a decision from the lowest ranks upwards to attach their seals to a proposal before it can proceed, is a weaker variant of 'groupism' (see Craig 1975: 17–24) which is often reflected in conventions of consultation in bureacratic systems.

Indeed, within organizations structures of reciprocity and group interaction are often claimed to be a viable alternative to a purely hierarchical style of management (in which the essence of organization is conceived as akin to the relationship between principal and agent and the control system is inherently limited by information asymmetry, that is, the ability of agents to conceal or distort the information that would be needed by their 'principals' for effective control). Horn (1995: 96) argues that the institutional design of conventional public bureaucracies is impossible to understand if we assume that legislatures or top-level executives aim to maximize their short-term influence on public servants (since commonly observed features like career tenure and merit appointment systems are hard to reconcile with such a 'principal-agent' viewpoint). But he says little about the way that interactive processes within bureaucracies can be used to regulate such organizations.

Accordingly, the mutuality approach makes the give-and-take of social-group dynamics the central element of control, emphasizing those features of organizational life. That approach to institutional design is familiar in clubs and communes, monastic organization, and traditional university government. It is central to the account of organizational control in the classic account of the senior British civil service given by Hugh Heclo and the late Aaron Wildavsky (1974), emphasizing mutual rating in an 'acceptance world'. And elements of mutuality are often observed in private business organization, for instance in William Ouchi's (1993) observation that many Japanese companies aim to harness such processes by putting their executives in a shared office, without even the physical barriers that people in 'open plan' offices elsewhere typically use to separate themselves from their colleagues. Indeed, it is common for that sharing to extend to desks, with several people working at the same table, and not simply rooms. In that way, the work of each individual is subjected to continual supervision from his or her co-workers.

The logic of groupism as a method of social regulation is not confined to intracorporate relations of the kind discussed by Ouchi. It can also be applied to the control of public-service provision by society at large. At that level, the formula implies maximum face-to-face group interactions between public-service producers and clients, and indeed as far as possible a dissolution of the difference between 'producer' and 'client' altogether. Its logical conclusion, as in contemporary 'dark green' visions of public management, is a vision of decentralized community self-government, in which differences between 'politics' and 'administration' and 'producers' and 'consumers' are minimized (cf. Dobson 1990: 122–9 and Goodin 1992: 146–56). As we will see in Chapter 6, a key doctrine for minimizing producer–consumer differences is the idea of citizen 'co-production' in public-service provision, with local 'communities' given a central role in oversight. It takes its extreme form in that model of community policing in which 'citizens' and 'police' are the very same people, a 'citizen army' view rather than the military-bureaucratic vision of professional policing.

Like oversight and competition, processes of organizational mutuality can take many forms and they have both radical and conservative champions. And again we can use the familiar two dimensions to distinguish mutuality inside a tight-knit group from reciprocal influence in a wider community, and ordered relationships from more *ad hoc* ones. For example, mutuality could be used to shape the quality of a public service by *ad hoc* mutual influence within an office or work group (such as two police officers working together in a patrol car, the subject of a thousand TV police dramas), by an *ad hoc* process of mutual influence across groups (as with Bentham's (1931: 415–16) example of combining mail delivery with carriage of passengers, so that travellers work to oppose delays), by a formal process of mutual responsibility through collegial processes within an organization (such as case conferences) or broader policy community (such as community-police fora). As with oversight and competition, there is no single way to bring group processes to bear to keep individuals in check in public management.

Like bossism and choicism, groupism could be understood as a mindset disposed to see mutuality, group norms, and reciprocal processes of interaction as the solution to every public-management problem—whether it be idleness, corruption, or policy fiascos. The stock assumption is that processes of mutuality like those observed by Ouchi or Heclo and Wildavsky will always produce greater effort and corporate zeal, and telling examples, such as the culture of successful Japanese business corporations, are readily available to serve as 'proof' of such a claim. But choicists will be sceptical of such ideas, because of the demanding cultural prerequisites for such an effect—namely, a widespread acceptance on the part of an organization's members of the

TABLE 3.4. *Four forms of mutuality*

| Rules of the game (Grid) | Locus of mutuality (Group) | |
|---|---|---|
| | Within groups | Across groups |
| Ordered | Activate formal mutual responsibility processes (e.g. classical Chinese law of mutual responsibility) | Activate formalized policy communities or community fora for public services |
| *Ad hoc* | Provide conditions for *ad hoc* mutual surveillance in offices or workgroups (e.g. in Japanese open-office tradition) | Provide conditions for *ad hoc* mutual influence of clients and producers (e.g. encourage police to live in the community) |

entitlement of the collective to hold them to account and to accept the priority of group decisions over individual wishes. Bossists are likely to be sceptical for a different reason. For them, the weak point in the groupists' logic of control is the assumption that mutuality will increase productivity and effort on the basis of a culture which sees shirking as dishonourable. They will point out that in other cultural contexts mutuality can have exactly the opposite effect, of *reinforcing* patterns of idleness and disruption in an anti-management stance, and thus making workers shirk rather more as a collectivity than they would when working alone. Similarly, mutuality in police forces is often portrayed as a potent force working against what new entrants are taught in ethics classes at police college. The effect of mutuality, like competition and oversight, will depend heavily on cultural and historical context.

## 4. 'Chancism': Control by Contrived Randomness

In contrast to 'bossism', 'choicism', and 'groupism' is what can be called the 'chancist' approach to control over public management, which is loosely linked to a fatalist world-view. While the mutuality principle of control makes group co-operation the be-all and end-all, contrived randomness takes the very opposite approach, substituting 'chancism' for 'groupism'. Much less familiar than oversight, competition, and mutuality, the control strategy favoured by 'chancists' is *contrived randomness*.

The late Northcote Parkinson (1965: 74–5) once suggested a way to beat Western income tax bureaucracy. The method he proposed was to predict the average time it took your individual tax file to rise from the bottom of the tax inspector's in-tray to the top of the pile, and estimate when your file was due to be looked at. Shortly before that time, Parkinson recommended, you should send a letter to the tax bureaucracy. What the letter actually said did not matter very much. The sole reason for sending it was simply to ensure that your tax file, with the new enclosure, gets put back down to the bottom of the pile again. Repeated application of the technique, Parkinson said, could ensure that your tax file is never looked at at all.

Anyone can see that one of the logical responses by the tax bureaucracy to the tactics recommended by Parkinson is to randomize the order in which it looks at tax files. And more generally randomness in some form is widely employed as the central feature of control systems. Public service organizations often use it as a way of dealing with their clients, as in the familiar example of random breath-testing of motorists by police, random tax audits, random bag checks (rather than universal or discretionary searches) for customs or security. In such conditions, the citizen is in effect being invited to play a game of roulette with the public authorities, and the outcome will depend on how different sets of clients respond to the risks of the game.

Elements of contrived randomness also frequently appear as a control device within organizations, for instance in random internal audits or unpredictable postings. We will explore this approach further in Chapter 7. As we will see there, it means combining a structure in which decision-making involves 'dual key' operations (that is, several people needed to commit funds or other resources, or separation of payment and authorization) with an unpredictable pattern of posting decision-makers or supervisors around the organization's empire. The rationale of moving staff around in that way is to avoid over-familiarity with clients or colleagues and the idea of unannounced random checks is also to reduce the motives and opportunities for corrupt collusion. Essentially, the aim of using elements of randomness as a control device within organizations is to discourage co-operation in the colloquial German sense of the word *organisation*, which means criminal co-operation or other anti-system 'networking' activity. It brings about this effect by aiming to make organizational operation, and therefore the pay-offs of competition among those who work within it—as bureaucrats, contractors, or other functionaries—as unpredictable as possible.

Such features are commonly and even typically built into contemporary multinational corporations as part of the way they control financial or field-group operations, and their absence is often associated with major control lapses. They are also part of the underlying logic of traditional imperial or tax bureaucracies. That logic is to turn the design structure of the organization into something more like a gaming machine (a 'fruit machine', in British parlance) than the orthodox slot-machine with which 'machine bureaucracies' are often compared. Again the response to such a structure will depend on how employees view the risks to which they are exposed. Putting a damper on co-operation within and across the boundaries of organizations, by making the effects of that co-operation doubtful and problematic, may well undermine 'legitimate' co-operative effort as well as the corrupt anti-system kind, and turning organizations into a gaming machine has the potential to foster fatalistic attitudes towards the underlying control system.

The idea of 'chancism' built into the contrived randomness approach is not confined to control of clients or control within organizations. It also has some potential applicability to control of public management by society at large, by introducing an element of unpredictability into who oversees public administration and how. The archetype is the selection of public auditors (and many other public officials) by lot from among the citizenry in classical Athens to avoid politicization or organized-group capture of oversight processes. It is reproduced to some extent in the American Grand Jury system which also involves a semi-random selection process and is sometimes used for public administration functions, as in the classic case of the institutional (and physical) reshaping of the California water-supply system after World War II (Ostrom 1965). More generally, politicians and senior public servants often complain about the processes of 'random agenda selection' (Breyer 1993: 19–20) to which they are exposed in modern democracies, making it difficult for them to predict what will capture public and media attention at any one time. While such an environment may be deplored from a bossist viewpoint as undermining the smoothness and consistency of rational policy-making, from a chancist perspective random agenda selection can be viewed as serving a beneficial purpose in making politicians unable to predict the environment in which they operate, in the sense of what questions will capture public attention and consequently where the spotlight of accountability will fall.

Contrived randomness and 'chancism' is the most problematic and least-explored of the four generic approaches to control and regulation in public management that have been identified here. As we will see in Chapter 7, 'chancism' is a public management philosophy more often used as a way of understanding what the world of organizations and public policy is like than a conscious recipe for designing institutions. And it is an open question as to how far it is necessary for control operations to be truly random in a strict statistical sense to achieve the intended result provided that they are widely *believed* to be random by those affected (indeed, it frequently happens that control systems intended to follow a quite different logic—for instance of co-operation—come to be perceived by some groups as a lottery or roulette wheel in practice).

Nevertheless, the use of planned chance for control is a recipe

TABLE 3.5. *Four forms of random controls*

| Rules of the game (Grid) | Locus of random controls (Group) | |
| --- | --- | --- |
| | Within groups | Across groups |
| Ordered | Random internal inspection processes | Random selection of functionaries by lot (e.g. jury service) |
| *Ad hoc* | Semi-contrived disorganized decision processes which make it hard to predict pressure points | 'Random agenda selection' for media/parliamentary/public scrutiny of politicians and public officials |

that is seldom completely absent from public management. And as with the other three main recipes discussed here, we can apply the same analysis to differentiate the approach one stage further, distinguishing the sort of randomness that is relatively rule-bound and organized (like random tax audits) from more *ad hoc* processes (like 'random agenda selection'), and distinguishing the sort of randomness that occurs within the boundaries of a group or organization from that operating across groups or organizations. Table 3.5 illustrates some of the different types, to which we will return in Chapter 7.

## 5. Ringing the Changes: Hybrids, Variants, and Alternatives

Each of the four polar types introduced above represents a distinctive—and, if cultural theory is correct, also a viable—approach to control by, within, and over public management. The next four chapters in Part 2 will examine historical and contemporary public management ideas from each of the four main biases of cultural theory. They will develop the claim made in Chapter 1 that there is a more or less explicit public management 'philosophy'—that is, a normative and explanatory account of organizational design—linked to each of the four 'polar' ways of life identified by cultural theory.

This chapter has aimed to show the 'architectural' potential of cultural theory in public management, indicating how it can be applied to the analysis of control and regulation both at a broadbrush overall level and at progressive stages of disaggregation. As the discussion in the preceding sections has suggested, each of the polar types may come in numerous variants. A first-order differentiation of each of the four basic types into a further four-part typology was explored in each of the sections above, in each case putting an additional grid/group 'lens' into the analysis. The sixteen sub-types identified there could be further divided by the same method.

This approach accordingly enables us to work at variable levels of detail and specificity in analysing control and accountability in public management. It highlights alternative approaches to control, and can thus serve as a 'variety engine' to aid institutional design, going beyond the one-best-way reflex that so commonly finds its way into thinking about management. And it also gives us a map on which to track changes in control structures, identifying new organizational forms as variants or new applications of the basic forms. For instance, contemporary tendencies in several English-speaking countries to 'delayer' management, encourage 'lateral entry' into the topmost management positions of many public organizations, and split up monolithic bureaucracies into smaller corporate 'chunks', can be analysed in terms of the framework introduced here. Those changes downplay some traditional forms of competition within public bureaucracies (by a relative weakening of competition for promotion as the central mechanism for control in public bureaucracy) while increasing competition between the new 'corporatized' units, or between them and private providers. The same processes may reduce the scope for traditional forms of 'contrived randomness' through unpredictable postings in ramified structures, while possibly introducing new forms of it through chance interconnections between newly-separated organizations or through organizational practices in multinational corporations to which parts of public services are outsourced. Mutuality in its traditional form of collegial professional self-government may be downplayed by the assault on professional dominance in policy domains like health and education and aspirations to build up the role of professional managers against professionals, but may appear in different forms, for instance in a vogue for team structures, management boards, or 'empowered' front-line workers. Oversight in traditional forms such as all-embracing authorization regimes by central agencies may decline with aspirations to provide more scope to managers to 'add value' to public services through their own initiative, but may reappear in different forms, for instance the regulation of 'quasi-markets' (Le Grand and Bartlett 1993; Hood and James 1997). To capture the fine grain of what 'managerial' changes in public management do to control structures, we need a framework for analysis that goes well beyond conventional dichotomies.

However, the polar types which were discussed above do not necessarily exhaust the possibilities of control in public management, even when extended from four to sixteen (or thirty-two, or any subsequent differentiation) to encompass the variants of each type. It will have already occurred to the reader that those types can—up to a point, at least—be linked up with one another in hybrid forms, and even from casual observation such hybrids seem far from uncommon. For example, in budgeting or financial allocation processes, we typically encounter competition (in the form of departments or other units engaged in rival bidding) together with oversight in the form of a Budget Bureau or Finance Ministry setting the rules of the game and refereeing the play. Often, too, there may be elements of mutuality (for instance in a 'Treasury Board' or ministerial committee concerned with expenditure) and even of contrived randomness, in the form of an approach to budgetary control which consists of unpredictable responses to requests by departments for authorization of particular spending items (cf. Parry, Hood, and James 1997). The relative emphasis and detailed configuration of these types of control may alter too, for example if an emphasis on 'strategic' oversight comes at the expense of unpredictable scrutiny or long-term financial planning reduces the emphasis on 'all to play for' rivalry between the main actors. We will return to the analysis of hybrid types in Chapter 10, when we examine six pairwise combinations of the four polar types discussed here.

If cultural theory is correct, the effectiveness of any one of the types of control discussed here cannot simply be read off from any 'objective' environmental conditions. Rather, as was noted in the first chapter, effectiveness will depend on the extent to which ideas and beliefs of the participants match the institutional structure of any control system. Such congruence cannot be taken for granted, and there are often self-disequilibrating as well as self-reinforcing forces at work in regulation and control. Moreover, cultural theory would suggest that no single approach to control and regulation can ever be expected to emerge as unambiguously superior to any of its rivals. On the contrary, in the very act of becoming dominant, any one of the polar approaches discussed here might be expected to regenerate and strengthen some of those rivals, however confidently they might have been consigned to the 'dustbin of history'. This theme will be pursued further in Chapter 9, where we look critically at the widespread claim that public management worldwide is in the throes of a transition to a new global paradigm.

# PART II

## CLASSIC AND RECURRING IDEAS IN PUBLIC MANAGEMENT

As noted in Chapter 1, the four chapters in this part of the book survey a range of what-to-do doctrines about public management, loosely arranging them according to the polar types of the cultural-theory typology. The aim of this part of the book is to bring out the variety of recipes for organization in government and indicate underlying themes that tend to recur across time and space, in spite of differences in detailed context. Accordingly, we look successively at 'hierarchist', 'individualist', 'egalitarian', and 'fatalist' themes in ideas about public-management doctrine.

# 4

## Doing Public Management
## the Hierarchist Way

'You are a young man, Leon,' he told me, 'And I am an administrator. I make no bones about it. I think like an administrator, you may have noticed that I eat like an administrator, and I don't mind telling you, Leon, just between ourselves, that I even make love like an administrator.'

(Jacobson 1987: 110)

### 1. What Hierarchists Believe

As discussed in the first chapter, hierarchism is an approach to organization which is high in both 'group' and 'grid'. High group means individuals are subjected to the dictates of the institutional structure and if need be individual wishes or desires are sacrificed to the needs of the whole. Hierarchist organizations tend to put a heavy stamp on their members, and hierarchists believe that when push comes to shove the collectivity must come first and the individual is secondary. Accordingly, like egalitarians, they will tend to embrace rhetorical themes that stress the transcendence of individual by organizational interests, for instance in likening firms or states to 'families'.

High grid means people are not left to work out how to behave in an *ad hoc* way. Instead, there are general ground rules (not necessarily written down) that are widely understood. Unlike egalitarians, hierarchists believe orderly rules of behaviour and authority structures are needed to avoid chaos, and have little faith in immanent self-organizing or self-steering processes. Unlike egalitarians, hierarchists are not afraid of differences of rank or remuneration, and tend to believe that society and organizations need to be directed by appropriate authority. Some people have to be field-marshals and others ordinary soldiers. But hierarchists' belief in rule-like behaviour typically works against giving arbitrary power to those in high authority (indeed, top-level leadership is often quite weak in hierarchist organizations). The rules are there to prevent every transaction from needing to be negotiated from a blank slate, for instance in specifying what is to be worn or eaten in what circumstances, how people are to be addressed, how communications and meetings are to be handled. The rules also provide a basis for who to blame when things go wrong—whoever didn't follow the rules.

Those two themes are summarized in Figure 4.1. Put them together, and you have what has, historically speaking, been an enormously successful formula for human organization, both at the level of whole societies and of discrete institutions like churches, armies, and state bureaucracies. Every textbook on organization

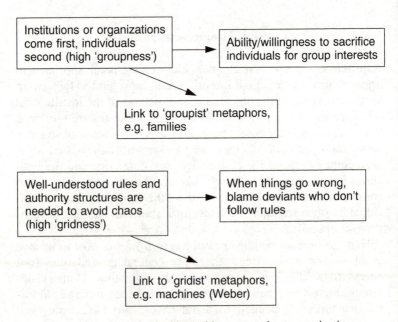

F ig. 4.1. Elements of a hierarchist approach to organization.

TABLE 4.1. *Some varieties of hierarchist organization*

| Type of group | Type of rules | |
| --- | --- | --- |
| | Immanent | Enacted |
| Task or profession-specific | Traditional professional organization | Weberian professional bureaucracy |
| Public-sector specific | Craft public-service organization | Juridified public-service organization |

theory has at least one category for hierarchism as a method of organization. The labels vary: common ones include 'machine bureaucracy', 'mechanistic organization', and 'Weberian bureaucracy'. And indeed a range of variants are possible—and commonly encountered—within a broadly hierarchist approach to organization. Some varieties of public management within this general approach are identified in Table 4.1, which distinguishes the extent to which the 'rules' are 'immanent' or 'enacted' and the extent to which the 'group' collectivity is defined in terms of a particular profession (which may transcend public and private organization) or of state service as distinguished from the rest of society. At the extremes of that categorization come the traditional professions (like law or medicine), with immanent rules of conduct and professional 'group' orientation, 'craft' public-service organization (as in the traditional British civil service), with immanent rules but a general 'state' orientation, 'juridified' public services (as in the traditional German civil service), combining a general 'state' orientation with enacted rules, and 'Weberian' professional bureaucracies (as with newer types of professions like accountancy), combining a professional 'group' orientation with enacted rules. Instead of thinking of hierarchism as a single form of organization, it may be more appropriate to think of a family of types.

Both in public and private organization, hierarchist doctrines have been heavily stressed, to the point where many people equate 'management' with a hierarchist approach and cannot conceive of how organizations or society could be 'managed' in anything other than a hierarchist way. Most US and European textbooks on public management begin the story with the development of broadly hierarchist ideas. Conventionally, the intellectual genesis is located in the late nineteenth century, with the identification of figures like Max Weber, Woodrow Wilson, or Frederick Winslow Taylor (who coined the term 'scientific management' in 1911 as a rhetorical device to lend greater authority to his ideas) as the 'founding fathers' of the subject. But fairly well-developed hierarchist ideas about how to do public management go back centuries (or even in the Chinese case more than a millennium) before what is conventionally regarded as the 'pioneer' age of Weber, Wilson, and Taylor.

This chapter looks briefly and selectively at four classic 'hierarchist' approaches to public management. Two of them (Confucian public management in classical China and the cameralist tradition of early modern Europe) rarely receive a mention in conventional public-management books. But those older traditions merit attention from present-day students of public management, and not just for pietist or antiquarian reasons. They show some of the different contexts in which hierarchist ideas have flourished, and their fate can help us to assess the strengths and weaknesses of doing public management the hierarchist way.

## 2. 'The Daddy of them All': Confucian Public Management

China, the world's most populous country, developed a public bureaucracy more complex than that of imperial Rome and more than five times larger than that of the current EU, some 2,000 years ago (see Creel 1964: 156; Kamenka 1989: 31). The structure survived in broad outline until the collapse of the Ching dynasty in 1911. Along with this remarkable system went a distinctive and enduring philosophy of public management which demands attention even in the present day, because it cuts to the heart of 'modernist' questions about what is out-of-date and what is special to our own age.

Max Weber (1948: 196), the great German comparative sociologist, distinguished 'modern' from 'traditional' bureaucracies. He claimed certain bureaucratic characteristics are only found in fully developed form in the 'modern' state (namely clearly established official duties, elaborate rules governing the exercise of authority, continuous and regular performance of tasks by staff appointed on the basis of regulated qualifications). But the Sinologist Harriet Creel (1964: 158) questioned Weber's traditional/modern distinction by claiming all three of Weber's features of 'modern' bureaucracy were in fact fully developed in Han China. She argues,

As early as the Han dynasties (BC 206–220 AD) the Chinese bureaucrat . . . depended for his professional advancement upon his evaluation by other officials on the basis of relatively objective criteria: grades obtained in examinations, experience and seniority, voluminous records of his performance in office, and merit ratings. The central government kept itself informed of local conditions by means of various systems of inspection and a voluminous flow of reports and statistics. It estimated its income and budgeted its expenditures. Like some governments of our own day, it sought to control economic activity . . .

This public management culture was intellectually self-conscious, with debates over issues such as the rival merits of rules-based versus discretion-based approaches to public service organization and the development of taxonomies of policy instruments, policy aims and criteria for evaluation, notably the 'three virtues' of straightforward government, strong government and mild government (see Kamenka 1989: 28, 33–4, and 38). And the system was robust. Imperial dynasties changed through invasion and rebellion, and the public service system was substantially modified in detail over the centuries. But 'the basic outlines of the Chinese bureaucratic system established by the Qin [221–201 BC] and supplemented with examinations and special education by the Han . . . remained those of Chinese administration for the next 2,000 years' (ibid. 32; Pye 1988: 42). Quaint and cumbersome as the system might seem today (Creel 1964: 183), it far outlasted any other system of public management yet devised and in sheer longevity was the most successful model the world has ever known.

Traditional Chinese political culture more generally has been characterized by Lucien Pye (1988: 39) as polarized between 'the orthodoxy of Confucianism and a heterodox blend of Taoism, Buddhism, and more localized belief systems'. But the public-service system largely embodied the 'hierarchist' way of life, and it was intellectually underpinned by Confucianism, which gained imperial patronage as the official philosophy during the Han dynasty.

Even the dominant Confucian tradition contained many rival schools and styles 'which provided a basis for the acceptance of an extraordinary range of individual behaviour between the extremes of engagement and withdrawal, on the part of the involved official and the withdrawn hermit, whether isolated scholar or protesting official' (ibid.). Nevertheless, the orthodox version of Confucianism contained at least seven themes which made it a definitive philosophy of hierarchist public management, offering a justification of the institutional arrangements as the inevitable product of 'reason and nature' (Douglas 1987: 45) rather than a quaint ragbag of happenstance and coincidence.

One is a view of human beings as fundamentally unequal in skill and talent, and above all in moral qualities. This proposition, anathema to egalitarians, served to justify the idea of a noble class selected on merit, the separation of social groups from one another according to highly elaborated gradations (Hsieh 1925: 40), and the subtle hierarchy of official ranks and titles. The latter was epitomized in the famous nine-grade official hierarchy introduced by the Tang dynasty in the seventh century and lasting until the twentieth.[1]

Second, human inequalities in wisdom and virtue were not claimed to be hereditary or given for all time. Those who are low in the social scale could raise their position, notably by absorbing wisdom and virtue from study, and those who are at the top might produce unworthy children or run off the rails themselves. Indeed, social corruption and degeneration were held to be most likely to develop in the upper ranks of society. On such assumptions, any system of caste, noble class, or inherited privilege is problematic, and a relatively short term of office (three years for all but the topmost offices in Imperial China), with no guarantee of re-employment, is the logical implication of the idea that ability and virtue are not necessarily enduring qualities.

Third, orthodox Confucianism suggests government can only be just when the 'artificial' hierarchy of state organization matches the 'natural' hierarchy of human wisdom and virtue. To prevent degeneration and ensure rule by the best (while they remain the best, at least), there has to be machinery for making appointments to

---

[1] Indeed, further demarcations, such as 'left' and 'right' and departmental pecking orders, applied to some officials with the same rank and title (Hsieh 1925: 116).

public office on the basis of 'merit', and for continuously re-testing fitness for office. Moreover, the most important qualities required of public managers are held not to be technical skills but high ethical standards. Ethical sensitivity is in turn held to be best fostered by studying the classics in philosophy and the humanities, not applied studies.

Such ideas served to justify the world-famous Chinese examination system first developed under the Han dynasty and relaunched in modified form under the Tang dynasty in about AD 630 (see Hsieh 1925: 180; Creel 1964: 156, fn. 6). The 'examination hell' (Miyasaki 1976) required children between 8 and 15 to memorize nearly half a million Chinese characters (the 'four books' and the 'five classics') in preparation for the civil service examinations (ibid. 16). Those Western countries which later imitated the Chinese system of examination as a method of recruitment on 'merit' for the public service adopted much less stringent systems.

Fourth, to ensure rulers put the interests of others before their own, those at the top were expected to take the blame for serious misfortunes. Chinese emperors were liable to be blamed and changed if popular satisfaction with government fell for any reason, including natural calamities (Hsieh 1925: 7). A notable variant of hierarchist approaches to dealing with system failure, this doctrine meant the failures or shortcomings of any particular emperor did not imply collapse for the institutional system as a whole, and that the official philosophy could readily accommodate whoever seized power and instituted a new imperial dynasty.

Fifth, for orthodox Confucians the relationship between state officials and the rest of the population was likened to that of parents and children (a key metaphor). The analogy was limited in that (as noted above) the 'children' were entitled to overthrow the 'parents' in some conditions, but otherwise the proper role of the mass public was held to be one of passive support of their rulers (broken by occasional violent insurrection when government failed to 'deliver'). Such a philosophy does not readily accommodate doctrines of continuous mass participation in government by the governed.

Sixth, the analogy between the state and a family was conventionally linked to advocacy of centralization of political authority (claimed to ensure peace) and of a high-discretion rather than legalistic approach to administration. That means the organization of the state officials amounted more to a 'craft public-service organization', in the terms of Figure 4.2, than to a juridified one. Stress on people of high moral character exercising discretion means the 'high-grid' element in orthodox Confucianism comes through convention and status rather than 'legislated' rules. A high-trust culture, built on continuous testing for moral qualities, was claimed to be a better basis for public management than either technical skills or fully enacted rules. 'The fact is, when a state is governed by men rather than by law, moral conduct as a quality of its workers should be above everything else' (Hsieh 1925: 125).

Seventh, it was conventionally held that no-one's authority should be absolute. 'Freedom to manage' had its limits. The powers of high officials, and even the emperor, were circumscribed by the institutional system, for example by the appointment of multiple examiners for civil service examinations, to check bias and unfairness. Though the emperor selected the best candidate in the final stage of the palace examinations in Beijing (which followed a winnowing process through provincial examinations), he could only choose from the ten candidates put forward by his fourteen assistants (ibid. 160 and 166). Similarly, the power of officials was checked by the Imperial Censorate, a powerful regulator which had the power to impeach officials, inspect their efficiency and integrity, and criticize the policy of the topmost officials or even of the emperor (Kamenka 1989: 32).[2]

As noted above, the Confucian tradition was far from monolithic and contained variants which span most, perhaps all, of the way-of-life categories of cultural theory. Moreover, classical Chinese institutions often failed to live up to high Confucian principles. Pye (1988: 40) notes the paradox that 'the mandarin elite proclaimed the Confucian creed of purposefulness in action while practicing the Taoist ideal of effortlessness, or leisurely non-effort; the masses believed in the Taoist creed of *wu-wei*, non-effort, but behaved in the spirit of diligent purposefulness demanded by Confucianism.' The mandarin system tended towards hereditary privilege when emperors gave degrees to the sons and grandsons of high officials, and the imperial Court weakened meritocracy by selling degrees

[2] To avoid conflicts of interest, close relatives of high-ranking officials could not be appointed as Censors and Censors were recruited at a low rank from fresh graduates to limit the risk of 'going native' from years of work in the bureaucratic system (Hsieh 1925: 98).

rather than awarding them on the basis of achievement (leading to the demise of the examination system in the closing years of the Ching dynasty in 1905, though it was resumed by the Nationalist regime in 1930).

Moreover, even when working 'to the book', this system of public management had some characteristic weaknesses. As in the traditional British civil service, the nature of the recruitment examinations and the subsequent system of short terms in office seems to have worked against the acquisition of technical skills and subject-matter expertise by the scholar-gentry, meaning real power was often corruptly exercised by under-clerks. (As Hsieh (1925: 179) graphically puts it, 'By excellence in writing essays, one got a degree which always brought him an appointment. But how many of the winners had learned anything about practical politics, or the art of governing? Yet, if one did not go through the grinding process of wasting his life in words and phrases, his hope of an appointment was only a hope . . .'). The narrow range of censored materials which formed the examinable corpus, together with the restrictive conventions according to which examination essays had to be constructed, meant the examination system seems in practice to have been less a test of the inherently hard-to-assess quality of ethical virtue or even intellectual adventurousness than of mechanical skills of literary composition. And the distinctive system of mutual responsibility, introduced in 1650, by which an official might be held jointly responsible for faults made by a subordinate, a *protégé* or a successor, and thus share in the blame and punishment, is said to have encouraged mediocrity, as officials 'played safe' and avoided risks (Hsieh 1925).

And yet . . . the overall institutional system had to have *something* that helped it to survive for nearly two millennia. Continuing cultural coherence seems to have been important, and one important ingredient for such coherence may have been continuing challenge to orthodoxy from a rival populist culture which 'idealized more egalitarian values, despised formal education and the pretensions of those who thought themselves to be the moral and intellectual betters of the common man, and placed great faith in elixirs and in magical slogans as formulas for political success' (Pye 1988: 39–40). As we have seen, cultural theorists stress the extent to which cultural identity is shaped by reaction against rival ways of life, and in this case there was always an egalitarian challenge to be resisted. Moreover, the institutions and ideas of orthodoxy seem to have fitted together and reinforced one another. That is, just as Confucian doctrine underpinned the institutions by offering a relatively coherent justification for their existence, so the institutional system bolstered the philosophy by making a knowledge of Confucianism essential for aspiring office-seekers cramming for their examinations, and consigning the works of rival schools to irrelevance. When parts of the system broke down and dynasties collapsed, there was a built-in remedy and blueprint for putting it back on track. When a dynasty collapsed, the successful invaders and rebels could be recognized as the new holders of the 'mandate of heaven'. When glaring corruption and serious mistakes occurred, they could be put down to the poor ethical standards or lack of wisdom of particular officials, calling for renewed efforts to make the hierarchy of the state match the natural hierarchy of human virtue, rather than to inherent defects in the system itself. Phoenix-like, the hierarchist structure could be reinvigorated by each particular failure.

### 3. The European State-Builders: Cameralism and 'Policey Science'

Cameralism is a second set of classic ideas about the art of the state which broadly fits into a 'hierarchist' frame. The term denotes a body of European public-management ideas and practices which developed from the early sixteenth century and flourished up to the early nineteenth, after which much of it suddenly disappeared from view. It is particularly associated with the German states in the era of Christian (largely Protestant) absolutism, but also developed in Sweden, Austria, and Russia.[3] Cameralist ideas about public management came largely from practitioners—those who worked as councillors, advocates, and chancellors of the post-Reformation German princely states (and, in the case of Oldendorp, one of the earliest cameralists, from the Hanseatic city-state of Hamburg).

---

[3] Raeff (1983: 29–30) also claims the Jesuit fathers who set out to establish Utopian communities in Paraguay and southern Brazil under Spanish royal sovereignty had many similarities in attitude and outlook with the ideas of the European cameralists in the late seventeenth and early eighteenth centuries, but cannot trace any direct link between the two.

Cameralism is conventionally regarded as the first attempt in modern Europe to systematize the study of public management and to try to develop 'principles' of administrative science. Curiously, even in Germany, which produced most of the cameralist writers, much of that tradition is forgotten and neglected today. But in its day it was an international movement, producing a massive literature, even by the standards of the present day (Maier 1980: 6, fn. 25), and in many ways anticipating later ideas.

The three main elements of cameralist 'science' were economics, public finance, and 'policey science' (*policeywißenschaft*). The word *policey* (later *polizei*, and conventionally translated as 'police', although that word has narrower connotations in English) is said to have been drawn from Aristotle's ideas about the conditions for promoting good order in society (Maier 1980: 25; Chapman 1970: 11). Early cameralists, like Melchior von Osse, Christian Friedlieb, Dietrich Reinkingk, and Ludwig von Seckendorff, took a view of 'good order' as denoting harmony among the various unchanging 'estates' of society achieved through feudal justice. But, paradoxically, considering its conservative social origins, cameralism later came to develop a quite different view of *policey* emphasizing the state's overarching role in transforming society, promoting general social welfare through state-led development linked to the extension of the state's administrative, economic, and military capacity.[4]

Each of the three main elements of cameralism met with a different fate. Cameralist economics, which were essentially mercantilist, were supplanted by liberal economics in the nineteenth-century German universities. Cameralist public finance, on the other hand, largely survived and developed. Even today in German public authorities the word *Kammer* still means the all-powerful finance department. But cameralist ideas about 'policey science' and the associated principles of good public management altogether disappeared from the vocabulary from the mid-nineteenth century, as a law-dominated *Rechtstaat* approach to government became the new received vision of good public management (paralleling the demise of absolutism), and as 'policey science' broke up, to

---

[4] This transformation in 'policey science' is complete with the eighteenth-century work of Johann von Justi, but the shift starts to appear long before (for example in Obrecht's *Fünff Underschiedlichen Secreta Politica* (1617) and Seckendorff's *Teutschen Fürsten-Stat* of 1656).

re-emerge later in different components and under different names such as administrative science and social policy.

Like Confucianism and the Chinese imperial system, cameralism and policey science helped to provide an intellectual underpinning for a particular type of regime—in this case, a state whose Christian princes aspired to be 'God's official' and whose fragile legitimacy rested heavily on their administrative and military capacity (Maier 1980: 149), since princely authority had to coexist with many other authorities (including the Holy Roman Empire and the free towns, as well as the nobility and the church). Accordingly, the study and development of public management developed under royal sponsorship and patronage, for example with the foundation of university chairs in Sweden, the German states, and Austria. Indeed, the Empress Catherine II of Russia (whose grandfather-in-law, Peter the Great, had developed cameralist principles in Russia with the introduction of administrative colleges or boards) herself produced a classic statement of 'policey science' in the form of her *Nakhaz*, or 'Instructions to her Civil Service Commissioners', in 1788.

It was no accident that the word 'cameralism' originates with fiscal management.[5] Just as fiscal pressure is often held to be a key 'driver' of public management reforms today, raising taxes and managing state apparatus and property was the central administrative problem for the struggling seventeenth-century German states, impoverished by thirty years of war between 1618 and 1648, much poorer than their wealthy Dutch neighbours, and vulnerable to military intervention from neighbouring great powers like France and Sweden. It was also no accident that fiscal management was linked both to economics and 'policey science', since taxability is linked both to economic prosperity and to the governability of the populace (not just in general contentment, but also in administrative infrastructure, particularly in the form of accurate population registers). The revenue-hungry governments of that time needed to develop an administrative technology for exploiting the public estate (in the form of mines, farms and forests) and for collecting taxes, especially duties like the *octrois* (town-entry taxes) which monarchs could raise without approval of the estates.

[5] *Kammer* denoted the chamber containing the king's money and was later extended to include the theories or doctrines on which tax administration rested, and to embrace state organization, economic regulation, and welfare policy as well as revenue raising and fiscal management (cf. Small 1909; Parry 1963).

The attraction of 'policey science' in such a context was that it purported to offer a design for the promotion of economic development (in the form of increasing wealth to underpin military strength) and for the construction of administrative systems which did not rely on the doubtful competence and loyalty of the traditional landed gentry. 'Policey science' itself had several components—including very broad principles of constitutional or policy design (*Verfassungslehre*), tactical 'advice to princes' (*Staatsklugheitslehre*), and more specific ideas about government and administration (*Staats- und Verwaltungslehre*). The last component, most central to public management, involved a broadly 'professional' and proto-bureaucratic vision of government. Good public management in this vision involves staffing the state bureaucracy by permanent salaried middle-class professionals, recruited by examination rather than by patronage or sale of office (as with the adoption of civil service examinations in Prussia from 1770), and with a college training in economics and public management. Professionalization goes with formalization, for good public management needs mechanisms for making sure that public officials carry out their duties properly and according to law. These themes form the intellectual background from which Max Weber (1948) drew his famous essay on bureaucracy in 1911, and anticipate the thrust of many later ideas about modern bureaucratic government.

Where the cameralists differed from later Weberian and other early twentieth-century ideas about organizational 'best practice' was their assumption that good public management would normally involve 'teams' collectively responsible for decision-making rather than single-headed hierarchies. Such structures—fashionable again today under different nomenclature—were widely used in European state administration in the early modern period and are said to have derived from the organization of the Roman Catholic church, such as the College of Cardinals, the curial organization, and the 'chapters' of cathedrals and monasteries (Johnson 1975: 20).[6] Certainly, as in other schools of thought in public

---

[6] Indeed, Raadschelders and Rutgers (1996: 71–2) argue the organization of the Roman Catholic Church formed a general model for early European public management, partly because of the Roman-law principles it embodied, notably separation of public and private, differentiation of government departments, law as the basis of supreme authority.

management, individual cameralists differed in emphasis and approach, and, as noted earlier, the meaning of 'good police' changed greatly between the sixteenth and eighteenth century. But much of cameralist 'science' rested on four key assumptions about state and society—assumptions which have often recurred more or less explicitly in later eras of public management.

First, the foundation of a strong state was assumed to lie in its degree of economic development, in the sense of overall wealth and the application of science and technology to agriculture and industry. This theme emerges explicitly in the work of the seventeenth-century cameralist Georg Obrecht, who acted as a financial consultant for the Holy Roman Emperor Rudolf II in his war against the Turks (Maier 1980: 124). Economic development was stressed because of its link with fiscal power (taxability), and also with what would today be called the state's 'human capital'. Thus Frederick II of Prussia wanted to improve the health of his peasants, not just out of royal benevolence, but to sustain an army whose strength and stamina would match that of its French, Russian, and British counterparts. Such concerns led naturally to a preoccupation with diet, agricultural development, and a general view of government as a scientific 'estate manager'.

Second, cameralists assumed economic development and social order does not happen spontaneously, but requires active management by government. Active management was needed to counter 'public sins' (identified by the early cameralist Oldendorp as religious unbelief, ignorance, and acquisitiveness) and to promote economic development. Such an assumption is a classic sign of 'hierarchism', and there are echoes of it in later ideas of state-led economic development through institutional 'miracle-workers', such as the aura surrounding the French *Commissariat General du Plan* and the Japanese MITI after World War II.

Third, it was assumed that to be equipped to promote development successfully, government needed a professional public service, unbeholden to any particular lobby or status group, and thoroughly schooled in the appropriate expertise—the sciences of public management and economic development. 'Relevant' subjects for state officials to master were defined by cameralists as administrative 'science' rather than older knowledge of feudal law for the adjudication of disputes or the Chinese emphasis on study of the humanities. The body of professional knowledge on which these technocrats' skills rested included within 'administrative science' the study of fiscal management, natural resource management (agriculture, forestry, mining, public works), and economic regulation, as well as comparative administration and administrative history. And it was held that such skills could not be picked up casually, but had to come from systematic instruction, just as in law or medicine. Hence the route to professional administration was claimed to lie through 'accredited' college classes rather than on the job (in contrast to the view that public management skills cannot be learned from books and that it is better to recruit highborn people to public and military service than the money-grubbing and politically unreliable middle classes).

Fourth, economic development was assumed to be a 'positive sum' game, from which everyone would benefit, not a process in which the gains of the winners come at the expense of the losers. As with the Confucian vision of good government, the society was portrayed as a family, indeed as a family farm, from whose development all the 'family' would benefit. Hence there could be no fundamental conflict between the 'managers' and the 'managed', and the interests of the two groups could not be separated.

These four assumptions, of course, were just what individualist liberals and egalitarian socialists challenged frontally in the nineteenth century, arguing instead that the interest of the rulers and the ruled may all too easily be diametrically opposed and that the whole problem of institutional design in government is to create structures which prevent the rulers benefiting themselves at the expense of the ruled. But they have proved remarkably tenacious. Like the Chinese ideal of meritocratic administration, cameralist themes have frequently been reinvented in later thinking about state management—for example in 'realist' international relations theory, in the idea of state-led development as the key to economic growth, in the frequent stress on improving administrative capacity, particularly for finance and revenue-raising, without questioning the broader parameters of social and political order within which public management operates, and in more general faith in strong leadership and technocracy. Indeed, though recently unfashionable, these doctrines of state-led economic development by a technocratic élite formed an orthodoxy of development nostrums for the Third World from the 1960s to the 1980s, were paralleled in socialist and communist ideas of development, and were even echoed in the vogue for *dirigisme* in some 'First World' countries too, following the French and Japanese 'miracles'.

One of the fascinating things about 'policey science' is why it achieved such impressive status and influence in its day and why much of it suddenly seems to disappear without trace in the nineteenth century. As with many public management doctrines, it seems difficult to explain either cameralism's dominance or its apparent eclipse in terms of conventional accounts of linear scientific progress. Certainly, cameralism laid claim to 'scientific' authority (albeit in the German sense of *Wissenschaft*, or organized inquiry, rather than laboratory-style experimentation), and if sheer bulk of published output is all it takes to make a 'science', it would certainly qualify. But its claim to 'science' was not unchallenged even at the time, and its propositions were based on the rhetorical device of selective examples rather than in systematic hard-data demonstration of the effects of alternative administrative design principles.

It seems more plausible that cameralist 'policey science' achieved its astonishing success because its ideas were rhetorically tuned to a particular time and space. The notion of promoting economic development and 'state-building' through a professionalized corps of middle-class technocrats fitted with the designs of monarchs who were locked in great-power conflict abroad, had good reason to doubt the loyalty and competence of their landed gentry as state officials and whose pretensions to 'absolutism' clashed with the authority claims of other institutions, notably the Church, the free cities, and the nobility. Cameralism's high-flown claims to general public interest were mixed with a programme calculated to appeal to the monarchs and the ambitions of the educated middle class, as well as providing a *raison d'être* for the cameralist professors themselves.

Equally, if we consider the dramatic apparent eclipse of cameralism in the nineteenth century, it seems hard to see that eclipse as following from some Popperian 'crucial experiment' showing the superiority of a juridical style of administration over a managerial one. There is no evidence of such an experiment, although Prussia's defeat by Napoleonic France in 1807 might be taken as a test of single-headed authority over a collegiate system (cf. Dunsire 1973: 66). Indeed, cameralism's fall from favour is conventionally interpreted as resulting not from scientific refutation but from a change in values reflected in the intellectual triumph of liberal ideas in politics and economics. The liberal slogan of the *Rechtstaat* and the development of a mechanical and rationalist 'new law' became the model for public management, with *Polizeistaat* and *Polizeiwissenschaft* altogether disappearing from the lexicon as symbols of a despised and outmoded past (Maier 1980: 5). The form of 'hierarchism' that cameralism represented waned with the development of individualist and egalitarian themes associated with liberalism and the revolutionary levelling state.

This case also suggests that cultural coherence may be important both in the demise and sustenance of received ideas about public management. Cameralism was always precarious as a public-management philosophy, precisely because its success lay in its apparent ability to reconcile opposites and present them as harmonious (the Enlightenment and absolute monarchy, conservatism and radicalism, the central state and the other bases of authority). The contradictions in 'policey science' were sharply exposed when the tide of middle-class opinion turned towards individualist liberalism.

But in another sense many cameralist ideas re-emerged in later thought about public management. One example was the cameralists' stress on group decision-making—often argued to be a device for testing assumptions and exposing possible bias and still applied in practice in many bureaucracies, including the Japanese *ringi* system in which bureaucrats collectively 'sign-off' on policy proposals. Others include the idea of state-managed economic growth and of scientific estate and forestry management, incorporating the concept of sustainable yield. Indeed, some (such as Horváth and Szakolczai 1992) have drawn comparisons between the state managerialism of the 'police science' tradition and doctrines about the role of the Communist Party in some of the post-World War II Eastern bloc regimes, and the dogmatic liberal counter-revolution in Eastern Europe in the early 1990s can also be compared with the *Rechstaat* revolution against absolutism in Western Europe in the nineteenth century. As an examplar of hierarchist ideas about state-led economic development by enlightened élites, cameralism has often been resuscitated in all but name.

## 4. Progressivism and Fabianism: 'Servants of the New Reorganization'

A third broadly 'hierarchist' strand of public-management doctrines, developing in the modern age of party competition and the mass franchise rather than in that of kings and emperors, is the faith in professional administration held by the Progressive and Fabian movements in the English-speaking world, beginning in the late nineteenth century and flowering in the early part of the twentieth. Very different in detail, what these movements have in common is a belief in what Beatrice Webb (quoted in Barker 1984: 34) conceived as a 'Jesuitical corps' of dedicated and selfless professionals to establish an orderly, well-planned world free of corruption and muddle.

Progressivism, unlike cameralism, is far from forgotten and will only be briefly discussed here. Though it is conventionally treated as a mainly US phenomenon, variants of the same ideas appeared in other English-speaking settler capitalist countries, notably Canada, Australia, and New Zealand. In the USA, Progressivism is normally interpreted as a middle-class reaction against the threat of rule by corrupt machine politicians interacting with organized crime bosses and big business 'robber barons', having as its programme three related themes: 'the elimination of monopoly capitalism by anti-trust legislation, the uplifting of the poor, and the breaking of the power of the plutocrats and bosses in government by the establishment of a merit civil service that would recruit the "college-bred"' (Merkle 1980: 20).

The Progressive recipe for good public management includes: independent regulation by enlightened technocrats; public administration as a middle-class profession rather than a set of jobs with which politicians could reward their friends and relations; and detailed procedural rules limiting opportunities for corrupt abuse of public office. In a variant of the doctrines promoted earlier by Confucians and cameralists, Progressives argued public services should be provided by professionals, normally engaged in a lifetime career, and recruited on the basis of merit and appropriate academic qualifications rather than political connections. To mark off the turf of these professionals from that of elected politicians, Progressives adopted Woodrow Wilson's (1887) famous doctrine of a 'politics–administration dichotomy'—the idea that politicians should concentrate on setting broad policy guidelines while professional managers work on the details of delivery and execution. The assumption is that representative democracy is only possible if policy decisions can be separated from management—otherwise, everything is 'politics' and the possibility of anything other than participative democracy disappears.

For Progressives, achieving greater honesty in government was seen as the route to greater efficiency:

After the muckraking of the nineties [the 1890s] it seemed clear enough that the cost of government was directly proportional to the dishonesty of politicians. Services were more expensive . . . because their accomplishment was padded with graft and corruption. Hence, 'honesty and efficiency' could lead directly to economy; an honest and economic government was obviously an efficient one; and if you could combine efficiency and economy, you could reduce . . . dishonesty. (Karl 1963: 18)

Now if a society is dominated by organized crime, a few giant business corporations and corrupt politicians aiming to use their public office for private gain, there is a certain logic in such a recipe. To dismiss Progressive ideas as outdated today (as so many contemporary 'new public management' advocates do) is to imply organized crime, political corruption, and the political muscle of giant corporations are yesterday's problems rather than those of today's enlightened times. Such a premiss is, to say the least, debatable in the light of the muckraking of the *1990s*. It is notable that Vincent Ostrom's (1974) trenchant attack on Progressivism, which he portrays as an alien import supplanting the native purity of the administrative design principles embodied in the US Constitution, makes no reference to the organized crime problem, and the same goes for Osborne and Gaebler's (1992) more recent and famous managerial attack on Progressive public administration.

What makes the Progressives' solution 'hierarchist' is its belief in certified expertise in both public and private management, by professional dedication allied to the authority of science. Progressivism embraced a faith in science in general (as did Fabianism) and notably in management science, which in that era embraced two linked elements. One was the 'scientific management' movement begun by the famous American engineer Frederick Winslow Taylor in the 1890s—a production-engineering approach to work organization which involved methodical observation and documentation of operations, and systematic measurement and central control of production processes by careful design of the physical layout of work and what we would now call ergonomics. The other was the so-called 'classical management movement', which broadly emphasized the virtues of hierarchy and specialization in large organizations and justified a role for management as co-ordinating, planning, and directing the work of those who are not managers. The two elements of management 'science' formed an orthodoxy in US public administration by the late 1930s, producing what Judith Merkle (1980) calls 'the cult of the engineer-administrator' (capable of applying technocratic politics-free production engineering skills, with objective measurement and redesign of work by managers replacing group and class conflict). The rhetorical power of that approach was reflected in the President's (Brownlow) Committee on Administrative Management in 1937 (that title itself representing an interesting transition between 'administration' and 'management' in linguistic usage).

The hierarchist ideas that this 'science' embodied were challenged politically after World War II, under the twin attack of radical fundamentalism and Chicago-school individualism, and thirty years ago were commonly held to be outmoded. 'Scientific management' was said to be out of line with modern ideas about motivation and communication as developed by the 'human relations' movement, while 'classical management' theory was challenged by the Nobel laureate Herbert Simon (1946), arguing that its principles were internally inconsistent, lacked any firm empirical background, and amounted to little more than a set of arbitrarily selected maxims and anecdotes. Indeed, the most fundamental assumption of Progressive public management—the idea that management or administration can be demarcated from politics—was challenged by political scientists like Paul Appleby (1949), who argued there can be no firm boundary line between politics and administration.

But these ideas have made a remarkable comeback in recent years. The doctrines of public-sector reform that came into currency in many OECD countries in the 1980s put heavy emphasis on the themes of scientific management, redolent of Taylor's doctrine of the worship of efficiency as a new 'civil religion' and the supersession of 'politics' by a focus on production engineering in organizational design (Schachter 1989: 111). Scientific and classical management has more academic defenders today than it had thirty years ago (cf. Drucker 1981; Schachter 1989; Hammond 1990). And the progressive public-administration doctrine of the separation of policy and administration has been revived with advocacy of processes of corporatization and contracting out which *do* imply that policy and management (or the delivery of services) can and should be firmly separated (see Overman 1984). Osborne and Gaebler's (1992) famous emphasis on the separation of 'steering' and 'rowing' in their *Reinventing Government*, while presented as an attack on Progressivism, is in many ways a reinforcement of its central doctrine.

Though rarely put into the same frame as Progressivism and developing in a different political context, the British tradition of Fabianism (which also became influential in India and other former British colonies) flourished in the same era, starting in the 1880s and beginning to wane after 1920 (Barker 1984: 28). Like Progressivism, too, the Fabian movement rested heavily on a faith in salaried middle-class professionals, and reflected a strong belief in science and disinterested professionalism, making it also distinctly 'hierarchist' in its recipes for public management.

Sometimes portrayed as the 'Boy Scouts of European socialism' (Beilharz 1992: 51), the Fabian society was founded by a group of socialist intellectuals in London in 1884. It took its title from a successful Roman general who preferred wearing down enemy forces by long-drawn-out tactics of attrition than attempting to defeat them quickly in a single decisive battle. Its aimed to follow such tactics to promote socialism (in the form of eventual state ownership of land and industry) and to reconstruct society in the light of the findings of enlightened social science. In public management, the principal early Fabian theorists were Sidney and Beatrice Webb, whose ideas on the subject appeared in their 1920 *Constitution for a Socialist Commonwealth of Great Britain*.

Like the cameralists before them, the Webbs saw states as engaged in a competitive struggle for survival. They saw government control over industry, educational reform, and the alleviation of poverty as ways of raising national efficiency to help Britain 'win the peace' after World War I, avoiding the muddle and anarchy which they saw as synonymous with unrestrained competition (Letwin 1965: 368). This rejection of spontaneous social organization or any faith in market solutions is captured by H. G. Wells (n.d.: 94) in *The New Machiavelli*: 'We got more and more definite that the core of our purpose . . . must needs be order and discipline. "Muddle," said I, "is the enemy." . . . "We build the state," we said over and over again. "That is what we are for— servants of the new reorganisation!" '

Also like the cameralists before them, the Webbs developed plans for a structure of government which elevated politics-free science and the professionalism of a small cohesive body of suppos- edly disinterested experts into a leading position, to displace the irrationality and special pleading of conventional politics. In con- trast to Joseph Chamberlain's view that democratic government meant giving voters what they wanted, 'Beatrice [Webb] preferred that social science, "a comprehensive knowledge of social facts, past and present", should come to rule' (Letwin 1965: 359). Indeed, Peter Beilharz (1992: 58) explicitly likens the Webbs' idealized view of professional experts to Georg Hegel's idea (in *The Philoso- phy of Right*) that a well-paid civil service can represent the 'general will' of society. Firmly rejecting the egalitarian socialist recipe of worker self-organization ('That the worker should decide the conditions of his work was unthinkable' (Letwin 1965: 370) ), they argued government-owned enterprises would only be effect- ive if directed and managed by expert boards, with a conventional ladder of authority reaching down to front-line workers. The boards themselves needed to be overseen and inspected, and for that purpose there would be a large expert bureaucracy (servicing legislative committees) to conduct audits, collect comparative stat- istics and undertake ratings exercises (ibid.). The salaried public- service professionals on which the whole system depended were implicitly assumed to be as earnest, selfless, and indefatigable in the pursuit of collective interest as were the Webbs themselves in following their own undeniably puritanical—and childless— lifestyle (see Barker 1984: 32–3).

To limit abuse of power and make public authority responsive to consumers in an extended state, the powers of government were to be divided up. There were to be two legislatures. One would oversee the traditional functions of government, like defence and foreign policy, which rested heavily on the traditional coercive power of the state. The other—a 'social' rather than 'political' parliament—would oversee the new and extended government functions of running the economy and the welfare state, for which the Webbs anticipated that the traditional coercive powers of the state would be largely unnecessary. Social affairs would be mainly conducted through 'non-coercive public administration' (ibid. 37), with the authority of the state further tempered by extensive social consultation in the process of policy-making.

These early Fabian ideas are, on the surface at least, unfashionable and largely forgotten today. The Webbs' imperialism and their admiration of the Soviet Union under Stalin seems anachronistic and seriously ill-judged today. The resurgence of individualist ideas about public management has prompted greater scepticism about professional experts as policy advisers and implementers, on the grounds that such experts are impossible to control if (as individualists would expect) they set out to look after themselves. The idea that experts and bureaucrats, rather than communities or front-line workers, should call the tune also sits ill with any egalitarian vision of good public management, as does the notion of government by social scientists, however well-intentioned.

Nevertheless, as with Progressivism, parts of the Webbs' recipe for public management have distinctly modern echoes. The idea of dividing the professional public service into two, with one half concerned with operational management and service 'delivery', and the other concerned with detailed regulation, inquiry, and oversight on behalf of the legislature, is heavily redolent of contemporary efforts to separate the 'regulatory' and 'service delivery' aspects of public management. The stress on applied social research as a politics-free basis for enlightened policy-making and management has frequently recurred, for instance in the foundation of the British Social Science Research Council in 1965 (see King 1997). The stress on what would now be called the 'subsidiarity principle' for the administration of the extended state, and on the importance of professional expertise in public management also links to themes which have come into prominence in the 'New Public Management' era. Much of current public management reform might be better interpreted as an attempt fully to develop the doctrines embodied in Fabian and Progressive ideas than (as they are conventionally painted) an out-and-out rejection of those ideas.

## 5. Conclusion

Hierarchist recipes for public management seem to have been dominant in thinking about the subject for much of its history. From the examination of three different strains of hierarchist public management in this chapter, three main conclusions stand out. First, hierarchist attitudes to public management are long-lived and tenacious. Those social scientists who tend to be suspicious of a stress on authority and differentiation in organization have emphasized the weaknesses and shortcomings of this style and, as we saw in Chapter 2, hierarchist organization is often said to be particularly prone to excessive faith and trust in organizational competence and inability to learn from experience. But if institutional success is measured in sheer longevity and tenacity, hierarchism as an approach to public management cannot be written off. The death of the various movements discussed here—at the hands of nationalist and later communist revolutionaries in China after 1911, the liberal *Rechtstaat* movement in nineteenth-century Germany, and the 'new right' attacking progressive and Fabian ideas in late twentieth-century USA and UK—is often exaggerated. Such ideas have a remarkable tendency to bounce back.

Second, hierarchist public management ideas have developed in very different countries and contexts, typically without very direct linkages and often as outright 'reinventions'. It is fascinating to speculate about how far Chinese administrative ideas directly influenced the cameralists, or whether there was a direct link between the ideas of the cameralists and those of the Jesuit rulers of Spanish America. But it is also possible that the ideas simply emerged independently with no direct contact, like the way football is said to have been spontaneously invented in different social contexts. Faith in professional expertise and a cohesive corps of dedicated public servants spans 'traditional' and 'modern' societies. Such ideas can also span different political programmes. They are not the exclusive property of the political 'left' or 'right' as ordinarily conceived. They have been espoused both by revolutionary socialists like Lenin (whose 1917 *What is to be Done?* is said to have been strongly influenced by the Webbs (Hobsbawm 1968: 255 fn.)) and by liberal-democrats like Woodrow Wilson, as well as by dynastic conservatives in an earlier era.

Third and relatedly, many variations on the theme are possible, as was suggested at the outset. Hierarchism is not a single organizational model but a family of related approaches, differing in the way that 'groupness' and 'gridness' are manifested. Classic Confucian ideas of good public management, involving a 'state service' group ethic but immanent rather than enacted rules of the game, developed in the context of imperial rule and a fairly static view of society and justice. Progressive and Fabian ideas developed in the context of mass-franchise democracy and a concept of the state as the key mechanism for promoting social development, and the Progressive formula involved more enacted rules and organization around professional specialisms. Cameralist ideas come midway between the Confucian and the Progressive approaches, since they are associated with the age of absolutism and began with medieval Christian ideas about harmony among estates but ended with a view of the state as a transformer of society in the name of general public welfare. But all of the three different approaches discussed here come up with the same, characteristically hierarchist, solution to the public-management problem. What they have in common is a faith in professional expertise dedicated to the collective good of society through an ethos of élite public service. The model is currently out of fashion, repeatedly challenged and prone to dramatic breakdowns, but faith in this approach is unlikely to disappear for good.

# 5

# Doing Public Management
# the Individualist Way

M'Choakumchild reported that ... she was as low down, in
the school, as low could be; that after eight weeks of induction
into the elements of Political Economy, she had only yesterday been set right by a prattler three feet high, for returning to
the question, 'What is the first principle of this science?' the
absurd answer, 'To do unto others as I would they should do
unto me.'

(Dickens 1985 [1854]: 95)

## 1. What Individualists Believe About Public Management

What can loosely be called individualist approaches to public management start from the assumption that the world is populated by
rational egoists who are bent on outsmarting one another to get
something for nothing. Rivalry and competition are central to the
individualist view of what the world of public management is and
should be like.

Taken to its logical extreme, the 'low group' character of individualism is perhaps incompatible with any sort of organization,
but we may still speak of an individualist *bias* in what-to-do ideas
about institutional design in public management. The individualist
bias embodies at least four basic propositions which contradict the
underlying assumptions of hierarchism (as discussed in the previous chapter) and of the egalitarian bias to be discussed in the next
chapter.

First, an individualist bias does not automatically begin with a view of public management from the apex of the state. It rejects the viewpoint (so to speak) of the chancellory or presidential palace and is not disposed to examine public management in the context of power-play among states (as did the cameralists or the Fabians) or even of collective perspectives like social justice. Instead, an individualist view of the public management problem is more predisposed to start 'bottom up'. That is, it takes particular concrete problems of collective action as its point of departure, like the organization of flood defences (see Hood 1986: 1–15) or the management of 'commons' such as water supply (see Ostrom, E. 1990). From such a point of departure, orthodox state bureaucracies do not necessarily form the central subject-matter of public management, since they can be seen as only one out of many different institutional ways to provide public services (and, for individualists, typically the least preferred one). Vincent Ostrom (1974: 19–20) argues that: 'When the central problem in public administration is viewed as the provision of [particular] public goods and services, alternative forms of organization may be available for the performance of those functions, apart from an extension and perfection of bureaucratic structures.' [1]

Second, instead of assuming that the interests of the rulers and those of the ruled can go together in a 'positive-sum game', an individualist bias is more likely to start from the assumption that rulers will tend to look after themselves at the expense of the ruled unless the institutions and incentive structures are very carefully engineered. To prevent the rulers from oppressing the ruled, a strong state is not necessarily a primary desideratum (as it was for the cameralists). On the contrary, those with an individualist bias towards organization may be keenly interested in ways of 'taming Leviathan' (a key focus of the 'Virginia' public-choice school: see Brennan and Buchanan 1985). A juncture of 'interest' and 'duty' can only be achieved if the rules of the game are devised in such a way that the pursuit of individual self-interest becomes identical with collective interest—an idea which was sketched by Adam

---

[1] Sproule-Jones (1982: 795) claims public choice is distinctive in employing three 'hard core' concepts: the analysis of transactions, individual preferences, and alternative institutional forms. These three elements together, but not in isolation, characterize public choice: if transactional analysis drops out, standard political science is left; if analysis of preferences is removed, standard public administration is left; if institutional analysis is dropped, standard economics is left.

Smith in his famous metaphorical concept of individual selfishness leading to social benefit through the market as if by the working of a 'hidden hand' and was elaborated for the design of state organization by Jeremy Bentham. Indeed, the bottom-up focus is epitomized in Jeremy Bentham's famous (though deeply ambiguous) slogan, taken from Joseph Priestley, that the proper basis of all morals and legislation should be the greatest happiness of the greatest number.[2]

Third, instead of assuming that economic development and social order require 'hands on' state administration guided by an enlightened technocratic élite (the guiding belief of cameralists and their latter-day equivalents), individualists will tend to assume that markets will ordinarily produce better results than bureaucratic hierarchies. A general distrust of collectivism, statism, and centralization leads those of an individualist persuasion to search for market rather than bureaucratic approaches to providing public services. In the face of most of the failures and problems discussed in Chapter 2, individualists tend to prescribe competition of some kind as the sovereign remedy. Even for those services which cannot be provided by orthodox markets because of the nature of the transaction, individualists will aim to introduce competition or market-like processes in *some* form, for example by the device of franchises or voucher systems for captive or insolvent customers (one of the cardinal doctrines of the post-World War II 'public-choice' movement).

Fourth, instead of assuming people are only corrupted by evil institutions (the central feature of the egalitarians' creed), individualists will tend to work on what Thomas Carlyle called the 'pig principle'—the assumption that human beings, from the highest to the lowest, are inherently rational, calculative, opportunistic, and self-seeking. Adam Smith argued: 'The brewer and the baker serve us not from benevolence but from self love. No man but a beggar depends on benevolence, and even they would die in a week were

---

[2] The slogan is deeply ambiguous in practice, for reasons often expounded: for example, what if the greatest happiness and the greatest number do not coincide, how do you compare happinesses across individuals or generations? Moreover, it is capable of being given an egalitarian bias to justify measures that individualists in general, and certainly Bentham in particular, would be likely to deeply disapprove of, for example in confiscating the wealth of the richest 20 per cent in society to give to the less wealthy 80 per cent.

their entire dependence on it' (Smith 1978: 493). Jeremy Bentham, the high priest of utilitarianism, took the analysis further, positing that human beings are calculating individuals who seek to gain pleasure and avoid pain and seeing political, constitutional, and administrative design as a problem of harnessing these two 'sovereign masters'. (Bentham elaborated the model with an impressive, if laboured, classification of pains and pleasures, and applied this analytic approach concretely to public management with rules for reward and principles of punishment that have seldom if ever been matched in terms of density of argument.) From this viewpoint, what is needed to tackle the public-management problem is to devise institutions that do *not* simply depend on benevolence to work properly, and in that sense 'economize on love', in a phrase coined by Sir Dennis Robertson (quoted by Buchanan 1983: 24).

These four assumptions taken together make a relatively coherent 'philosophy' of institutional design for government. It is the first two assumptions that mainly distinguish the individualist bias in public management from the hierarchist approach considered in the last chapter, and the second two which mainly distinguish it from the egalitarian approach to be considered in the next.

## 2. Individualist Approaches, Old and New

Individualist ideas in this sense have been one of the major sources of intellectual dynamism in public management over the past thirty years, and continue to be influential. That goes both for the 1980s vogue of New-Right ideological ideas about 'government by the market' (Self 1993) and for 'positive' explanations of organizational and political behaviour couched in terms of institutional economics. Such themes have been a notable growth point in public management over the past generation, in a renewed challenge to the functional-bureaucratic approach which is the hallmark of hierarchism. There is now a large group of related approaches within the individualist family, including: general theories of representative government and collective choice processes (as developed by such luminaries as James Buchanan, Mancur Olson, and Gordon Tullock); the economics of bureaucracy and budgeting (as explored by theorists like Anthony Downs, William Niskanen, Albert Breton, Patrick Dunleavy, and Murray Horn); the analysis of law, law enforcement, and regulation (including the work of Gary Becker, Harold Demsetz, Sam Peltzman, Richard Posner, and George Stigler); and analyses of the boundaries and structuring of organization, for example in 'make or buy' decisions or the use of markets versus hierarchies (notably the work of Oliver Williamson, building on that of Ronald Coase). The latter approach contains several variants which have developed into major distinct specialisms,[3] but they are related in the sense that they take the exchange or transaction as the basic unit of analysis (rather than goods/services, as in classical economics), and focus on exchange or transaction costs, involving contracting under conditions of incomplete knowledge as the central issue in organizational design.

This family of approaches to analysing organization and explaining its development contrasts sharply with the exposition of 'modern' bureaucracy by Max Weber. Indeed, it has to a large extent displaced the Weberian approach as a ruling orthodoxy for public management analysis in the English-speaking world, and to some extent beyond. It is hard to make a convincing claim to be educated in public management today without knowing something about this approach because many of the important developments in public management doctrine over recent years have come from this intellectual stable (notably the theory of performance-related pay as an optimal incentive structure for managers, coming from principal-agent theory). But for all the Nobel-prizewinning intellectual development and sophistication of the contemporary individualist world-view of public management, many of the basic *doctrinal* ideas are not new in substance. Like most what-to-do ideas in public management, many individualist doctrines of how to

---

[3] Including at least six varieties, namely: transaction cost analyses which view organizations as devices for cutting down on uncertainty and opportunism (recently developed for public bureaucracy by Murray Horn (1995) ), principal-agent analysis developed from the economic theory of the firm and focusing on problems of how managers could be prevented from shirking in conditions where corporate ownership and control were divided (Leibenstein (1976) ), theories of incomplete contracts (viewing organization against the extent to which activities can be specified in contingent contracts), property-rights analysis concerned with the difference that ownership makes over other forms of relationships, informational economics and the theory of strategic interaction in organizations.

manage public services have had a previous life and times, both in practice and to some extent in theory.

Indeed, an individualist bias in thinking about public management can be identified as far back as Spinoza and Montesquieu. Such an approach can also be found in the works of Adam Smith, the father of modern economics, and (perhaps compounded with authoritarianism, in the eyes of many commentators) in the work of the utilitarian philosopher Jeremy Bentham and his disciple, the 'administrative gadgeteer' (Finer 1952: 56) Edwin Chadwick. Of course, these earlier writers developed their arguments in a rhetorical style very different from the modernist approach of contemporary economics, using dense prose and classical tags rather than algebra and equilibrium diagrams. But utilitarian ideas about public management, largely developing out of the ideas of the eighteenth-century Scottish Enlightenment, anticipated many of the doctrinal themes associated with today's 'New Right' economic rationalists. And, like most ideas about public management, those doctrines developed as a reaction to a status quo and a prevailing orthodoxy which was seen as unsatisfactory. In large part, the utilitarian vision of public management grew out of a rejection of the cameralist doctrines of 'policey science' (the ideas of economic management and state organization that were discussed briefly in the last chapter), and in particular the implicit assumption in those doctrines that economic progress generally required state-led economic development and that the interests of the rulers and the ruled were essentially synonymous.

## 3. Recurring Themes in Individualist Public Management

One brief chapter cannot chart contemporary individualist approaches to organizational design in detail, let alone their precursors. What it can do is to pick out three recurring and (broadly) shared what-to-do ideas about the design of public-service provision within this tradition (namely ideas about how to design reward and incentive structures, ideas about how to contrive competitive provision of public services and ideas about how to constitute and operate units of administration), and explore how these themes relate to a broader individualist vision of public management.

*Reward and Incentive Structures*

For individualists, material incentive structures tend to be identified as the central design factor of public management. Since those who provide (as well as those who consume) public services are seen as broadly self-regarding and opportunistic, the most important management tool for influencing them is the design of the cost–reward structure. The assumption is that if you want to change or improve the performance of individuals in organizations, go for the 'bottom line'—what and how they are paid, or their pattern of rewards more generally.

Such an approach to public management can be traced back at least to Adam Smith (1937: 678) who declared, in one of the all-time classic dicta of public management: 'Public services are never better performed than when their [= public officials'] reward comes only in consequence of their being performed, and is proportional to the diligence employed in performing them.' Smith's underlying institutional design principle (according to Rosenberg 1960: 559) is to put each individual under an optimum degree of psychic tension, to encourage maximum effort. 'Optimum' tension comes somewhere between a level of stress so burdensome that people buckle under the pressure and a level of security so comfortable as to produce complacency. And pay on performance is conceived as a cardinal instrument for achieving that tension, by rewarding individual diligence and good performance, achieving a wider collective benefit through the pursuit of personal self-interest.

Smith stated the individualist perspective on the problem with unequalled clarity, putting personal pay and reward into the centre of the public-management problem. But he did not get past 'first base' when it came to elaborating the sort of incentive structure he advocated. He recognized some of the practical difficulties of devising performance pay systems which did not fatally distort the behaviour of those subject to them (ibid.), but did not work on the problem in any detail. It was left for Jeremy Bentham to develop the idea into systematic rules for reward in the 1820s and for Frederick Winslow Taylor to produce another twist in 'scientific payment' systems from the 1890s.

Bentham made the 'duty-and-interest-junction' principle central to his vision of good public management, producing a 'philosophy' of public-management reward structures which dwarfs most later work on this subject. The philosophy included a general preference for performance contracts rather than direct management and careful design of incentive structures by measures such as not paying profits to government companies until their other entitlements had been discharged. Edwin Chadwick followed Bentham in strong advocacy of 'piece work' payment rather than fixed salaries in public management in order to link pay to performance, and put those principles into practice in the British Poor Law Board in the 1830s (Chadwick 1854: 217).

Bentham's ideas are developed in his famous 1825 essay on 'The Rules of Reward' (Bentham 1962) and also in his *Constitutional Code*, begun in 1822. The former offered seven rules of reward, which can be summarized as follows

1. Rewards for office should be designed to make duty coincide with personal self-interest (the cardinal principle of an individualist bias in organizational design).
2. Rewards should be attached to offices to maximize the quality of service offered (a modification of the first rule).
3. No more should be paid in salaries than what is strictly needed to recruit and retain able people (a principle that might imply honorific service rather than paid work for many public offices).
4. The nominal and real amounts of salaries ought to be the same (to ensure transparency Bentham argued there should be no hidden perks or hidden deductions, for example in the form of taxes on public offices, which were common at that time).
5. As far as possible, the expenses of an office should be paid by those who are the direct beneficiaries of the service performed (for instance, professors' salaries paid by students) to ensure there are built-in performance chasers and monitors.
6. High salaries should be paid where office-holders are exposed to peculiar temptation, for example when they have substantial financial responsibility (a form of 'honesty bond' principle).
7. Retirement pensions ought to be an important part of the reward package, partly out of humanity but also to give an

extra incentive for proper discharge of duty (effectively in the form of an 'honesty bond') that salary might not provide.

Rules 1, 5 and 6 are developments of Adam Smith's ideas. Smith had advocated high pay for positions of trust (for example in the handling of money or sensitive information) and argued that in general the immediate community of beneficiaries should assume the primary burden for the provision of public services, to limit what the present-day Virginia School call 'rent-seeking' and distortion of preferences. (Hence Smith's principles lead to a preference for special-fund financing of public services through user fees rather than general fund financing out of pooled tax revenue or capital endowments.[4]) But Bentham devised some ingenious applications of Rule 1, the cardinal principle of making duty and interest coincide. Those applications included payment of salaries on a daily basis, for example to judges and professors, to ensure they actually attended at their place of work regularly (something professors are not always known for) and performance-based rewards devised with elaborate detail. Pay on performance for Bentham (as for Frederick Winslow Taylor seventy years later) was not conceived as variable pay at the discretion of the boss—the form of 'performance pay' most commonly adopted for top public servants today—but rather pay based on some objective measurement of work or results, including 'piece-work' and payment based on poundage or commission.

Rule 2 is intended to ensure quality rather than single-minded cost-cutting or mechanical provision. It is illustrated in Bentham's plan for a performance-based reward system for prison governors which included an 'insurance' principle designed to ensure that governors had an interest in promoting prisoner welfare as well as incarcerating their charges at the lowest possible cost.

The governor of the prison undertook to feed and care for each prisoner for a fixed sum, smaller in amount than the cost of transportation [to the colonies, the main alternative form of punishment in the UK at that time] or imprisonment on the old plan. In return, he was to have whatever profit he could make from the labour of the prisoners . . . Another principle, that

---

[4] When he wrote *The Wealth of Nations*, Smith was a professor at Glasgow University, which was much less well-endowed than Oxford University (where he had been a student), meaning that professors' salaries depended on fees for their classes rather than on endowments, thus creating much greater incentives for academics to be responsive to student demand (cf. Rosenberg 1960).

of insurance, was called in to make certain of the governor's interest in the well-being of the prisoners. A normal death-rate was to be agreed upon between the government and the contractor-governor, the rate to be lower than that actually existing in the old prisons. The contractor then insured the lives of the prisoners, so that he faced heavy penalties if the death-rate rose. Thus his profits would depend on his keeping the man in good health and at productive work. (Everitt 1931: 177)

The first part of the reward structure gave governors an incentive to keep costs down, but the second part gave them an incentive to avoid doing so by starving their charges or treating them with a degree of inhumanity likely to threaten their lives.

In practice, Bentham changed his position over the detail of several of these rules, for example over the principle of retirement pensions, and also had difficulty in deciding whether government ministers should be paid salaries or whether they should be hired on the principle of honorary reward (which would fit the logic of Rule 3, the salary-minimizing rule, if a stream of sufficiently able candidates would still be attracted to those positions even without a salary). The 'duty-and-interest-junction' principle led Bentham to a preoccupation with prizes and honorary rewards as a method for encouraging effort and mobilizing talent for public service at minimal cost (though in fact he kept shifting his ground on the principle of 'honorary reward' owing to the difficulties, pointed out by Max Weber a century later, of obtaining reliable work, appropriate skill levels and discipline from unpaid volunteers in public service). Indeed, like Adam Smith's famous canons of taxation, Bentham's 'rules' may in many concrete cases be contradictory, in particular the salary-minimizing rule and the duty-and-interest-junction rule. But the extent of Bentham's achievement in working out these doctrines is remarkable, because it anticipated both late nineteenth-century 'Taylorist' principles of pay for performance and ideas of optimal incentive structures in late twentieth-century institutional economics.

Indeed, Frederick Winslow Taylor took these individualist ideas about incentive pay to another stage in his famous 1895 paper on 'scientific' payment systems (Merkle 1980: 2 ff). Against the general social background of late nineteenth-century American worries about cost-cutting competition from abroad, increasing labour union organization and fears that the USA would catch the European 'disease' of class conflict by militant industrial workers,

Taylor was one of several thinkers who saw the fundamental problem as lying in the design of payment systems. His argument was that the standard 'day wage' system of that time encouraged workers to organize collectively, giving them an incentive to shirk (or 'soldier', as he called it) when working in teams, and differentiated society into antagonistic classes. Accordingly, replacement of the day wage by a system of pay related to performance was called for. Taylor was not alone in thinking along such lines. But what was distinctive about Taylor's ideas, as compared to other designs of the time for performance-related pay, was that he aimed to link performance to pay on an *individual* rather than group basis, by measuring the work effort of each separate individual. Albeit unconsciously, Taylor was building on two earlier Benthamite principles of reward, namely the 'separate work' principle (with the related assumption that work in teams inevitably meant shirking and the consequent need to devise systems that separated the individual from the group) and measured piece work, with reward related to effort or results.

What made Taylor's system distinctive from Bentham's, however, is his ideas about how those work-related rewards were to be set. The essence of his system was a variable relationship between performance and rewards: performance below a quota of the standard expected work pattern was heavily penalized by loss of earnings, while performance above that quota attracted extra pay, but at a *falling proportional rate*. The quota had to be set in such a way that workers could beat it if they worked hard or 'smart', and there had to be an incentive for going over quota. But the more they went over the quota, the more profit accrued to the employer, because the workers' wages fell proportionately relative to the extra output.[5] Accordingly, much depended on how the rate and the quota was set. But Taylor argued that adopting such a system would make everyone better off, because the removal of incentives to shirk meant workers could achieve higher wages in shorter hours. Taylor claimed to have demonstrated this principle 'scientifically', by a crucial experiment in which he reorganized the working methods of a docile and allegedly stupid worker called Schmidt in his job

---

[5] Taylor believed, just as Bentham had done, that anything over a modest (30 to 60 per cent) increase in workers' wages would tend to be spent on drink (Merkle 1980: 13)—an assumption which is perhaps more hierarchist than individualist.

(shovelling pig-iron), so that Schmidt's output rose 200 per cent and his wages 40 per cent. But Judith Merkle (1980: 28) suggests this crucial experiment may have been largely or wholly faked and indeed that some of Taylor's other experiments may have been faked too.

A third wave of enthusiasm for individualized performance-related pay in public management has come in the contemporary era (another 'reinvention' of the idea, in that it has little or no direct link to the work of Bentham and Taylor). As mentioned earlier, modern principal-agent theory, originating from developments in the theory of the firm in institutional economics (Liebenstein 1976), has produced a more formal justification for performance-related pay for corporate managers through deductive economic reasoning. But the measures it advocates, in the form of individualized performance-related pay, are not essentially different from those developed by those earlier writers (nor has it solved any of the practical problems Bentham and Taylor had to grapple with over measurement of work). Certainly, 'performance-related pay' schemes were adopted for senior public servants in a number of OECD countries in the 1980s and 1990s (ostensibly in imitation of private-sector schemes). This development constituted a 'policy boom' which combined strong faith in the merits of individualized performance-related pay as an established technique for improving public-sector performance with a complete lack of attention to the many studies giving a negative assessment of performance-related pay in contemporary public management (cf. Ingraham 1991 and 1993) or of the problematic historical record of previous attempts to pay by results.

## Competitive Provision of Public Services

Along with a preference for individually varied pay, an individualist bias in public management tends to be marked by a commitment to competition rather than ordered hierarchy in public-service provision. Such a bias leads to an instinctive suspicion of terms like 'co-ordination' or 'planning' wherever such ideas are used to argue against rivalry or competition in the design of organizations. But, as has frequently been pointed out, pure competition of the textbook type is often infeasible in public management, and there is no single all-purpose form of competition that can be used in public services.

Indeed, like the hierarchist bias considered in the last chapter, the individualist approach to public management may be better seen as a family of approaches to institutional design rather than a single one. For example, the late Kieron Walsh (1995: 46) distinguished 'quasi-markets' (limited competition within an organizational structure) and 'quasi-organizations' (cases where a market structure starts to approximate to an organization, for example through regulation) as two different forms lying between pure markets and pure organization, and Dunleavy and Dowding (1996) have also identified a range of competitive forms of provision. Some of the variety of possible types is illustrated in Table 5.1, which distinguishes six different types of competition in the supply of public services. One dimension refers to the extent to which rivalry to supply users is continuous or only periodic. The other distinguishes

TABLE 5.1. *Six forms of competition in the supply of public services*

| Relationship of user (at point of delivery) to producer | When competition occurs | |
|---|---|---|
| | Continuous rivalry | Periodic rivalry |
| The user pays directly | (1) Orthodox market competition | (2) 'Contestable markets' and franchisable user pays public services (e.g. airports, railways) |
| An independent third party pays | (3) Competitive services funded by compulsory insurance (e.g. some health-care systems) | (4) Franchisable services paid for by third parties (e.g. licensed broacasting financed by advertising) |
| The state pays | (5) Quasi-markets, league-table rivalry and 'Tiebout competition' among states or local government (e.g. rating exercises for rival service providers) | (6) 'Franchisable' services which are free at point of delivery (e.g. garbage collection; Benthamite 'patriotic auction' schemes for public office) |

cases where payment is made at the point of delivery by the user from those where a third party pays, dividing the third party into quasi-independent bodies (like advertisers or insurers) and the state.

As noted above, competition in public management can come in many different forms and at a variety of levels. Accordingly, for those with an individualist bias towards public-service organization, 'market failure' will rarely mean that all forms of rivalry are impossible. If one form of competition is infeasible for a particular public service, an individualist bias will prompt a search for another. But not all the 'great names' in individualist-type thinking about public management have advocated exactly the same doctrines of competition in public services. For example, Adam Smith in general seems to have advocated competitive provision of public services, but he did not offer the blanket 'ideological' market solutions beloved of so many of those who operate under his name today. Indeed, he argued that ostensibly competitive contract arrangements for public services might in some circumstances be much less efficient than directly managed state monopoly. In the specific case of tax administration, he argued that state bureaucracy could far outperform private franchise arrangements.[6]

On the other hand, Jeremy Bentham (who, unlike Adam Smith, had no family connection with the state bureaucracy, and hoped to take a leading role in government contracts and franchises, notably in prison management and poor relief) took the principle of competition in public services much further than Smith. In fact, he 'out-Smithed' Adam Smith on this point in at least two ways. First, he offered a broader defence of 'farming' (that is, franchising or contracting-out of service provision, along the lines of cells (2), (4) and (6) in Table 5.1), for example in showing that a general principle of contracting-out public services such as poor relief was more consistent with Smith's underlying principles than the direct government provision which Smith had advocated for tax administration. Second, and even more boldly, Bentham offered a reasoned

---

[6] Whether this uncharacteristically rosy view of public bureaucracy was coloured by Adam Smith's family connection with British tax administration is interesting to contemplate (he was, after all, the son of the Judge Advocate and Collector of Customs in the Scottish town of Kirkcaldy, and always expected to get a lucrative position in the Scottish revenue service, which he indeed secured in the later years of his life).

defence of 'venality', or sale of public offices. This idea is perhaps the high point of individualist doctrine in public management, and Bentham, except for Montesquieu, is the only major philosopher to have advocated it.

Bentham's plan was for a two-stage system of competition for judicial office, which he grandiosely termed a 'patriotic auction', or 'pecuniary competition' for positions—that is, an open competitive auction of public offices among qualified candidates. The first stage of competition was an examination to weed out the candidates who were technically or otherwise incompetent for office (the scheme was originally developed for appointments to the judiciary). At the next stage, the competition became a financial one, with the candidates invited to bid for their offices or at least to compete for who would serve for the lowest salary (what he called 'reductional' as distinguished from 'emptional' bidding), combined with bonding requirements (that is, the lodging of financial security) for positions of trust. Bentham saw this design for competition for office as one of his most original contributions to political economy. Certainly it is one of the ways in which his ideas about organization in public management diverge most radically from those of Max Weber; and it goes much further than the range of privatization doctrines conventionally argued for even by the most extreme advocates of the contemporary 'new right' (cf. Hood 1991*b*).

Edwin Chadwick, Bentham's disciple, took the argument for 'competition for the field' further than Smith or Bentham (the principle of allowing rivals to bid for the exclusive right to supply some good or service over a fixed contract or franchise period, as in the right-hand cells of Table 5.1). Chadwick first formulated this principle in 1859, anticipating one of today's key 'new right' formulae for providing public services, and also late twentieth-century ideas in economics about 'contestable markets' as an alternative to classical regulation. Chadwick argued that the principle of competition for the field under 'consolidated management' brought the advantages of competition without the waste that competition produced in conditions of natural monopoly (such as the 'network industries' like gas, water, railways). Indeed, he extended the same principle not just to natural monopolies in a narrow sense but also to any case where there were high information and search costs to consumers, for example funeral services. In principle, there was a competitive market for such services (with six undertakers available to compete for each funeral in London in the 1850s, according to Chadwick), but in practice high search costs meant there was no real competition. The result was exorbitant charges and 'home funerals' leading to health and sanitary hazards (see Crain and Ekelund 1976).

Contemporary individualist approaches to public-service provision have rediscovered most of the recipes for competition advocated by Chadwick and Bentham (with the partial exception of the 'patriotic auction' principle, which has been applied for purposes such as allocation of TV franchises, but not to open sale of public office in the way Bentham proposed). And contemporary thinkers have added others. For instance, the nineteenth-century utilitarians did not explicitly formulate what is today known as the 'Tiebout theorem' (Tiebout 1956), following a landmark paper in public choice; that is, the important idea of local governments competing for mobile taxpayer-customers in their tax-and-service mix, which has developed into broader theories of 'competitive government' (Breton 1995). And much of today's enthusiasm in public management for disaggregation of monolithic institutions into separate corporate units, 'internal markets' for services like health care and fragmentation of government seems to go well beyond what Bentham seems to have had in mind (particularly since he thought uniform specification of accounting standards was a prerequisite for effective competition).

## Other Aspects of Public Management

Relating reward to individual performance and introducing competition into the provision of public services are central to any individualist vision of public management. Individualists may also be disposed to see some aspects of private business practice as the model for government, as did Chadwick in the 1850s[7] and countless enthusiasts for 'businessizing' government ever since. They may prefer special-purpose authorities to provide public services rather than general government, as did Adam Smith, on the grounds that it is normally easier for aggrieved citizens to pursue legal remedies

---

[7] Criticizing the Northcote–Trevelyan scheme for general examinations for the British civil service, Chadwick (1854) declared: 'The proper official specialties are those which are common to private as well as public business and are for the most part derivable from the best private practice.'

against special-purpose authorities than against general government (because of the legal problems surrounding a challenge to 'policy' in the latter case). Like Smith, too, individualists may well prefer smaller rather than larger units of government, believing that large institutions are prone to inefficiency because remoteness from the general community of beneficiaries gives greater scope to senior officeholders to distort organizational activity. (Smith's analysis in *The Wealth of Nations* of the built-in institutional failings of the British East India Company, the colonial development company which came to rule India through its role as a multinational tax-collecting contractor, contains themes redolent of twentieth-century 'economics of bureaucracy' analysis, since it shows how information asymmetry coupled with a no-profit incentive structure produced an inherently inefficient and corrupt organization.) But none of these positions seem to be exclusively linked with an individualist bias towards public management. For example, hierarchists may well find aspects of private business practice to admire and egalitarians may also prefer smaller to larger units of government administration.

However, it is worth noting one well-worked-out theory of management that falls somewhere between the world-view of individualism and that of hierarchism—namely Bentham's ideas about how to achieve efficiency in organization (or, in his language, how to maximize official aptitude and minimize official expense). We have already noted how Bentham applied his 'duty-and-interest-junction principle' in designing individual incentive systems which make interest run with duty, but the doctrine of pay on performance was accompanied by a set of other management principles in Bentham's thought. Worked out almost a century before the supposed 'pioneers' of modern management thought in the late nineteenth and early twentieth century (Hume 1981: 161), some aspects of Bentham's management theory fit more closely with a hierarchist world-view than with an individualist one, but nevertheless several of its principles fit with an individualist approach to institutional design.

For instance, one of Bentham's cardinal principles was that physical design was of central importance for effective public management. Such a principle could be argued to reflect the view that, since people are assumed to be calculating opportunists (prone to shirking and malversation whenever they get the chance), the best way to limit rule violation is to shape the physical environment such that individuals have no option but to follow the rules. Such ideas are commonplace today, for instance with speed bumps and other physical alterations to road layout (rather than exhortations or speed-limit rules) as the favoured approach to 'traffic calming' in many cities. But Bentham perhaps took them to their logical conclusion with his famous 'panopticon' design for prisons (originally taken from a design for naval stores, and later also applied to the design of workhouses). That scheme, later stressed by Michel Foucault (1977) as a paradigm of a particular form of power, involved a circular design which served to separate every individual inmate from every other, thus making collusion among prisoners physically difficult while exposing all of them to inspection from a central point. (Bentham (1863: 173–248) tried without success to convince the British government of his day that panopticon-style penitentiaries at home would be a cheaper and better approach to penal policy than shipping convicts out to Australia.)

Second, Bentham laid heavy stress on transparency and publicity as a general principle of public management, and this theme also fits with individualist (as well as egalitarian) distrust of discretion in the hands of authority. Rejecting Weberian notions of 'status honour' or *noblesse oblige* among public officials, Bentham argued that 'the more closely we are watched, the better we behave' (Bahmueller 1981: title page). To prevent abuse of power by office-holders, every decision and document was to be recorded, by a registrar located in every major organization, and all secret decisions and arbitrary proceedings to be forbidden. (For example, in Bentham's proposal for a 'National Charity Company' all official business was to be done in the 'common room'.) Likewise, all fees of office and official accounts were to be published, in the most accessible form rather than in obscure language or special hieroglyphics (Bentham 1983: 265), in order to achieve maximum exposure of potential miscreants to general scrutiny—a process in which, as Bentham (1931: 410) put it, '. . . the worst principles have their use as well as the best; envy, hatred, malice, perform the task of public spirit'. Another means of opening up public management to scrutiny from as many quarters as possible, according to Bentham, was the design of multiple-use service-delivery systems. His main example was the combination of mail service and passenger transport (the post-bus principle, still commonly used today), which meant that passengers acted as *de facto* inspectors of the mail service, speeding up mail delivery by witnessing and complaining about every needless delay on the part of the driver (ibid. 415–16).

Related to transparency was Bentham's stress on what might be called (following Loughlin and Power 1992: 133) the 'accountingization' of public management—the division of public-service organization into separate cost centres, with costs and performance minutely documented. Recording, accounting, and reporting were central to Bentham's vision of good public management (as shown by the fourteen different account books he prescribed for each government department in his *Constitutional Code*); and though this principle too might be thought to have more affinity with an hierarchist world-view, much of the importance of standard reporting conventions for Bentham was to further the thoroughly individualist aim of promoting 'yardstick competition' through data which could be compared across units of management in order to produce ratings and league tables across the range of performance indicators.

A third theme in Bentham's approach to public management is the principle of separate work and of putting responsibility on to a single individual for each function rather than spreading it among a committee or board. At the same time, Bentham (and his disciple Chadwick) were wary of the consequences of giving any single individual a monopoly of any particular function through minute specialization of work, favouring instead the principle of 'consolidation' of different kinds of work (the so-called 'sundry-trade' principle). Again, the principle of individual responsibility and separate work is perhaps an hybrid of individualist and hierarchist themes, but stands in stark contrast to the egalitarian focus on group responsibility and decision-making (and indeed to the cameralist style of collegiate management as noted in the last chapter). For Bentham, collegiality and boards tended to operate in practice as 'screens', that is, devices for evading clear accountability. Anticipating one of the primary themes of classical management theory, he argued for a single responsible person in each position of authority rather than a group, on the grounds that individuals cannot shift blame onto their colleagues, cannot evade decision by non-attendance at committee meetings or abstention and can be made responsible to an outside body for everything done by the office. (Similarly, Bentham (1983: 214) argued that complication, delay, and cost would be minimized by flat 'delayered' hierarchies, without substantial layers of middle management between top officials and front-line workers.) Bentham (ibid. 174) argued that unity of authority can reduce 'delay, vexation and expense', because collegial authority was more likely to cause delay, mixed messages, lengthy debates, and quarrels. But this unqualified advocacy of 'single-seated' management is not quite consistent with another argument by Bentham (ibid. 181) that boards and committees were 'completely apt as a security for misrule'—one of the many cases in which he did not resolve the apparent contradictions among his management precepts.

As Leslie Hume (1981) points out, such principles are part of a relatively coherent theory of management—which in many ways anticipates scientific management and contemporary ideas of public management reform through cost centres and individualized pay—embedded in a relatively well worked-out philosophy of government and its place in society (stressing the importance of devising rules which ensure that the public officeholders, conceived as 'trustees', act in the interest of the citizens, conceived as 'beneficiaries'—by means such as rules for transparency, short fixed terms of office, elections, receipt of anonymous information, liberty of the press, and publication of the reasons and facts on which the laws and administrative acts are founded). Certainly, as applies to any complex thinker, Bentham's ideas cannot be fitted neatly within any single cosmology. His stress on the primacy of law and rules (opposing what he called the 'anarchical fallacy', the belief that formal rules are unimportant) might be considered more hierarchist than individualist; and his advocacy of a welfare state (rejecting the argument that poor relief should be left to private charity, which would be a 'tax on humanity'), might be considered more egalitarian than individualist. Nevertheless, what is interesting about his management theory for those who hold an individualist bias towards institutional design is that it puts into the centre of the frame individual work and reward, within a strongly competitive institutional environment, and spells out the infrastructure and institutional requirements of such a system in far more detail than is contained in most contemporary treatises on public management.

## 4. Conclusion

Like hierarchism, the individualist approach to institutional design may be better seen as a family of approaches rather than a single one. As we have seen, enthusiasm for rivalry and competition as the watchword of public-service provision does not imply a single organizational form. Franchising or outsourcing, as indicated in Table 5.1, can come in many different varieties. But franchising does not exhaust the possibilities of competition in public-service provision. Apart from institutional competition (such as in quasi-markets, quasi-organizations, overlapping bureaucratic jurisdictions, or competition by local or national governments, in fields like regulatory or tax/service policy), individual competition for public office and competition for promotion within public bureaucracies constitutes a different dimension of rivalry in public management. As noted in Chapter 3, the problem for those predisposed to individualist solutions to the public-management problem comes at the point where different forms of competition may not be compatible with one another, leading to potentially painful trade-offs. For instance, Murray Horn (1995: 111) has argued that individual competition among bureaucrats for promotion within a career civil service structure (a system derided by those like Niskanen (1971), who focus on 'monopoly bureaus') may in fact be the most potent mechanism for economizing on the legislature's costs of monitoring bureaucratic behaviour and ensuring bureaucratic responsiveness.[8] Ironically, the 'old model' of merit bureaucracy may have stronger elements of individual competition within it than the stereotype suggests.

The discussion in this chapter has suggested that individualist approaches to public management may look like another case of 'reinvention' in ideas about public-service provision. At least quasi-individualist ideas, unfashionable for much of the twentieth century in government, returned to dominate the field in many countries in the 1980s, bringing what seemed to be a new perspec-

---

[8] But, as Horn (1995: 129–30) comes close to pointing out, the way that rivalry between bureaucrats works may be indeterminate from an orthodox rational choice perspective. The working out of such rivalry is likely to be mediated by culture, in that we might expect collusion within an egalitarian culture and excessive rivalry, perhaps carried to the institutionally damaging extent of sabotaging the work of potential rivals for promotion, in a truly individualist culture.

tive on the subject. Much of that 'novelty', however, seems to have come from the application of a 'modernist' style, with the elaboration of metaphors drawn from mathematics in the form of algebra and geometry, rather than in the underlying content of the ideas (cf. McCloskey 1985). To make that observation is not to dismiss metaphorical elaboration as a form of intellectual innovation, simply to note that the public-management doctrines that have been drawn out of the apparently fresh ideas of the contemporary Chicago School and Virginia School had well-developed nineteenth-century precursors, even though the style of argument was rather different. Moreover, the contemporary relaunch of individualist ideas with fresh metaphors for new times seems to fit better with the rhetorical account of public-management development sketched out in Chapter 1 (and to which we return in Chapter 9) than the notion of linear scientific progress with each generation standing 'on the shoulders of giants' of an earlier era.

As with the case of cameralism, briefly discussed in the last chapter, the apparent disappearance of the earlier tradition of individualist writing about public management may simply show that 'nothing fails like success', in the sense that many of the ideas of nineteenth-century utilitarians were received into official doctrine in many countries, notably the idea of a welfare state built on the Benthamite principle of 'less eligibility' (i.e. the idea that individuals supported by state welfare needed to be worse-off than the 'working poor', to preserve incentives to work). But many were not, particularly in the field of public-service payment systems. Accordingly, the waning of the approach after its nineteenth-century peak must either be put down to disappointing practical experience with schemes like pay-for-performance in public services or, more generally, that the approach came to be 'out of tune with the times' in the sense that it did not match the collectivist (often quasi-militarist) culture that dominated thinking about public management for most of the first half of the twentieth century. But the current revival of fashion for individualist themes in public-management doctrine suggests that, for some at least, the tune has regained its appeal.

# 6

# Doing Public Management
the Egalitarian Way

At Oodnadatta, after Sir Alex Snedden had delivered a
famous speech in defence of formal grammar, insisting that
the paragraph was the last bastion of civil discourse, the Students' Union banned punctuation and declared every day
until the end of the century a Day of Outrage.

(Jacobson 1987: 261)

## 1. What Egalitarians Believe

Egalitarians believe 'management' in the conventional stereotyped
sense of overpaid power-suited executives organizing everyone
else, is not a solution for making public services work properly.
Rather, it is part of the problem. The solution for egalitarians is to
find ways of 'managing without managers', to use the title of an
iconoclastic book by Shan Martin (1983).

Richard Rose and Guy Peters (1978: 217) quote Assar
Lindbeck's remark that 'it may be possible to make a strong case
against either markets or bureaucratic systems, but if we are against
*both* we are in trouble'. But egalitarians are indeed against both.
They deny the conventional assumption in social science that organizational design comes down to an ineluctable choice between
conventional markets or orthodox hierarchies. Instead, communitarianism and participative organization, in the form of radically
decentralized self-governing units rather than conventional
large-scale state structures are believed by egalitarians to be a
distinctive alternative. Perhaps predictably, that alternative started

to come back into fashion in the 1990s as a reaction against the 1980s vogue for individualist doctrines of 'government by the market'.

Like hierarchism and individualism, egalitarian forms of organization come in several variants. One variant currently figures large in international development literature, as a backlash against the 'hard market' approaches fostered by the World Bank in the 1980s. It is epitomized in the 'Sustainable Human Development' approach, much in vogue with the UNDP and international development agencies in the 1990s (cf. Speth 1994), which advocates the 'empowerment' of supposedly solidary poor communities through participation and bottom-up decision-making over aid projects in developing countries (quite what happens when poor communities are not solidary, participation is weak or biased, or entrenched local power structures run clean counter to these lofty ideals, tends not to be discussed in official literature). Such doctrines have also re-emerged in domestic policy debates in developed countries, also as a reaction against 1980s individualism. One example is Amitai Etzioni's (1993: 249) *The Spirit of Community*, which argues for a high-participation approach to public life: 'Individuals' rights are to be matched with social responsibilities. If people want to be tried before juries of their peers, they must be willing to serve on them . . . Voting is not enough.' Etzioni's communitarianism is by no means a pure or radical form of egalitarianism (as we shall see, contemporary 'dark greens' and some radical feminists push the logic far further), but the stress on mutuality and participation and the hostility to government 'usurping' community functions are distinctly egalitarian themes. Even in mainstream management literature, a weak egalitarian strain is detectable in currently fashionable ideas such as empowerment of front-line staff, 'hot desking' and team-working, and a stronger one in William Ouchi's (1980) analysis of 'clan' structures of organization as alternatives to conventional lines of corporate command.

When things go wrong in public management (as in the sample of failings which was discussed in Chapter 2), egalitarians tend to see the root of the problem as the self-serving behaviour of those at the top of big organizations. From this perspective, it is the gulf between the amoral and manipulative 'executive suite' level of big corporate structures and the virtuous but oppressed organizational rank-and-file or surrounding community that corrupts the whole structure and leads to fiascos. So egalitarian recipes for better public management normally consist of more group participation to limit the large-scale errors and damaging power-plays that conventional hierarchist organization is believed to foster. The preferred recipe for making individuals respond to the needs of the institution or community is to use group solidarity more than top-down restraint. After all, if everyday public management works mainly through the 'subsidiarity principle' (that is, providing as many public services as possible through low-level organizations, voluntary organizations, self-help associations rather than central state bureaucracies), those who do not share the faith can always move to different forms of organization. The problem for egalitarians comes in conditions where expulsion or small-scale organization, or both, is inherently difficult.

Like individualism and hierarchism, egalitarianism embodies a particular vision of control of public management both within organizations and by the society at large, as was sketched out in Chapter 3. That approach to organization can be linked to a broader vision of good government, which takes 'groupism' rather than 'bossism', 'choicism' or 'chancism' as the point of departure or central organizing principle for co-operative behaviour. The egalitarian approach to organization involves at least three closely interrelated elements. They are group self-management, control by mutuality, and maximum face-to-face accountability.

### Group Self-Management

Egalitarians share with individualists a distaste for 'statism' and professional management. Instead, they tend to prefer *group self-management*, which has at least two possible implications for public management. One is the notion that wherever possible the producers and consumers of public services should be the same people. 'Co-production' of public services means that citizens (or 'prosumers', in language used by some contemporary Green advocates (Dobson 1990: 124) ) are not passive consumers of what professionals or specialized organizations provide, but a crucial part of the production process. The egalitarian bias is to distrust professionalism in service production and to resist the conventional managerial doctrine embodied in the US Progressive-era idea of a 'policy-administration dichotomy' (as discussed in Chapter 4). The idea that democracy should be confined to the 'big issues' or general policy settings decided by the general electoral system, with policy execution and public-service organization controlled by professional managers, is anathema for those biased towards egalitarian approaches to organization. They are inclined to deny the central proposition of conventional public administration and management theory that a dichotomy between 'policy' and 'administration' or 'management' is essential to make democracy effective. Perhaps the ultimate egalitarian ideal is of what Robert Hunt (1984: 363–7), discussing the anti-bureaucratic strain of early Marxism, labelled 'democracy without professionals'.

This idea of limiting professionalism and maximizing collective citizen participation in the production of public services is a long-established one. Citizen militias rather than standing professional armies, as in the Swiss or French Revolutionary tradition, are perhaps the most important traditional form of public-service 'co-production'. The underlying idea in classical political theory is that a citizen army can avoid the development of a potentially dangerous separation between military forces and the population at large, which can lead a professional army to execute *coups d'état* against a popular government in pursuit of its sectional interest or its own vision of what good public policy should be. But there are many other forms of public-service co-production. 'Neighbourhood watch' in its various forms (that is, co-operative neighbourhood organization to watch for crime and report suspicious circumstances) and community approaches to crime prevention and control more generally, which have been widely adopted to counter the perceived failures of military-bureaucratic approaches to crime control, is another well-known case. A third example is the efforts at communal self-provision of public services that developed at the height of the 'counterculture' movement in the 1960s and 1970s, and particularly in the US 'Great Society' programme of the 1960s, as discussed in Chapter 2.

One of the more 'mainstream' examples of communitarian self-provision of that era was 'Community Free School' in Boston. CFS developed as a reaction against the perceived failings of professional educators (that is, a believed tendency for teachers to advance their own interests at the expense of their students, notably by abandoning the front line of classroom work to pursue greater comfort, fame, or fortune through research and consultancy). In a move to 'empower' parents against educational experts, CFS involved all the parents in the school as the decision-making body: 'The parents said we, and not the educators, will run the school, and three-quarters of the educators who were at the meeting left. In this way we eliminated people who wanted to be researchers, consultants, and so on' (Davidson 1983: 170). Dislike of professional domination and emphasis on participation by the affected group shows the fingerprints of radical egalitarianism in public management (though the stress on a decentralized pattern of provision is also compatible with 'Tiebout' principles of organizing public services, as discussed in the last chapter).

Just as egalitarians typically aim to minimize the distance between producers and consumers, they normally seek to limit the difference between top officeholders and the rank-and-file in organizations, and this theme is the other commonly occurring element in the egalitarian preference for group self-organization. Even egalitarians recognize there are tasks which unavoidably require some formal leadership, like chairing meetings to stop everyone speaking at once. But in such conditions, egalitarians prefer to establish leadership on terms that minimize the distance between officeholders and the rest. Typical prescriptions for limiting the differences between 'management' and 'rank-and-file' include: sharply limited terms for those in executive positions; the rotation of those positions among group members (rather than assigning positions permanently to those who show the most disposition or talent for running things—society's 'born organizers'); election and recall procedures for top officeholders rather than appointment from above for a secure term; and conditions of work that require officeholders to do their share of the organization's 'real work'— even, in some cases, expecting them to share the living conditions of those they serve. Many of these features are found in the management of traditional universities (for instance in the allocation of positions like deanships or departmental chairs), and most of them were briefly adopted by the (West) German Green party after its success in getting over the 5 per cent vote threshold to obtain representation in the federal parliament in 1983.

Clearly, a central problem for any egalitarian organization is how to limit shirking and free-riding. The ever-present risk is that, in the absence of hierarchic assignment of duties, the least-preferred kinds of work will be avoided by group members, with the result that important tasks will not be carried out. Egalitarian organizations have to counter that problem either by relying on commitment to the cause that the organization represents, or by some other incentive system. An example of the latter kind is given by the management guru Rosabeth Moss Kanter (1972: 24 ff), in an examination of 'Twin Oaks', Virginia, a US communal organization founded in the late 1960s. Each member of the organization (numbering about forty-five people in the early 1970s) had to earn every week a number of non-transferable work points, based on the number of available people and the jobs to be done. Before each work week, 'everyone ranks, in order of preference, a list of up to sixty-three tasks, ranging from laundry to morning milking to washing the supper pots. Jobs ranked one to three (the most preferred) have a labor credit factor of .9; jobs ranked four through ten have a labor credit factor of 1.0; eleven through eighteen, 1.1; and jobs ranked fifty or over carry a maximum factor of 1.5. Thus, a person assigned to less preferred work earns more credit for it' (ibid.). Returning the job preference sheets before the start of each work week itself earned work points, and after job preferences were stated there followed a complex three-day process of constructing a matrix matching members to jobs, in most cases resulting in members getting the work that they preferred. What seems to have been evolving here was something between an orthodox labour market (but without the differences in market power represented by varying investment in education and training) and administrative allocation of work, minimizing hierarchical allocation of tasks—but still leaving open the problematic issue of how work quality is to be monitored and enforced.

## Control by Mutuality

Second, the key egalitarian prescription for control within organizations is to lay stress on the process of *mutuality*. Mutuality as a polar type of control is distinguished from competition (the individualist way), regulation and oversight from the top (the hierarchist way) or by randomized processes (the 'fatalist' way, to be discussed in the next chapter). Mutuality, as briefly discussed in Chapter 3, puts co-operation into the centre of the frame as a control strategy and elevates 'groupiness' into the cardinal organizational virtue. The logic of mutuality is that organizations and public services should be run on the basis of maximum participation and minimum differentiation of rank or status, with each individual continually subjected to mutual surveillance and veto from the rest of the group.

Such processes can work at several levels. One is enforcement of collective norms through informal group criticism of and influence over individuals, as in the practice referred to in Chapter 3 in which employees are placed together in large open-plan offices in an attempt to discourage shirking, or the common practice of pairing police officers on patrol in an attempt to reduce the scope for corrupt behaviour by one officer acting alone. Alternatively, group processes can be used to check individuals in a more formal way, for example when performance appraisal is conducted by fellow-workers (or fellow-students) rather than assessed by a boss or instructor in the conventional bureaucratic style. Such practices are by no means uncommon. For the USA, Shan Martin (1983) claims that group self-organization for relatively low-status workers at the 'sharp end' of public-service delivery in practice often makes line supervisors redundant and even dysfunctional, and she gives many examples of public-service providers who are organized in that way in all but name.

Indeed, this form of organizational control is by no means limited to far-left politics of the type associated with the Chinese Cultural Revolution of the late 1960s. As noted in the discussion of cameralism in Chapter 4, the classic *collegium*, said to have originally derived from medieval church organization and widely used in Europe for organizing public administration until the eighteenth century, builds on the notion of each member having a 'seat and voice' to control the others. The same goes for the traditions of the academic world, satirized by Francis Cornford (1908: 9–10) as a structure designed on the principle of 'never allowing anyone to act without first consulting at least twenty other people who are accustomed to regard him with well-founded suspicion' (as to motives, ethics, and competence). And, as noted in Chapter 3, Heclo and Wildavsky's (1974) famous portrayal of the 'village world' of the top British civil service also depicts a system in which the behaviour of high-flying bureaucrats is controlled by continual exposure to the judgement and assessment of colleagues over a working life-time of forty years or so. 'The number of people involved is at most a few hundred, and they change but slowly. They all know or have heard of one another, and they all enjoy rating one another . . . The ratings work by slow accretion. It is difficult to get a high rating and equally difficult to lose one. But over the years events reveal to colleagues that some . . . are bright and others dull; some strong, others weak; some trustworthy and others not' (ibid. 14–15).

Such a system requires group members to accept the entitlement of the collective to hold them to account at any time and to accept the priority of group decisions over individual wishes—conditions which are not likely to be accepted by individualists or hierarchists, and which fit uneasily with 'Chicago School' ideas of public officials and bureaucrats as rational self-regarding individualists. Mutuality hardly fits into the common 'economic' notion of control over public administration as essentially a two-person game played between a 'principal' and an 'agent', but for all that, peer-group accountability is a recurring theme in the literature on public ad-ministration control and accountability. Indeed, control of this type is often identified as a viable alternative to the intractable informa-tion-asymmetry problems which otherwise beset any principal-agent model of public management (see, for example, Hague, Mackenzie, and Barker 1975 and Kaufmann, Majone, and Ostrom 1986). More generally, the boundless contemporary political-science literature on policy communities and neocorporatism puts a strong emphasis on mutuality as the central process governing complex institutional systems.

### Maximum Face-to-Face Accountability

Third, the same egalitarian logic is applied to control over organi-zations from the outside, in the form of maximum face-to-face accountability[1] of public service 'producers' to their 'clients'. The underlying idea is that 'authority resides in the collectivity as a whole, in a group of consenting decision-making individuals rather than in an all-knowing figure or in a set of elected or appointed officials' (Baker 1982: 324). Accordingly, egalitarians will tend to favour structures which not only put leaders under maximum scru-tiny from the led, but put all public officials under the strongest possible popular scrutiny. Typical parts of the repertoire include

---

[1] My LSE colleague Brendan O'Leary refers to this phenomenon as 'hyperaccountability'.

procedures for recall of officeholders by popular vote (as embodied in many of the US states), mandatory disclosure of all aspects of the conduct of public business, frequent scrutiny in community fora with strong sanctions. Maximizing outside scrutiny implies a highly decentralized approach to government, to make the distance between officeholders and citizens as small as possible.

A fourth idea often associated with egalitarianism is the view that the *process* by which decisions are reached in an organization or group is just as important, if not more so, than the *results* or outcomes in a narrow sense (cf. Kanter 1972: 3; Baker 1982: 324). That is, the achievement of the substantive policy goals of egalitarians (which might include greater income equality, gender equality in employment or even species equality in 'dark green' politics) is not held to be more important than reaching the process goal of decision-making through high-participation, weak-leadership structures. For example, an authoritarian or fascist state which successfully enforced gender equality or environmental conservation by fiat from above, accompanied by draconian sanctions, might be considered feminist or green in terms of substantive policy outcomes, but would still be anathema to egalitarians in organizational terms. Though such a propensity to hold process goals as important as substantive goals is often remarked as a feature of egalitarian ideas, it seems doubtful if such a propensity is really confined to egalitarians alone. On the contrary, it could be argued that much the same applies to all the other polar approaches to organization. After all, individualists can face a similar difficulty with the possibility that the process goal of competition might not always produce the substantive goal of choice. And those of a hierarchist persuasion may often prefer ladder-of-authority decision processes (a process goal) even when such processes work against their preferred substantive goal of orderly management of society. They are likely to have just as much difficulty with the possibility that social order might be achieved by mutuality as egalitarians will with the idea that equality might be achieved by hierarchist structures.

## 2. The Managerial Critique of Egalitarianism

Egalitarianism as summarized above is frequently satirized as a sure recipe for chaos (as in the epigraph to this chapter). As a way to organize, it tends to have powerful enemies, even—perhaps particularly—in movements aiming to improve equality of outcomes in the society at large, and goes against the grain of most management orthodoxy. Critics of organizational egalitarianism point to the many historical instances of egalitarian designs for communitarian public management that have collapsed in a heap and to the recurrent tendency of radical egalitarian forms of organization to self-destruct through splits, expulsions, and reactions against real or perceived 'personality cults'. There are plenty of nineteenth-century examples of such processes, including the 'villages of co-operation' started in New Lanark, Scotland, by the Christian Socialist Robert Owen in 1817; the wave of nineteenth-century American egalitarian communities influenced by ideas of human perfectability through better institutions as advanced by European thinkers such as Robert Owen, Charles Fourier, and Étienne Cabet (Kanter 1972: 6–9) and the famous 1871 Paris Commune that fascinated Marx and Lenin. But in more recent times the most dramatic cases have been the turmoil and disorganization of the 1960s Chinese Cultural Revolution and the communal experiments in the USA in the 'maximal feasible participation' era of the 1960s and 1970s.

The egalitarian model of organization is conventionally criticized on at least four grounds. One of the most commonly observed difficulties with egalitarian organization, stressed by critics with different cultural biases, is that such structures tend to be 'greedy' in their demands on the time of their members. Geoff Mulgan (1988: 25) claims the time and energy claims of the endless face-to-face meetings required for egalitarian decision-making accounts for 'why periods of intense politicisation tend to be short, why pure democracies often degenerate into control by self-appointed cliques and why Oscar Wilde said that socialism would never come because there are not enough evenings in the week'. A second is that the egalitarian model ignores variations in human leadership ability, condemning organizations to a 'talent lottery' in selection of top officeholders. A third, noted above, is that the egalitarian model is critically vulnerable to shirking and deadlock on the part of those who do not share egalitarian fervour for collective effort. After all, the practice of pairing police on patrol may well have the effect of *reinforcing* rather than discouraging idleness or corruption if corrupt police dominate the force. Fourth, egalitarian forms of organization are often held by those adhering to other cultural biases to be a structure quite unsuited for the complexities of modern life or to government on a large scale. The egalitarian bias towards small-scale non-technocratic organization may be adequate for a limited range of services, critics say, but it cannot be reconciled with the running of complex technologies unavoidably demanding an element of secrecy, a high degree of professionalism, and large-scale operation.[2]

Such arguments, and particularly the last, are used by Robert Goodin (1992) to attack egalitarian ideas of public organization in his well-known critique of dark green political theory. He claims (ibid. 168) the 'green theory of value' (the substantive goals about environmental protection that greens espouse) is not consistent with the 'green theory of agency' (that is, dark green doctrines of egalitarian organization). He argues that the egalitarian organizing principles espoused by dark greens—notably participatory democracy, rotation of office, radical decentralization—make it impossible to achieve the substantive environmental changes that greens demand. Specifically, Goodin (ibid. 146) argues: that rotation in office is incompatible with political effectiveness (especially if political rivals, notably the mainstream 'brown' parties, continue with permanent officeholding and the cumulative policy experience which it brings); that only centralized co-ordinating mechanisms can solve what would otherwise be the intractable problems of collective action among the decentralized communities preferred by green theorists as an alternative to large cities; and that such central co-ordination is in fact the only possible way to realize the green slogan to 'think globally, act locally' (ibid. 163).

Goodin presents his criticisms as if there could be no cultural variation in the handling of co-ordination and collective action. But his critique comes down to the unsurprising claim that it is just as possible to have a hierarchist approach to green politics as an egalitarian one (just as applies to feminism or socialism more generally). Indeed, Goodin's green hierarchism might be viewed as the environmental equivalent of Marian Sawer's (1990) defence of

---

[2] This issue is at the heart of the late Maurice Cranston's (1968: 132) imaginary dialogue between Karl Marx and the anarchist Mikhail Bakunin about how to run the railways. Cranston's Bakunin wants the railway workers to elect the guards and signallers and calls for application of the principle that 'people would take it in turns to do the work and enjoy the comfort, by mutual agreement', while Cranston's Marx argues for a much more managerial top-down approach.

hierarchist feminism through 'sisters in suits': that is, the realization of feminist goals through conventionally organized state agencies and bureaucracies, rather than the radical feminists' preferred (egalitarian) route of stateless organization in small communitarian groups. Culturally, the obvious weakness of Goodin's position is the assumption that substantive green policy goals are necessarily to be preferred to egalitarian principles of organization and that greens must necessarily be prepared to trade the latter for the former. But, as noted above, egalitarians (like the devotees of other polar ways of life) often hold process goals at least as important as end-states.

A similar point can be made about the undoubtedly high time demands made by egalitarian organizations on their members. Such demands may be a drawback from different cultural viewpoints—as in the 'not enough evenings in the week' quip noted above. But viewed from an egalitarian perspective, those demands may be an *advantage* rather than a cost, because the continuous participation is a key to self-development in learning civic skills and is an important part of what sustains an egalitarian group. So what to some might seem a 'transaction cost' might for egalitarians be more properly placed on the benefit rather than the cost side of the transactions-cost ledger. Indeed, that shows some of the difficulties in taking 'transactions costs' as a culture-free way of reasoning about organizational design. It has often been argued that one of the important effects of radical groups taking over every aspect of their member's lives and uniting them in a common lifestyle as well as a common set of goals and beliefs, is to heighten commitment and isolate members from exposure to competing ways of life (cf. Bittner 1963).[3]

Moreover, the conventional technology-based critique of egalitarianism starts from the debatable assumption that technological change is to be taken as a given and community structures as what have to be adapted. But the egalitarian approach starts from the opposite assumption. Technological changes should be selected and applied according to their ability to reduce rather than increase differences among human beings. Contrariwise, if certain types of

[3] Whether such emphasis on communal lifestyle also prevents defection, as Bittner claims, is perhaps more debatable: it may actually encourage it, by creating a highly-charged atmosphere in which accusations of betrayal of the faith and personality cults are more rather than less likely to develop.

technology (of which nuclear power is usually claimed to be the prime example) inherently require secrecy and centralization and thereby embed hierarchism, they should be rejected. Egalitarians will naturally claim that contemporary developments in society and information technology (like increasing leisure and today's 'internet society' of globalized computer networks) are inexorably working to make their preferred approach to public management ever-more viable than in the past and mean history is on their side after all.

Undoubtedly, egalitarianism as a way of doing public management has its limitations. Radical egalitarian forms of organization are indeed prone to self-destruction, particularly once an initial group of zealots draws in other participants less committed to core egalitarian values. But pure forms of the other polar approaches to organization in cultural theory tend to self-destruct too. The radical egalitarian ideal of 'democracy without professionals' may be a triumph of hope over experience. But so is the radical individualist ideal of unfettered government by the market and the radical hierarchist vision of social order created through enlightened expert regulation. Moreover, the hope keeps on coming back.

### 3. Varieties of Egalitarianism

As with hierarchism and individualism, egalitarianism is better seen as a 'family' of related approaches to organization rather than a single model. One indication of the range of types that can be found within the family is given in Table 6.1. It distinguishes those types of egalitarian organization which are devoted to a revolutionary or transformational agenda and those more oriented towards self-maintenance, and also distinguishes self-contained or sequestered forms of organization from those extending across a whole society or community. Such distinctions are admittedly crude, but it is important to stress that egalitarian forms of organization are not to be equated with socialist political views as ordinarily understood. Socialist debates about public management have always contained egalitarian voices. But if socialism is defined as the doctrine that social progress in modern capitalist societies can only occur by modifying the system of property ownership, not all socialists have advocated egalitarian forms of public management. As

TABLE 6.1. *Some varieties of egalitarian organization*

| | Change orientation | |
| --- | --- | --- |
| | Self-maintaining forms | Revolutionary forms |
| Self-contained or sequestered forms | (1) Example: Traditional *collegia* (e.g. professions, colleges, some élite clubs and communities) | (2) Example: Radical alternative lifestyle communes or service organizations |
| Community-wide or whole-society forms | (3) Example: Privileged élite democratic communities (e.g. government of classical Athens) | (4) Example: Transformational whole-society organization (e.g. Chinese Cultural Revolution) |

we saw in Chapter 4, the Fabians who founded the LSE in the 1890s had a relatively hierarchist view of how the state should be organized, and the same goes for the administrative architecture of the former communist states against which the 1960s 'New Left' reacted with different visions of public organization (Baker 1982: 324). Moreover, egalitarian ideas about management often appear in rather privileged settings, not proletarian ones. Accordingly, at least two different strains of egalitarianism need to be briefly explored.

### Élitist or Sequestered Egalitarianism

As noted above, some forms of egalitarian organization are found in highly privileged or sequestered social settings, like monasteries, 'alternative lifestyle' communes or some forms of collegial academic institutions. Indeed, exclusive clubs and top residential complexes are sometimes run by their members on this basis too, with minimum internal differentiation of rank. Egalitarian groups of this type have no general 'project' for social transformation, and may simply wish to preserve their privileges or seal themselves off from the corrupting influences of the rest of society. But the markers for egalitarian organization are still there, in the form of weak leadership structures, emphasis on participation in communal activity and control of individuals through processes of mutuality.

One classic case (cell (3) in Table 6.1) is that of Athenian government in the fourth and third centuries BC (but it had other distinctive features too: we will reserve until the next chapter a discussion of its use of random selection for office, which might be considered a quasi-fatalist recipe for organizational design). Still influential in contemporary thinking about institutional design, this much-discussed 'democracy' was élitist, in that slaveholding and subjugation of women was combined with an egalitarian participative approach to public management on the part of the 20,000 to 40,000 adult males who formed the citizenry (Jones 1957: 50). It incorporated all three of the central themes of egalitarian public management discussed above—management without managers, co-production rather than professionalism in administration, and the exposure of those performing public duties to intensive face-to-face scrutiny in powerful community fora.

'Athenian democracy was direct, not representative, in a double sense; attendance in the sovereign Assembly was open to every citizen, and there was no bureaucracy or civil service, save for a few clerks, slaves owned by the state itself, who kept such records as were unavoidable, copies of treaties and laws, lists of defaulting taxpayers, and the like' (Finley 1985: 18). Citizens had equal rights to speak and vote in the Assembly and all were eligible for selection (by lot) to the Council which met every day. The Assembly met about forty times a year—almost once a week—under a chairman who was selected by lot and held office only for a single day (Jones 1957: 106–7). Public officers were either elected (as in the case of the ten generals, who were elected annually) or selected by lot, as in the case of public auditors, or the members of the legislative commissions.

The result was a structure designed to prevent the development of an institutionalized political élite or political parties in the modern sense (Finley 1985: 25), and also to avoid other familiar organizational features of contemporary liberal democracies. Courts were not autonomous from the legislature, but committees of the *demos*—involving large juries of citizens chosen by lot. There was no sharp distinction between politics and administration or management, because most public officers were selected by lot, and therefore citizens voted on policies which they themselves might have to implement.

Part of the control structure of this extraordinary system of public management, involving a minimum of bureaucracy in the conventional sense, came from processes of mutuality. Generals and other public officers were subject to scrutiny by the citizens at large in the Assembly, and the Assembly could vote for ostracism or exile as punishment for errant citizens, including those who had misled the Assembly through demagoguery or demonstrated poor judgement (ibid. 26–7 and 118). This society remains the best-known example of a relatively privileged structure of a high-participation, weak-leadership structure applied to public management as a whole, and it lasted in that form for about eighty years (interrupted by two brief oligarchic counter-revolutions). But parts of the recipe, albeit in less pure form, have recurred in later 'élite egalitarian' structures, such as the oligarchic democracy of Venice or some of the Hanseatic cities, the New England town-meeting tradition, and the Swiss tradition of citizen-initiated legislation (reflected in Jean-Jacques Rousseau's recipe for good government, which included the prescription of election as the basis of public office and the entitlement of citizens to recall their deputies at any time). And, as has been noted before, contemporary enthusiasm for quasi-egalitarian forms of working can be noted in a range of settings from development theory to corporate management theory.

*Radical Egalitarianism and Public Management:*
*Some Contemporary Varieties*

In contrast to the élitist or sequestered variety of egalitarianism, 'radical' egalitarianism involves a transformational agenda, in which the development of high-participation and non-hierarchical forms of organization are taken to be an essential step towards overall social justice. Today, two of the major sources of egalitarian thinking about public management come from radical feminism and green politics.[4] In their current form, both movements stem from 1960s New Left ideas about restructuring society through

---

[4] The two movements are to some extent linked through 'ecofeminism', the view that depletion of the world's resources and exploitation of women by men are part of the same oppressive social order (see Dobson 1990).

anti-bureaucratic, democratic forms of organization for all human relationships, including government. These ideas were reflected in a range of 'alternative lifestyle' forms of organization—residential, educational, therapeutic—which developed in the USA and other wealthy countries at that time as a conscious reaction against Weberian hierarchist principles of bureaucracy, particularly impersonal relations, hierarchy of authority, technical competence, and specialization (Davidson 1983: 166).

Dark green politics aims to change the world in a way that makes 'speciesism'—the subordination of animals and plants to the interests of human beings—as much of a crime as 'racism' or 'sexism' (Goodin 1992: 12). The classic modern statement of green organizational principles is ordinarily taken to be the 1983 manifesto of the (West) German Greens (see Capra and Spretnak 1984), which was referred to earlier. What set off the Greens from mainstream political parties was not only the strength of their commitment to protection of the environment (expressed particularly in opposition to civil and military uses of nuclear technology, logging, expanded road transport, and conventional economic growth more generally) but also in their espousal of egalitarian principles of organization. The most important features of those ideas for public management are commitment to radical decentralization of power to small-scale communities (between which some sort of spontaneous co-ordination is expected to occur), together with grassroots democracy, for which the Green Party itself offered a model, notably in its principle of participative democracy. The recipe included decision-making through endless open meetings in which everyone attending had a say and a vote and the famous principle of rotation in office (adopted in 1983, abandoned three years later (ibid. 188–9)), under which Green parliamentary representatives were expected to hand over their Bundestag positions to designated 'understudies' after only two years in office, to prevent them developing a 'cult of personality' and becoming corrupted by the manipulative mind-set and backdoor dealing of mainstream politics (Dobson 1990: 137–9).

The key elements of contemporary green thinking for public management are community empowerment against professionals or large business interests, and decentralization of population into small communities (of a few thousand, in most accounts) which are capable of self-administration through face-to-face participation.

For Goodin (1992: 149–50) the assumptions underlying those precepts are that:

People must feel a part of their community in order to participate meaningfully in deliberations regarding its future. They must be able to meet together with all other members of their community, face to face, to discuss the problems and options before them. They must be confident that their participation might make some material difference to the outcome. They must be able to comprehend, reasonably fully and completely, what is actually going on in their community; and they must understand its workings well enough to form a reasonable estimate of how various alterations might affect it. Finally, they must be able to survey the community as a whole, rather than just having a sense of their own small corner of it, if they are to judge the general good rather than pursue narrow sectional interests.

Such an organizational structure is often seen as reflecting 'caring/sharing' attitudes. But it is not necessarily a formula that is 'soft' on opportunism. On the contrary, dark greens claim close surveillance through mutuality in decentralized communities would make opportunistic lawbreaking like tax evasion far more difficult than it is in large impersonal societies (cf. Dobson 1990: 124–5).

Green ideas of this type were partly influenced by the development of the new wave of feminism from the 1960s; and radical feminism offers the main other contemporary example of polar egalitarianism in ideas about organization and management. Radical feminists like Kathy Ferguson (1984) reject the strategy of their 'liberal' feminist sisters to achieve feminist aims through 'femocracy'—that is, to build 'state feminism' in the Swedish style, through organizations dedicated to the pursuit of the feminist agenda, through 'representative bureaucracy' and the appointment of women to key positions in the state structure. From this conventional liberal feminist viewpoint, hierarchy is acceptable as long as women are adequately represented on the upper rungs of the ladder. But radical feminists see such a strategy as self-defeating, because it leaves unchanged the very features of 'patriarchy' they most dislike—hierarchy, gigantism, impersonality, power-play, coercion, and manipulation.

Accordingly, for the radicals, the answer is not for women to colonize inherently oppressive male organizations and structures, but to reject them in favour of non-hierarchical forms of organization which build on what they claim to be the special skills of women, rooted in their historical experience of oppression, to achieve co-operation without élitist forms of management. Ferguson (ibid. 27) claims that is what makes radical feminism different from the other general organizational recipes of the 1960s 'New Left' counterculture. Ferguson's recipe is drawn in part from the structures developed by women in their traditionally 'private' domestic sphere and partly from the consciousness-raising women's groups of the 1960s and 1970s (cf. Randall 1987: 255). The aim, in true egalitarian fashion, is to devise high-participation, weak-leadership forms of organization, making decisions by consensus and sharing out the menial work by 'dividing the work process into areas within which each individual has responsibility for both the creative and the routine aspects of the task' (Ferguson 1984: 205). And characteristically egalitarian methods are identified for combating the problems of 'zealocracy', or rule by the most articulate activists, such as rotation of leadership positions and the election of delegates to canvass the less active members (ibid. 207).

Such approaches were central to the organization of a mid-1970s US lesbian-feminist community documented in a landmark study by Andrea Baker (1982). Baker claims the radical feminists and lesbians of that era added at least four elements to egalitarian assumptions about organization, namely:

(1) leadership potential resides in every woman, regardless of her background, formal education, or training; (2) this potential can be optimally encouraged by women banding together in feminist activities; and (3) the more confident 'leaders', those women with experience in various collectivities, can expand their ranks by becoming 'role models' . . . to change novices from 'followers' to leaders. Thus, feminist power is not domination, but a transferable source of energy or initiative . . . Furthermore (4), if leaders or members have to act independently of the entire group membership, they must remain 'accountable' . . . to all involved individuals by justifying and explaining decisions and by being 'open' to criticism and revision of plans. (ibid. 325)

How far the idea that everyone has leadership potential is really novel (let alone valid) is debatable; but at the least such themes put a new feminist 'spin' on more general egalitarian approaches to organization outlined earlier. Moreover, a broadly egalitarian feminist perspective has also been applied to the debate over citizenship, one of the most problematic aspects of contemporary government. For egalitarians, citizenship has to be understood as something more than being a consumer of public services provided by business (or on a business model), but citizens' obligations to co-produce public services traditionally involve mainly the obligation to undertake military service (and the administration of justice in the common-law countries). Now you do not exactly need to be a radical feminist to view a concept of citizenship as the obligation to die for your country in uniform as both largely obsolete in an age of Cruise missiles and of doubtful relevance to at least the female half of the human race. Diemut Bubeck (1995*a*) has suggested that a modern and inclusive concept of citizenship should be built on obligations to participate in caring rather than military duties. She defines caring (Bubeck 1995*b*) as face-to-face activity to meet needs that those being cared for could not possibly meet for themselves, such as looking after small children, the sick, or infirm elderly. Her argument is that citizenship based on obligation to contribute to caring would represent a way of tackling simultaneously three problems that confront the contemporary state: the lack of any clear modern concept of citizenship to replace the outdated and male-oriented role of military service; the fiscal crisis occasioned by the cost of caring services borne by the state; and the continuing problem of gender inequality comprised of unequal sharing of caring duties. She argues (1995*a*: 259–60):

Rather than follow the welfare state model of social provision, one might conceive of care as part of a citizen's obligations to contribute her share to one of the most, if not the most important function any self-governing society has, namely to ensure the well-being of its members. Citizenship would be redefined to comprise care as much as, or even more importantly than, defence, as every citizen's obligation ... Such a universal caring service ... makes care more visible; it gives care the central place and social recognition that has been denied it for so long; it is a 'school for carers' for both men and women and may thus have an important role re-educating fighters into carers by fostering the skills and virtues of care in everybody; it abolishes the gendered division of labour and morality; it may be cheaper than ... state provision [on an orthodox welfare state model].

This policy prescription has egalitarian features in so far as it is centrally concerned with reducing inequality and recasting citizenship into a more participative mode, in a 'caring' equivalent of the Swiss army, and thus represents an interesting egalitarian 'slant' on citizenship from a feminist perspective. But the 'caring' organization itself need not necessarily be egalitarian in form (indeed, if it were, it is not difficult to imagine the difficulties it would encounter). Nor is there any reason in principle why 'caring' should be more important to egalitarians than to those with different world-views.

## Precursors of Contemporary Egalitarian Ideas about Public Management

Such contemporary debates almost exactly parallel nineteenth-century arguments among socialists about public management, indicating how recurrent is the egalitarian viewpoint in public management debate. Like today's greens and feminists, yesterday's socialists argued fiercely about whether putting different kinds of people behind the desks of the bureaucracy would make any essential difference to the way public services work. Several nineteenth-century anarchists (notably Mikhail Bakunin, challenging Marx in the 1870s) argued that replacing middle-class bureaucrats by working-class ones would make no real difference on its own to the way state organization worked, but would simply elevate a new bureaucratic class to power. Like today's greens and feminists, yesterday's socialists disagreed about what state functions needed to be carried out to achieve their social agenda, and how they should be carried out, with state-centric versions of socialism clashing with visions of spontaneous collective action without state coercion. Like today's greens and feminists, yesterday's socialists disagreed about whether existing forms of public management could be reprogrammed to pursue a socialist agenda, or whether such structures were essentially part of the problem rather than of the solution. Like today's greens and feminists, yesterday's socialists argued about how much centralization and concentration of authority was needed to pursue their aims, both in their own political organization and in the new public management structures that they needed to establish.

Moreover, just as today's egalitarian feminists tend to take their model of ideal organization from little-known women's communes in the Third World, egalitarian socialists had their own model of public management from the Paris Commune of 1871. The Commune was the short-lived 'workers' government' of a large part of Paris after the Prussian occupation in the Franco-Prussian war,[5] and it is famous mainly because it aimed to take egalitarian doctrines of public management to their logical conclusion.

The Paris Commune was founded on four doctrines of good public management (see Rihs 1973) which have often resurfaced later. First, all public officials—both elected and unelected—were paid no more than the standard wage. This pay structure was intended to produce solidarity between those at the top and the community at large, by forcing the rulers to share the conditions of those they rule. Second, there was no permanent tenure in office for anyone. The route to positions of authority was generally by election (for instance, army officers were elected by the soldier-citizens in each *arondissement* and magistrates were elected at large). And all officials, both elected and unelected, were subject to recall at any time—that is, they could be voted out of office if a sufficient number of electors were dissatisfied with their performance. Third, there was no real distinction between 'policy' and 'administration' or 'management'. Those who made the laws were expected to help enforce them. Elected members of the Commune had the 'administrative direction' in their own *arondissements*, including defence and military operations. Fourth, and relatedly, there was no professional military or police force. Instead, there was a 'citizen' army and police force, with policing undertaken on a rotational basis by all citizens.

Despite, or perhaps because, it lasted less than a year, the Paris Commune has been enormously influential as a public management ideal for egalitarian thinkers within the socialist tradition. Its short duration means that egalitarians can argue it was never really tested properly (while those from other cultural biases can argue it was tried and failed, in that it did not secure the new 'state'). The model fascinated Marx, who endorsed it as a recipe for radical public management in *The Civil War in France* (1871) and to some extent in the *Communist Manifesto*. Lenin rejected it in 1905, but flirted with it again during the Kerensky government of 1917, when he published *State and Revolution*, arguing that ordinary citizens were perfectly capable of carrying out the administrative tasks of

---

[5] It was set up by a central committee formed by the various batallions of the French National Guard, comprising some 300,000 men who were left in arms after the armistice with Prussia.

the modern state, once those tasks had been stripped of 'official grandeur'.[6] The Commune was still a beacon for the French student revolutionaries of the 1960s and the ideas of the Commune were to some extent reflected in the Chinese Cultural Revolution of the 1960s under Mao Zedong and the Gang of Four, with their attack on senior managerial and planning tasks as 'not real work' and their attempt to destroy all the 'élitist' features of the Chinese public bureaucracy and educational system.

## 4. Conclusion

Egalitarian ideas on public management have a long history, and continually reappear in new contexts, such as the dark green and radical feminist ideas of the contemporary world. Nor do such ideas only exist on the outer fringes of 'loony leftism', as is sometimes supposed. Themes such as a stress on 'networking' approaches to organization, community empowerment, and the avoidance of producer/consumer splits in public services, are recurrent themes in public management and have featured strongly even in the relatively mainstream contemporary approaches to 'reinventing government' commended by Osborne and Gaebler (1992) and the advocates of communitarianism and 'sustainable human development', as we saw at the outset.

As noted earlier, egalitarianism as an approach to public management organization has obvious and well-known weaknesses. It is more difficult for egalitarian than hierarchist organizations to sacrifice individuals for the collective good, because weak leadership and high-participation decision-making rules give each potential sacrifice an effective veto. For the same reason, it is hard to resolve disputes, and egalitarian organizations which are unable to expel deviants and heretics may be peculiarly vulnerable to long-running feuds and civil wars, as in the Birmingham hospital case referred to in Chapter 2 (cf. Thompson, Ellis, and Wildavsky 1990:

[6] Though Lenin's administrative practice in office was far from the ideals of the Commune (particularly the re-establishment of the secret police only six weeks after the October revolution, and his open endorsement of rule by terror), some of its features were formally built into the administrative architecture of the former Soviet Union, notably the principle of recall, the fiction of 'workers' wages' for politicians, and the antipathy to professional politicians.

6). And when egalitarian organization goes beyond a dedicated core of like-minded participants to embrace a more culturally diverse membership, it becomes extremely vulnerable to opportunistic free-riding tactics which Mancur Olson (1971) identified as the core of collective action problems where there is no power of coercion.

But the egalitarian recipe for public management also has some major strengths. In some circumstances mutual surveillance can be a powerful antidote to corruption. Avoiding a sharp split between producers and consumers likewise can provide a check to abuse of office and a formula for making public services responsive to their clients. If egalitarian organizations at the 'street level' of public-service provision frequently collapse in a welter of mutual recrimination, they also often spring up again in some different form. Modern technological developments like information superhighways are quite capable of being exploited in an egalitarian direction, as new forms of 'town meeting'. Weak leadership structures may be the only way to organize in circumstances where it is easy for key players to 'exit', and high-participation structures develop social boundaries around themselves, which may in turn (unintendedly) produce beliefs and attitudes that underpin the egalitarian structure.[7]

Moreover, egalitarian principles of public management keep recurring, as we saw in briefly examining contemporary dark green and radical feminist ideas about organization. Indeed, the late Aaron Wildavsky and Brendon Swedlow (1991: 63) have claimed that, in spite of the stereotype view that rampant individualism is the dominant trend in modern societies, the growth of radical egalitarianism in the USA since the 1950s is at least equally dramatic, as measured both by the numbers of people holding egalitarian beliefs and by the intensity of their views. Wildavsky and Swedlow argue that the strongest signs of growing egalitarian

[7] This functionalist argument is developed by Douglas (1987: 38–40), claiming the emergence of egalitarian, high-participation structures is compatible with conventional Chicago-School assumptions about self-regarding calculating individuals. Ease of exit from a latent group produces weak leadership, weak leadership involves high participation in decision-making, high participation produces common beliefs in internal and external threats. Hence, as she puts it (ibid. 40): 'Instead of using the beliefs to explain the cohesion of the society, we have used the society to explain the beliefs, and they certainly needed a better explanation than by reference to real cosmic conspiracies and satanic dangers.'

ideas are to be found in the sphere of culture, media, popular music, literature, and art, rather than in economic outcomes. They point to growing support for civil rights, animal rights, children's rights, the rights of the aged (reflected in trends such as the removal of mandatory retirement ages), and argue that the combination of these trends has substantially weakened US individualism (ibid. 98).

Even if Wildavsky and Swedlow's more general argument may be exaggerated, egalitarianism seems far from dead as a source of inspiration for models of public management. But perhaps the paradox of egalitarianism in public management is that it often seems to last longest in relatively privileged social settings, in its élitist form. The more long-lived organizations with egalitarian aspects, notably the upper reaches of the professions and collegiate public services, often seem to be of this type. Perhaps such organizations are better able to maintain a distinctive culture and have a stronger resource base to underpin it. It may be easier to be more equal than others when the menial tasks are done by other people.

# 7

# Doing Public Management the Fatalist Way?

Numbers are fuzzy. . . . And if numbers are fuzzy, everything
is. And everything is.

(Kosko 1993: 125, quoted by Morçöl 1996: 318)

## 1. Beyond Markets, Hierarchies, and Solidarity:
## A Fatalist World of Public Management?

Can there be a fatalist approach to public management? If cultural
theorists are correct to identify fatalism as a *viable* way of life, there
ought to be. But if there is, it does not figure prominently in conventional accounts of how to provide public services. Ordinarily we
are presented with markets and hierarchies as the main alternative
forms of social organization, though sometimes a third type is
identified in the form of 'solidarity' (the currently fashionable
communitarian solution of group self-organization, as discussed in
the last chapter). The standard assumption is that we have to
choose among those major options, but if we do not like any of
them there are no other alternatives.

Certainly, the pursuit of a fatalist way to do public management
takes us into less familiar territory than we traversed in the last
three chapters. Although cultural theorists see fatalism as one of
their most important 'finds', only a few cultural theorists have given
detailed attention to fatalism in practice. Michael Thompson and
his associates (Thompson, Ellis, and Wildavsky 1990) frequently
leave fatalism out in their discussion of alternative ways of organizing derived from their cultural grid. Instead, they give the most

attention to the three other 'active' categories, as discussed in the last three chapters.

It is easy to see why. At first sight, fatalism might seem hard to reconcile with any kind of management, even on the broadest construction of that term. Fatalism is usually portrayed as essentially an 'anti-organizational' attitude, and though that can be counted as a management philosophy of a kind, it is on the face of it a negative one without obvious implications for better design. Certainly it is not what the power-suited denizens of the top executive suites in public-service organizations are conventionally supposed to believe in. And yet, you do not have to work for very long in or around such organizations to come across the widespread—albeit typically informal, semi-articulated, and 'off the record'—belief that public organization and policy is inescapably unpredictable and chaotic, defying any clear-cut theory.[1] Such a belief—epitomized by Scott Adams' (1996) best-selling *Dilbert Principle* satirizing contemporary management fads and organizational practices on the basis that 'managers are idiots'— often prompts an attitude of private and underground detachment in the face of public enthusiasm for this week's favoured managerial path to salvation.

Such attitudes and beliefs are sometimes to be found even— perhaps especially—among those at the very top of major public institutions, even though they may only be what Helena Eilstein (1995: 71) calls 'closet fatalists'. Fictional and dramatic accounts of the working of large bureaucracies and institutions also often highlight the way randomness and chance interconnections produce unintended and often bizarre outcomes. And, as Gerald Mars shows in a famous study of cheating at work (Mars 1982: 70; Mars and Frosdick 1997), people whose work is highly regulated in some way but who do their jobs in relative isolation from others (the high-grid, low-group characteristics of fatalism) often find ways of reacting against management-imposed rules by individual 'fiddles' (stealing time, money, or goods) and even sabotage.

In a classic sociological study, Edward Banfield (1958) analysed what seems to have been a whole society of fatalists, the inhabitants of a poor peasant village ('Montegrano') in southern Italy in the

---

[1] On a stricter definition, 'fatalism is a doctrine according to which, for everything that occurs, there never was an instant of time at which its non-occurrence in the future was possible' (Eilstein 1995: 73).

1950s. The central feature of 'Montegranesi' behaviour, according to Banfield, is lack of co-operation in community welfare and collective action. Banfield interpreted this feature, which he termed 'amoral familism' (ibid. 85), as a product of beliefs and values, not income per head, or educational level. He argued poverty alone could not explain the chronic lack of co-operation which he observed among the Montegranesi. After all, equally poor agrarian societies like the early European settlers in North America had produced far more collective community-oriented action than Montegrano. In a society like Montegrano, according to Banfield, public management will be narrowly bureaucratic and 'statist' because only paid officials will be concerned with public affairs. The citizenry at large will be cynical about the motives of public officials, believing them to be corrupt and self-serving even when they are not.

But even in spite of that widespread belief, there are likely to be few effective checks on public officials in a fatalist society. Because fatalists reject participation and collective action, any checks there are can only come from other paid officials, not from the general public. Any zeal on the part of those paid officials is hardly to be expected. The lack of trust and collective loyalty which is the hallmark of fatalism means that 'officeholders, feeling no identification with the purposes of the organization, will not work harder than is necessary to keep their places or (if such is within the realm of possibility) to earn promotion' (ibid. 91) and indeed will take bribes if they can get away with it. Such attitudes produce a self-reinforcing fatalist syndrome of public management which is depicted in Figure 7.1

Such a syndrome of related attitudes and beliefs is recognizable in many societies, and perhaps present to some degree in most. Nor is it necessarily outdated: Banfield's 1950s portrait of the Montegranesi is echoed in more recent studies of the culture of southern Italy, such as that by Robert Leonardi (1995: 171–3), who links it to a culture of 'criminal capitalism'. The fatalist syndrome depicted in Figure 7.1 is at the very opposite pole from the co-operative community spirit noted by Alexis de Tocqueville (1946) as a hallmark of early nineteenth-century America, and to the extent that it exists it is likely to undermine the egalitarian recipe for effective public management through community participation. But it may undermine hierarchist and even individualist

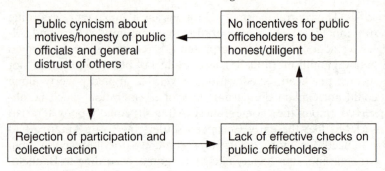

Fig. 7.1. The fatalist syndrome of public management (from Banfield).

approaches too. It involves rejection of what in German parlance is termed *Beamtenethos*—that is, a sense of moral mission among public officials, going well beyond what is written down in the relevant rule book or public-service statute. But fatalist attitudes and beliefs do not involve any evangelical faith in market competition either, to the extent of prompting entrepreneurial zeal by producers and agressive pursuit of self-interest by consumers. The central principle on which a fatalist society operates is a rejection of co-operation in any form, as something likely to have unpredictable and possibly unpleasant results. The approach is taken to its logical conclusion in Howard Jacobson's (1987: 198) satire on 1970s Australian universities, in which two academics run a 'Futility Unit' in Canberra, accepting no students and encouraging no research 'since these would breach the spirit of the discipline'.

Such attitudes are naturally deplored by those, like Banfield, who see fatalism as a social pathology bound to produce social backwardness and stagnation. For fatalists, on the other hand, it is the only rational way to cope with an inherently insane and unpredictable world.[2] An egalitarian, hierarchist, or individualist bias prompts action of some kind to make things better, but a fatalist bias assumes there is likely to be 'a problem for every solution' (to

[2] As in the Buddhist idea of passive acceptance of success and calamity, which '. . . offers a solution to every conceivable problem and removes every reason for outcry or rebellion. It is, by this account, a vade-mecum and panacea, and hence all tears are by definition idle and the heart cannot break, except through weaknesses that no one would wish to boast about or from causes so illegitimate or childishly unreal that no one would care to set them down in print' (Enwright 1969: 186–7).

paraphrase a famous characterization of the attitudes of the British civil service, said to have come from Lord Samuel).[3]

Cultural theory is ambiguous on whether fatalism can be a *viable* basis of organization in the sense that a Montegrano-type society can survive and reproduce itself over time, given the appropriate conditions. Nor is it clear from the work of cultural theorists exactly what fatalists' focus on *karma*, or the random working of unknowable forces, amounts to. Is it simply a device for understanding the world—or at least for understanding why it can never be understood? Is it a device for passively allocating blame (to ill-luck, Act of God, blind chance, 'one of those things') when plans fail or disaster strikes? Or is it linked to more positive recipes for good government or management?

The last possibility—that fatalism might link to how-to-do-it ideas about organizational *design*, as distinct from a view of the world as ineluctably ruled by the fickle goddess of fortune—has had little attention. From conventional cultural-theory accounts, it would seem the most appropriate role for fatalist social science in public management would be like that of the chorus in classical Greek theatre (see Hood 1996a: 160). The chorus relates to the drama as a periodic commentator on the decisions made by the active players on the stage. Its comments underline the inherent folly, futility, and unpredictability with which all human affairs are conducted. They stress the tendency of the best-laid plans to fail, the most highly educated élites to err, the most confident forecasts and predictions to be wrong, the greatest of schemes to go awry because of apparently small but unexpectedly disabling errors, while unexpected (and typically undeserved) fortune and success may come to apparently much less promising enterprises.

Even if that *was* all there was to a fatalist approach to public management, it would still be important. After all, the role of commentator-critic is a far from trivial one. Some of the classic books on public affairs and public management in recent decades— like Barbara Tuchman's (1984) *March of Folly*, David Halberstam's (1972) *The Best and the Brightest*, or Daniel Moynihan's (1969) *Maximum Feasible Misunderstanding*—have adopted just such a role of underlining the deep in-built irony and fatal flaws in large-scale public projects. For Tuchman (1984: 473),

---

[3] See *The New Penguin Dictionary of Quotations*. London: Viking, 1992: 336.

for instance, lack of intelligent thinking is a 'universal' among those in high public office, and inevitably produces results that are unexpected and contradictory to their policy aims. So an approach which brought no more to public management than a deep sense of humility about anyone's capacity for controlling organizations or tracking their environment, would still add a distinctive perspective to the drama.

The next section examines such a perspective on public management, looking particularly at one influential strain of 'new institutionalist' literature which portrays the functioning of organizations as a highly unpredictable process, involving eclectic decision-making unavoidably dependent on chance connections. After that, the chapter moves on to build on the recipe for 'contrived randomness' briefly introduced in Chapter 3. It argues that a fatalist perspective can at least in some sense be taken beyond commentary and criticism into a positive prescription for conducting management and designing organizations to operate on the basis of chance.

## 2. Fatalism as a Greek Chorus in Public Management

As noted above, acting as a 'Greek chorus' is a minimum role for a fatalist science of management. The job of the chorus is to underline the many instances in which widely shared assumptions turn out to be false, powerful empires spring up from nowhere while confidently backed plans produce outcomes quite different from, and even the very reverse of, what was expected. Such an approach serves to highlight the defects and shortcomings of the other three polar approaches to public management discussed in previous chapters, both as explanations of cause–effect relationships and as ways of designing organization.

The theme of the unpredictability of human affairs and the large part played by small chance events, each trivial in itself and whose significance is not recognized by the participants in advance, is an age-old one. It is the stuff both of comedy and tragedy, and central to the 'what if' games historians like to play, focusing on little events with big consequences—what if Cleopatra's nose had been a centimetre shorter or longer (McCloskey 1990: 88), if the temperature had been a few degrees warmer when the ill-starred space shuttle *Challenger* was launched on that fateful day in January 1986

(Bovens and 'tHart 1996: 6–7; Vaughan 1996), if the disastrous 1986 Chernobyl experiment had been conducted during the shift of Yuri Tregub as shift foreman of No.4 reactor rather than that of Aleksandr Akimov (Medvedev 1991: 90)?

The consequences of putting such an approach into the centre of the frame in thinking about management are potentially far-reaching. After all, if every tiny event can potentially have far-reaching consequences, the outlook seems bleak for any approach to management or institutional design aiming to predict or control behaviour on the basis of a few key variables (cf. Hood 1976; Coram 1996). Popular scientists like Edward Tenner (1996) argue that 'revenge effects' are pervasive in modern society as new technologies (like pesticides) tend to 'bite back' in the form of unpredicted new problems. And as we noted in Chapter 2, Marshall Meyer and Lynne Zucker (1989: 9) argue the normal 'rational' expectation that organizations which fail to achieve their goals will disappear is often not fulfilled: 'we are surrounded by organizations whose failure to achieve their proclaimed goals is neither temporary nor aberrant, but chronic and structurally determined'. Wolfgang Seibel (1992) also speaks of 'successfully failing' organization in the 'third sector' of public-service provision, and any such world is also a potentially rich soil for the growth of fatalist attitudes. But in contemporary writing about public management, the approach which most closely fits a fatalist 'Greek chorus' role is the work of James March and Johan Olsen (1989) and their associates, who represent one distinctive strain out of a number of contemporary analytic approaches that have (confusingly) come to be dubbed 'new institutionalism' (see Hall and Taylor 1997). Their work fits that role because its central theme is the inherent complexity of organizational process. The implication is that we cannot make any useful predictions about the policy process unless we had access to a social-science equivalent of 'Maxwell's demon', an imaginary and omniscient entity which is capable of seeing each individual atom and observing its movement over each nanosecond (and consequently would be able to predict whether any given coin would land heads or tails on the next spin).

March and Olsen are less inventive than physicists like Maxwell, in that they do not specify precisely what a 'demon' would need to know to make predictions about organizational behaviour. The March/Olsen strain of new institutionalism is primarily sceptical, criticizing what they see as 'simplistic' deterministic approaches to explaining and predicting how politics and public organizations work. What they have in their sights is the perspective offered by some influential strains of economic and sociological analysis of organization—namely that organizations largely reflect their social or class contexts or that they can be understood through a few key variables as the product of rational action by narrowly self-regarding individualists. On the contrary, March and Olsen and their followers claim that factors inside organizations comprise complex intervening variables making it impossible reliably to predict organizational behaviour from outside with reference to a few key variables, and that predictions based on simple concepts of rational self-serving behaviour are unreliable too because preferences cannot be abstracted from the institutions which shape them. Rather, this school of thought sees the working of institutions as a product of a complex of interrelated variables so rich that they typically defy simple predictive models or recipes for intervention. As Jan-Erik Lane (1993: 172–3) comments: 'The positive side of the argument about institutional dynamics is the notion that organizational change is a contested process involving *accidental* outcomes and *random* activity, meaning that results *cannot be predicted* and change *cannot be controlled* by fiat' (italics mine).

The telling metaphor chosen by Cohen, March, and Olsen (1972) is of the operation of organization as a 'garbage can'—a chance accumulation of relatively unconnected phenomena, like the disparate bits of refuse that happen to end up beside one another in a rubbish bin. That metaphor of what organizational decision-making is like applies to what Cohen *et al.* call 'organized anarchies'. Organized anarchies—of which universities are held to be the pre-eminent example—are organizations or decision situations which involve problematic preferences rather than well-defined agreed goals, unclear technology rather than well-understood relationships of cause and effect, and fluid participation rather than clear organizational boundaries. Decisions are thus a product of 'a collection of choices looking for problems, issues and feelings looking for decision situations in which they might be aired, solutions looking for issues to which they might be answers, and decision makers looking for work' (ibid. 2). The only way to understand the working of such institutions is through interpretative hermeneutics, not deterministic models (Lane 1993: 174).

Although often criticized, the garbage-can metaphor still 'resonates' because it exactly fits with a fatalistic view of public management as driven by unpredictable happenstance and coincidence (and, according to Lane (ibid. 173), because it fits with what he calls 'a new phenomenon: the negotiation society'). And John Kingdon (1984) has adapted the garbage-can model to produce an equally well-known model depicting the opening of 'policy windows' (opportunities for policy change) as a product of the coincidental interaction of problems, political environments, and solutions. But Kingdon is less 'fatalist' than Cohen, March, and Olsen, because he sees more of a role for strategies of anticipation: in his account, far-sighted 'political entrepreneurs' may be able to steer events by judiciously waiting for the relevant policy windows to open and then quickly seizing the opportunity to advance their favoured projects.

This perspective is not just an abstract vision of organization—one of those angels-on-the-head-of-a-pin debates that 'ivory tower academics' are constantly being accused of indulging in. It has some very practical implications, not least for the question of how far organizations can be designed to avoid egregious damage to life and limb—like accidental deployment of nuclear weapons, transport crashes, building collapses in earthquakes or typhoons. According to Scott Sagan (1993), the 'garbage-can' approach is an important foundation of the influential theory of 'normal accidents', associated with Charles Perrow's (1984) famous book of that title. It forms one side of an important debate about how to maximize safety and avoid accidents in the management of high-technology systems in contemporary society. The other side of the debate is constituted by what has come to be called 'high reliability systems theory' (HRST). HRST claims that accidents in risky technologies are avoidable by adoption of organizational designs incorporating features like high redundancy, an entrenched 'safety culture', and continuous learning processes feeding back experience from errors or near-misses into ever-more-effective operating procedures (Sagan 1993: 13–28). Such a design implies strong goal consensus within organizations, reflected in willingness to commit large resources to furthering safety by organizational leaders and/or governments.

But Perrow's controversial argument runs clean contrary to this comforting perspective, with its hierarchist faith in expertise, well-understood rules and meticulous organizational design on the basis of recognized 'best practice'. Perrow claims serious accidents with risky technologies (like the Chernobyl case considered in Chapter 2) are in fact bound to occur, given the way most human organizations operate in practice. The argument is that real-world organizations always operate to a greater or lesser extent in a 'degenerate' mode, whatever their corporate propaganda may say. Such typical degeneracy arises from 'normal' slackness, dishonesty, and unofficial arrangements which diverge sharply from the formal rule structure, avowed objectives, or official procedures. Personality clashes, conflict over resources, petty (or worse) corruption, and contradictory pressures are a fact of life in most organizations, irrespective of what top managers may declaim in public about their commitment to togetherness and clear-cut goals. Given the capricious way in which real organizations subvert formal design procedures, the only way to avoid risky high-tech accidents, according to Perrow (mixing egalitarian prescription with fatalist diagnosis), is to ban technologies which involve a combination of 'tight coupling' and high complexity rather than to indulge in the forlorn hope that perfect organizational design can ever solve the problem. Sagan's (1993) own study of the history of nuclear weapons safety in the USA suggests the balance of the evidence in that case seems to lie with normal accident theory rather than the rival high-reliability organization theory—implying that a fatalist perspective may indeed be a more accurate predictor of organizational behaviour than its main rival.

Of course, the garbage-can metaphor is not the only reflection of the 'Greek chorus' approach as a fatalist perspective on public management. The long tradition in social science of analysing the unintended consequences of social action also fits that perspective to some extent, in that: '. . . in social science the role of irony is to draw attention to shocking (or "mocking") *discrepancies between intentions and consequences*, goals and realities' (Sztompka 1986: 252, paraphrasing Louis Schneider). That tradition, stretching back at least to ideas of the eighteenth-century philosopher David Hume and in this century most closely associated with Robert Merton's (1968) stress on the unintended consequences of social action, highlights the various ways in which social interventions in public policy can unexpectedly produce side-effects or even reverse effects. We shall be exploring such processes further in Chapter 9, in considering ways in which excessive emphasis on any one organizational 'way of life' may unintentionally produce reverse effects.

The fascination of such analysis lies in retrospective understanding of the catastrophically false assumptions—often made by highly reputable experts at the top of their professions—which prevent 'reverse effects' from being anticipated by the organizations and individuals who bring them about. Viewed from a hierarchist perspective, the study of such instances can be expected to provide 'lessons' which can be codified and cumulatively incorporated into better knowledge and more adequate causal theories, so that next time planning or management will be better-informed and less likely to fail for the same reasons. From a fatalist perspective, on the other hand, hindsight analysis of unexpected disasters or triumphs simply shows that unpredictable failure or success is part of the human condition and not likely to be avoided no matter how well-qualified the experts or how carefully-researched the plan. The difference between those two perspectives concerns how far we can systematically 'learn from history', and that in turn relates to the number of independent factors which are held to be capable of changing at once.

Indeed, the fatalist perspective is capable of being expressed as a mathematical metaphor which goes rather beyond the garbage-can image in complexity and elaboration. Contemporary natural science ideas about 'fuzzy logic' and chaos theory are potentially a rich vein for fatalists to mine in conceptualizing the world of organizations. Fuzzy logic challenges the conventional positivist assumption that things and events have clear-cut boundaries, while chaos theory challenges the assumption that there is a linear relationship between things and events (Morçöl 1996: 317). Chaos theory was originally devised for the purpose of discovering underlying order beneath the 'noise' of apparently disorderly patterns of events (like stock-market prices or weather changes)—a theme which fits with a hierarchist view of the world and was picked up with characteristic astuteness by the management guru Tom Peters (1989) in his bestseller *Thriving on Chaos*. But there is a 'flip side' too, because chaos theory is also capable of chiming with fatalist ideas about the inherent unpredictability and uncontrollability of human affairs (Mulgan and Leadbeater 1995: 2).

The reason why chaos theory fits well with a fatalist cultural perspective on organization is that, while it offers an analytic technique for finding underlying patterns in apparently random data for low-dimensional dynamic systems, it also shows why such a result is inherently impossible for high-dimensional dynamic systems (that is, where the number of independently changing dimensions is more than about four or five). And the world of organizations could in principle constitute a high-dimensional dynamic system in that mathematical sense. As Deirdre McCloskey (1990: 87) put it: 'The point is not that great oaks from little acorns grow . . . and the right acorn is impossible to see before the event . . . The point here is rather that in some modeled worlds an acorn produces by itself a great tree in an instant. The models need not be complicated. As students of "chaos theory" have pointed out, simple models can generate astonishingly complicated patterns in which the slightest perturbation can yield an entirely different history.'

Originating in recondite areas of natural science, chaos theory rapidly 'crossed over' into popular thinking about society and organization, to the point where it has become 'a favourite of bar-stool philosophers', in the words of Geoff Mulgan and Charles Leadbeater (1995: 2). And that instant popularity no doubt reflects the rhetorical power of a new 'scientific' metaphor for what not just 'bar-stool philosophers', but also historians, policy analysts, and organizational theorists of a fatalist disposition, already thought about the inherent indeterminacy and fuzziness of social processes. It produced a new 'warrant' for those who believe that organizational development is more akin to the plot of *War and Peace* than to the propositions of eighteenth-century physics, or to the 'traffic accident' theory of the causes of war (Blainey 1973: 127 ff.), as a product of chance contingent events which have large but inherently unpredictable consequences. Indeed, ironically, the development of such approaches suggests that traditional social science is perhaps more a model for contemporary natural science than vice versa (Morçöl 1996: 317). It is therefore not surprising that fuzzy logic and chaos theory is beginning to make its appearance as a way of modelling processes of public and private management (cf. Priesmeyer 1992; Syvantek and DeSchon 1993; Zimmerman and Hurst 1993; Kiel 1994).

Hence we could redefine a fatalist perspective on public management as one which assumes that public policy and institutions inescapably involve high-dimensional dynamic systems, while the other approaches discussed in this book are more inclined to view it as capable of being understood in terms of a few key dimensions. And as the link with chaos theory shows, such a view is not to be equated with a pre-scientific outlook—what might be considered the ignorant or pre-modern superstitions of the primitive Italian peasant community studied by Banfield fifty-odd years ago. Fatalism is just as capable of being presented in modern scientific dress as any of the other major approaches to public management. Indeed, with the advent of chaos theory, it might be argued that its time may finally be arriving as a serious and rigorously based way of analysing public management.

### 3. Fatalism as a Recipe for Good Public Management: Lotteries as an Organizational Way of Life

More controversially, it can even be claimed that a fatalist approach to public management can be—and often is—taken well beyond a Greek chorus role or commentary in the vein of 'What's the use?' or an apathetic Montegranesi-style philosophy of opting out of every form of co-operative action. Fatalism in a certain sense can be linked to recipes and prescriptions for positively designing institutions, using chance as the central part of the organizational architecture.

At a fairly superficial level, what might be considered to be quasi-fatalist recipes for running organizations appear in currently popular 'New Ageist' approaches to management, which Andrez Huczynski (1993: 54–8) claims to be the major management fad of the 1990s. Among the fashionable business practices which Huczynski highlights are the pursuit of Zen, *aikido*, the use of the American Indian medicine-wheel and Chinese oracle and fortune-telling methods (ibid. 56)—approaches which are at the opposite pole of conventional rational decision-making models. And the introduction of a deliberate element of anarchy into corporate decision-making might also be considered as a rejection of orthodox ideas of rationality: in 1995 Britain's major privatized airline (British Airways) appointed a 'corporate jester' (Paul Birch, a former management consultant), reintroducing some of the vagaries of medieval court life into its operations.[4] As this chapter was first drafted (Spring 1996), media stories were circulating of the UK security services using a mystic seer to predict the terrorist actitivities of the IRA.

There might well be a fatalist cultural streak behind the corporate Zen warriors or the reintroduction of the court jester's cap and bells into contemporary boardroom life, in so far as they link to the fatalist idea that human activity is controlled by mysterious forces that cannot be changed and can only imperfectly be understood and harnessed. But at best such practices are a weak or hybrid form of fatalism. The 1990s 'management New Ageism' of which Huczynski writes may be more accurately interpreted as a cross between fatalism and other ways of life, in that preoccupation with star signs and getting in touch with inner forces are really linked to ideas about individual self-help or building trust and solidarity within a team on the basis of shared rituals and beliefs.

But there may be more to fatalism than offering a way for individuals to conduct themselves and understand their predicament in a bewildering world of complex multi-organizational interactions. Potentially at least, it also offers a positive recipe for institutional design based on advocacy of lotteries as an organizational way of life. Looked at this way, the fatalist approach to organizing public management is to build an element of randomness into the process at every level, as was noted in Chapter 3 (Table 3.5), when four different forms of randomized controls were briefly examined. The reason for linking 'contrived randomness' to fatalism is that, as has been noted already, the distinctive characteristic of the fatalist way of life is its rejection of co-operation with others in any form, on the grounds that the effects of co-operation (and indeed the consequences of any action) are likely to be inherently uncertain and problematic. A strategy of building randomness into organizational design turns such a belief into a self-fulfilling prophecy by making the pay-offs of co-operation among the consumers and producers of public services—be they bureaucrats, contractors or other functionaries—as unpredictable as possible.

---

[4] See *Independent Magazine*, 2 Oct. 1995, p. 7, which scoffed at the move as further evidence of 'the tide of loony management nonsense currently sweeping the country'.

Built-in randomness is a more common feature of organizational design than conventional organization theory allows for. Although Max Weber (1948) produced what is ordinarily seen as the definitive characterization of bureaucracy as a machine for applying determinate rules for the promotion of the rule of law, organizations which are too predictable in their operation are apt to be highly vulnerable to exploitation by opportunists. If all public organizations were fully developed Weberian 'slot-machines', they might well produce a society of lawyers or Parkinsonian-type opportunists (trying to beat the system through methods akin to Northcote Parkinson's scheme for defeating the tax bureaucracy, described in Chapter 3). Perhaps that is why real-life organizations often incorporate substantial elements of chance in the way they work. Accounts of the way powerful leaders operate often reveal an unpredictable element in their behaviour, and indeed some game theorists have developed strategic models in which a random element is included to 'faze' the opponent—just like a tax bureaucracy randomizing the order in which it looks at tax files to defeat Parkinsonian tactics built on ability to predict the bureaucracy's behaviour. What looks like a predictable slot-machine in fact works more like a gaming-machine.

As we saw in Chapter 3, contrived randomness as a controlling device in public management can operate in a variety of ways and at different organizational levels—including control exercised by public-service organizations over their clients, control within organizations, and control over organizations. It is perhaps best-known at the organization–client level, in the form of deliberate randomization of scrutiny procedures like security searches or regulatory compliance checks. The relative advantage of random testing for deterring crime and its diminutives is that it can avoid the tendency of generalized checking procedures to involve wasteful 'overkill' or degenerate into perfunctory rituals, for example where security guards or customs officials search every traveller's suitcase. It can also avoid the distortion by social filtering to which selective checking conducted on any other principle is so notoriously vulnerable (if, for example, police breath-test units would be disinclined to pull over other police drivers, and especially their senior officers, for spot checks in the absence of a random-testing regime). Nevertheless, the logic of random-testing systems is often deeply controversial, and although frequently derided, the search-every-suitcase approach to control in public services very often wins the day, even at the point where public organizations meet their clients and hence social distance between inspector and inspected is likely to be at its greatest.

Contrived randomness also applies to the internal structuring of organizations. It can be used to create the kind of organization in which no one can know exactly who their boss, subordinates or workmates may be for very long into the future; when the next check on their activities will come and what it will consist of; and whether the people they think are ordinary clients or workmates are really plain-clothes internal inspectors from some oversight unit. (Or perhaps volunteer inspectors from the population at large: Ayres and Braithwaite (1992: 13) note that in the last days of the former Soviet Union over a fifth of the adult population was engaged in voluntary inspection for the People's Control Committee or the trade unions, adding a further dimension to the game of 'roulette' played by would-be miscreants.) The aim of such a design is to discourage individual malfeasance by placing the individual within a network where their ability to predict the behaviour or attitudes of those with whom they have to transact business is minimized, because they cannot know with any precision what the membership of that network will be at any one time. Introducing an element of randomness into who does what and with whom is designed to raise the barriers against corrupt collusion or other 'networking' activity designed to jump over 'Chinese walls' separating different parts of an organization, such as regulatory and policy responsibilities or audit and operations.

As noted in Chapter 3, the logic of such an organizational design has seldom been fully explicated, but it can be represented in the metaphor of a traditional 'one-armed bandit' gaming-machine (known in British parlance as a 'fruit machine' (cf. Hood 1976: 160–1)). Modern gaming machines are electronic, but in their earlier mechanical form they worked through three wheels turning on their own axles with independent timing devices but activated by a common ratchet. Before the machine will deliver the 'jackpot' to the gambler, the three wheels need to come into a common configuration, whose improbability is built on the fact that probabilities combine multiplicatively rather than additively. As amateur gamblers know, that is why such machines are hard to beat.

The gaming-machine metaphor conveniently captures a set of

key features which were built into the structure of traditional tax bureaucracy as it began to develop from the eighteenth century (combining separation of different aspects of a transaction into different authorities, unpredictable postings around the field structure, snap inspections).[5] Such features were also to be found in many colonial administrative structures and other traditional forms of public management, such as the US forest ranger service as depicted in a classic account by Herbert Kaufman (1967). Gaming-machine features have by no means disappeared from public bureaucracies (for instance, rotation of senior staff among jobs is often said to be an important element in the remarkably successful anti-corruption strategy of the public service in contemporary Singapore). But the thrust of conventional managerial reforms may be tending to remove some of the prerequisites for such a structure within public bureaucracies (such as large size, extended field structure, dual-key methods for doing business). Indeed, this method of internal control, once a hallmark of public organizations, is perhaps now more characteristic of private multinational corporations, seeking to control their financial or field-group operations by posting their employees around their empires to prevent them 'going native', installing 'firewalls' between related elements of decision-making (to prevent fraud) and operating unpredictable inspection or audit systems on the activities of their scattered managers.

Such a model of organization, diagrammatically summarized in Figure 7.2, involves the combination of two main features. First, authority to perform key functions is divided up. Such division may take the literal form of 'dual key' structures, where two or more people must act in combination to take important actions, for instance when two separate keys and a combination lock secure a safe containing valuable assets, with two people holding one key each and a third who is the only person knowing the number of the combination lock. But often the 'dual key' effect is secured metaphorically by separating responsibilities functionally. Historically, important functions that have been separated in this way in public services are responsibility for making or receiving payments, responsibility for authorization of payment (or tax assessment), itself

---

[5] Indeed, the greater incidence of 'gaming-machine' features in the traditional organization of tax bureaucracies, in the UK at least, than in those of prison or police services may account for the typically lower incidence of corruption in tax bureaucracies than in prisons or police.

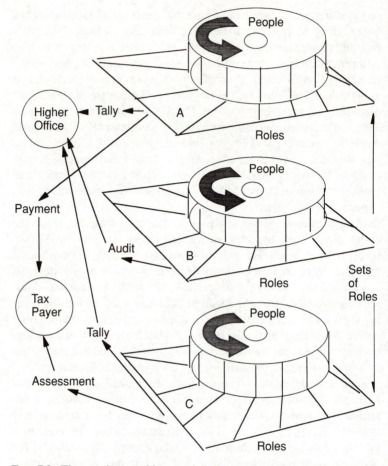

Fig. 7.2. The gaming-machine model of organizational design in traditional tax bureaucracy.

*Source*: Hood 1976: 161.

sometimes separated into dual-signature systems, and responsibility for internal audit or inspection of the activities of each unit. Like opening the safe with the three separate locks, the achievement of unauthorized private gain in such an organization thus requires collaboration among those occupying those three different roles, who can also be conceived as the fruits on a gaming-machine which need to be lined up for a jackpot payout.

However, separation of roles or 'multiple-key' operations do not on their own guarantee that the different functionaries involved will not collude to open the 'lock' or trigger a jackpot payout for themselves. Such collaboration might well occur if the occupants of each of the roles stayed in the same post for life and got a chance to know their opposite numbers very well. That is where the second feature of the 'gaming machine' model of organization comes in. That is, the organization is designed to limit the possibilities of collusion among those occupying different roles. To do so, the organization is operated on the basis that no one in a position of major responsibility has indefinite tenure in any one posting, and that such staff are rotated around the different parts of the organization's territory to avoid over-familiarity with their clients, colleagues, or subordinates. Other typical parts of the recipe include semi-random postings of employees to countries or cities other than those in which they were born and brought up, together with unannounced random checks, in order further to reduce the motives and opportunity for anti-system co-operation (military 'snap inspections' or their analogies, for example in unannounced inspections of prisons or fire safety).

A variant on the gaming-machine form of organization as described above is Susan Rose-Ackerman's (1978: 183–6) model of 'disorganized' bureaucracy, a structure in which decision procedures are inherently uncertain and changeable. For Rose-Ackerman (ibid. 184), an element of contrived randomness built into the structure of 'disorganized bureaucracy' can act as an anti-corruption shield in some circumstances, because the key pressure-points in a decision system are harder to identify in advance by would-be extortioners or bribers than would apply to organizations with stabler and more ordered procedures. For example, in a police force where some police are honest and others are corrupt, making it unpredictable whether beat police will work alone or in pairs and if the latter, with whom they will work at any one time, may decrease the opportunities for the dishonest police to receive bribes or practise extortion.

A quasi-fatalist recipe of contrived randomness does not only apply to control over clients and within organizations. The same implicit administrative philosophy of 'chancism' is also capable of application to the control over public management by society at large. Even Jeremy Bentham, the arch-advocate before Weber of 'rule-of-law' processes in organization, argued in his *Constitutional Code* (1983: 281): 'The Legislature, the Prime Minister, and the Minister will have in consideration the advantage, derivable in some cases from the use of *chance*, for the purposes of securing unexpectedness to inspection visits, and thence constancy of good order in the places visited.' An element of deliberate unpredictability in who oversees public administration and how, is held to reduce the risks of systematic bias, for the same reason that juries are selected by a notionally random process in the common-law countries. Certainly the classical model of democracy put randomized processes into the centre of the stage for social oversight of public administration, as reflected in Aristotle's view that selection by lot is the purest form of democracy. In classical Athens of the third and fourth centuries BC, public auditors (among other officers) were selected by lot in an attempt to avoid politicization or organized-group capture of oversight processes.

Moreover, at least two important contemporary thinkers have put a variant of the same process at the heart of their recipe for better control over government, as we will see in Chapter 10 when we look at hybrid forms of the four polar types of control in public management which were identified in Chapter 3 and have been discussed *seriatim* in the four chapters of Part II. One is the 'New Right' guru William Niskanen (1971), who advocates random assignment of programmes and bureaucracies to legislative oversight committees. Niskanen's aim is to prevent 'accountability conspiracies' (in the words of Dowding 1995: 70) between bureaucrats and orthodox legislative oversight committees, to expand public services and programme expenditure beyond the level desired by the legislature as a whole. The other is the philosopher John Burnheim (1985), who advocates 'demarchy' as a design for public management. His proposal is to divide government bureaucracy into a number of specialized authorities to be overseen by committees of citizens selected by lot from those who were willing to serve. Burnheim argues that in such a structure hardly any large-scale public bureaucracy would need to exist, because corruption, the main problem associated with contracting-out public services to private firms, would be difficult to sustain in such circumstances. His argument (ibid. 167) is that corruption depends on the ability to combine power with secrecy and a network of reciprocal favours, and that such a combination cannot be achieved in circumstances where people in power have no control over who their colleagues will be—which would be the consequence of dividing up power and selecting the overseers by lot.

Some important features of Burnheim's model seem to have been present in the organization of public finance in classical Athens—a system of government which was briefly discussed in the last chapter, in relation to its features of 'élite egalitarianism' in public management. That system is also of interest from the perspective of a 'gaming-machine' approach to organizational design in public management, because it involved both of the two features of that model, as described above. First, it involved division of responsibility in financial management among different departments and officeholders—such as treasurers who paid out money, receivers who collected it and allocated it to the spending departments, the magistrates who were responsible for farming the taxes and the other public service franchises. As the late Arnold Jones (1957: 103) put it, 'The system seems unnecessarily complicated, with its many boards, each dealing with one stage of the process. The object probably was to make peculation or improper expenditure of public funds or slackness in exacting State dues difficult by making the money and accounts pass through many hands.' Second, all of these separate functions were until the second half of the fourth century BC overseen by boards of magistrates selected by lot. And those randomly-selected magistrates reported to the Council (which was also selected by lot from the citizen Assembly) and were audited by public auditors (plus a Council committee of auditors), who were selected by lot as well. The system is reported to have been 'tolerably efficient' (ibid. 101), lasted for nearly a century, and has been (admittedly in less extreme form) reproduced in aspects of later organizational design in public management.

## 4. Conclusion

At first sight, the fatalist quadrant of cultural theory looks like a rich field for satirical treatments of management theory (and perhaps of unofficial philosophy too) but not a source of any workable doctrines of public management. Certainly, in terms of behaviour and attitudes, fatalism is a major and commonplace element in public service organization. A 'chaos theory' view of how public management works seems to be widespread in practice (even though 'garbage-can' theory on the part of management practition-ers is often advanced in a relatively incohate way). And, as we have seen, it extends even to such fundamental issues as the prediction of how major accidents and disasters are generated. Moreover, organizational designs which are intended to have quite different effects, such as the dismantling of hierarchies aimed at increasing individualism, may unintentionally produce an increase in fatalism instead (cf. Thompson, Ellis, and Wildavsky 1990: 79).

However, it has been tentatively argued in this chapter that the application of fatalism to public management in one sense goes well beyond interpretation of what the process is like and attribut-ing blame when things go wrong. It also lends itself to some degree to a positive doctrine of how to organize in public management, and how to exercise control as between organizations and their clients, within organizations, and over public administration by society at large. In this extended sense of positive design, the fatal-ist recipe for organizing public management centres on ways of deliberately making public-service organization unpredictable to those who work in and with it. And in some cases at least, any organizational system based on contrived randomness may in turn tend to generate or reinforce fatalistic attitudes—and as an inevitable by-product lead to major deficits in entrepreneurship, 'proactivity', or innovativeness, of the kind discussed in Chapter 2. After all, in such a system an individual's whole career success or failure may very well be attributed to one throw of the organiza-tional dice, and any sort of co-operation outside what is formally required may lead to personal disaster. But, as was noted in Chap-ter 3, the extent to which the operations of an organization are *perceived* as random is likely itself to vary with cultural bias, and indeed a fatalist structure of beliefs and attitudes may even act as a substitute for strict mathematical randomness in organizational design.

The 'gaming-machine' model of organizational design which can loosely be related to a fatalist world-view, has received little atten-tion. Its shortcomings as an all-purpose approach to public man-agement are not hard to see. But such a recipe cannot be fully dismissed either. As was suggested earlier, one of the underlying paradoxes of the Weberian view of bureaucracy as a determinate slot-machine applying rules to cases is that it is difficult to see how such an organization could ever collect taxes or fight crime, to the extent that its world is substantially populated by (low-group) opportunists. The paradox is that at least in a certain sense, 'rationality' in institutions (faced with Parkinsonian-type opportunists trying to exploit them) can sometimes only be achieved by designing in an element of arbitrary randomness.

# PART III

# RHETORIC, MODERNITY, AND SCIENCE IN PUBLIC MANAGEMENT

After the survey of classic and recurring ideas about how to organize public services in Part II, the three chapters in the final part of the book return to more general themes of rhetoric, modernity, and science in public management which were discussed in Chapter 1. Chapter 8 explores what a cultural theory framework can add to the analysis of public management as an arena for rhetoric. Chapter 9 returns to the theme of 'modernization' and 'global convergence' which was introduced in the first chapter, to explore what obstacles might lie in the way of these apparently ineluctable processes. In conclusion, Chapter 10 returns to the sixth and seventh propositions advanced in Chapter 1, assessing the role that the analysis of cultural variety can play in the study of public management and exploring the strengths, weaknesses, and 'stretchability' of cultural theory as an analytic approach for that purpose.

# 8

# Public Management, Rhetoric, and Culture

> ********* so conceived is not a series of self-consistent theo-
> ries that converges towards an ideal view; it is not a gradual
> approach to the truth. It is rather an ever increasing ocean of
> mutually incompatible (and perhaps even mutually incom-
> mensurable) alternatives, each single theory, each fairy tale,
> each myth that is part of the collection facing the others and
> all of them contributing, in this process of competition, to the
> development of consciousness
>
> (Feyerabend 1975: 30)

## 1. Do Ideas Develop Cumulatively in Public Management?

The missing word in the extract from Paul Feyerabend quoted
above is '*knowledge*', and the passage is part of Feyerabend's argument against the idea that science progresses in a cumulative way
(that is, building steadily on established modes of analysis and
understanding). David Stove (1982: 12) correctly points out that,
strictly speaking, to make the word 'knowledge' the subject of the
two sentences in the quotation turns the whole proposition into
nonsense. 'Knowledge entails truth, and truth entails possible
truth, and possible truth entails incompatibility. These are facts
about the meaning of common English words . . . and because they
are, you might as well say that knowledge is a poached egg, as say
what Feyerabend says about it here' (ibid.).

As Stove also points out, Feyerabend's proposition seems to be
nonsense in more than a formal sense, for at least some branches of
knowledge. No reputable geographer now believes the earth is flat.

No serious contemporary astronomer thinks the sun goes round the earth every day. Orthodox scientific beliefs in their day, the flat-earth paradigm and the Ptolemaic astronomy may still attract a few cranks, but those early ideas have been decisively refuted and are not likely to re-emerge from the garbage heap of discredited scientific theories.

It seems harder, however, to say the same thing about the progress of knowledge in public management. As noted briefly in the first chapter, ideas about what constitutes good organization or 'governance' do not seem to change as a result of a cumulative development of knowledge akin to that which caused flat-earth ideas to be abandoned. And if (as would be concluded not only from cultural theory but from many other 'system' perspectives), 'what works' in public management depends on how attitudes and structures mesh together, it is difficult to see how any major set of ideas about good government and management can be wholly discarded for all time. The chapters in Part II suggested that each of the polar types of organization has contemporary 'modern' applications.

Indeed, each of those four ways of reasoning about how to organize government and public services can sustain a workable rhetoric of public management. By 'workable rhetoric' is meant a persuasive discourse based on some sort of 'logic' (albeit typically with some key propositions kept implicit) and on a set of plausible stories and metaphors. For that reason, we could insert the words 'public management' in place of 'knowledge' in Feyerabend's quotation, and the whole passage would make much better sense than the original version.

This chapter aims to do three things. First, it briefly expands on a now familiar argument (noted in the first chapter) that shifts in what counts as 'received' ideas in public management works through a process of fashion and persuasion, not through 'proofs' couched in strict deductive logic, controlled experiments, or even systematic analysis of all available cases. Second, and more ambitiously, it aims to bring together the analysis of rhetoric in public management with the four ways of doing public management which were explored in Part II, to show how each of those approaches can have its own rhetoric, in the sense of foreshortened 'proofs', analogies, and parables. The aim is to put a cultural theory perspective to work in a different way, to identify multiple rhetorics of public management. Third, it briefly develops the suggestion made in Chapters 1 and 2 that shifts in received ideas about how to organize typically occur in a reactive way, through rejection of existing arrangements with their known faults, rather than through a positive process of reasoning from a blank slate.

## 2. The Rhetorical Dimension of Public Management

The idea of science as cumulative progress towards truth is the optimistic 'Whig' view of intellectual development. It holds that, over time, knowledge replaces ignorance and better theories replace worse ones (that is, those which are better able to explain observed facts without anomalies). The process is ordinarily supposed to work by a mixture of competition among scientists, institutionalized memory (involving the convention that current scientific work must take previous work as its point of departure), and controlled experiment or systematic analysis of cases, which carefully test rival theories according to their explanatory power and drive out the weakest.

Even in natural science, this once orthodox view has been challenged by those philosophers who see changes in prevailing ideas as more discontinuous and less mechanically rational than the traditional philosophy and historiography of science allows for (cf. Kuhn 1970: 19 and 151). Some have even argued that 'institutionalized forgetting' rather than cumulation is built into the social structure of science, because of the premium on 'discovery claims', meaning that scientific propositions are forgotten almost as much as they are 'discovered' (Douglas 1987: 69–80; Merton 1965).

Whatever may be the truth of that, the traditional view seems particularly hard to apply to the development of 'what-to-do' ideas about social organization of any kind. Arguments about how to organize and manage are rarely if ever closed by facts and logic alone. Indeed, often they cannot be, because the issues at stake are at best 'trans-scientific' in nature. 'Trans-scientific' issues are those which come somewhere between science and politics because, although they can be stated in scientific terms and could in principle be addressed by the orthodox methods of science, crucial experimentation is in practice not feasible (Weinberg 1972; Majone 1989: 3). Consider, for instance, the difficulty of mounting a controlled experiment to explore the effects on public-service corruption of staffing the police force exclusively by millionaires, or of testing Bentham's idea that the best way to solve the identity problems that plague most administrative systems is to tattoo all babies at birth.

The general difficulty of conducting controlled experiments in laboratory conditions applies to all the social sciences. But if, as was suggested in Chapter 3, the success of any management recipe for organizational performance depends on cultural context (ideas and beliefs matching structures), all such recipes must be highly contingent. And such contingency becomes still greater if cultural context in its turn is capable of being shaped by the rhetorical power of those advocating a recipe. Compound contingency of that type implies high complexity if not indeterminacy, in identifying the circumstances in which a recipe works. And it also may imply high instability through self-exciting changes in cultural configurations and the waxing and waning of different forms of rhetoric. High contingency and the possibility of high-dimensional dynamics (for example through self-reinforcing or self-destructive processes) may serve to produce a high incidence of 'trans-scientific' questions in public management. Indeed, Giandomenico Majone (1989) argues that contemporary policy analysts are more like lawyers than like natural scientists. Just as most developed legal systems consist of a set of contradictory precepts, rules and precedents, and the skill of the lawyer lies in which precept or precedent to stress and which to downplay, so the skill of advocacy in public management lies in finding and stressing those elements that support the particular argument in hand and downplaying the others.

How then can persuasion be achieved without systematic analysis of cases or the deployment of irrefragable formal logic? In the science of rhetoric, definitively defined by Aristotle (1984: 2155) two millennia ago as 'the facility of observing in any given case the available means of persuasion', persuasion involves three basic elements: 'speaker', 'speech' and 'audience'.[1] The analysis of persuasion accordingly needs to focus on: the personal character of the 'speaker' (the personal 'credibility' factor), the creation of an appropriate emotional atmosphere to put the audience in an appro-

---

[1] In modern telecommunications language, we might speak of a 'sender', a 'receiver', and a 'message', since persuasion may occur by means other than speech alone, such as dress, hair, architecture, or pictures on TV.

priate frame of mind ('mood music', in popular parlance), and the substantive arguments used ('the proof, or apparent proof, provided by the words of the speech itself').

When argument has to rely on methods other than exhaustive logical proof or strictly controlled experiment, it needs to draw on example, story (real cases or invented fables selected to support a particular case), and more generally on what Aristotle called 'enthymeme'. The term means a foreshortened chain of reasoning, with key premises suppressed, so the conclusion flows swiftly and apparently effortlessly from a few stages of argument. For Aristotle enthymeme is the key feature which distinguishes deliberative rhetoric from formal logic: the key to the construction (or deconstruction) of deliberative argument lies in the choice of which initial premises to argue from, which steps of the argument to expose and which to suppress. Ricca Edmondson (1984: 20) defines an enthymeme as 'an inference whose communicative effectiveness depends partly on the hearer's conception of the speaker's qualification for making his or her remarks; whose form is adjusted to its hearer's presumed capacities for response; and which is based not on some genuinely universal empirical generalisation but on an assumption about what is probably the case or can reasonably be expected. This type of assumption (technically known as a *topos*) is a generalisation with an everyday standard of rigour, not purporting to hold for every single example possible, but applicable to most cases, sound enough to ratify the arguments it generates'.

Three well-known examples of enthymeme in organizational argument include: simple dichotomies or trichotomies of alternatives, such as 'rule-boundedness' versus 'discretion', 'theory X' versus 'theory Y', 'proactivity' versus 'reactivity', presented as if the alternatives are mutually exclusive or jointly exhaustive (using apparent opposites to make a case, one of the devices of rhetorical argument); casual attribution of motives to opponents which are different from the public arguments they are making (the familiar 'hidden agenda' argument that surfaces so often in debates about public management reform); and the *post hoc, ergo propter hoc* argument (that is, the casual attribution of causality).

The latter, noted by Aristotle, is a familiar type of argument about management and organization, since it is often used to make claims about success or failure of a particular method of organization—like privatization or restructuring—by reference to selected 'before' and 'after' aspects of an organization's perform- ance on some dimension or other (like numbers of complaints or of financial surpluses or deficits). Steps in the argument which are suppressed in such reasoning typically include the possibility that the performance changes might have nothing to do with the altera- tions in the management system, or that the effects of the manage- ment system are impossible to disentangle from other concomitant changes in the organization's circumstances, or that *any* manage- ment change might have had the same effect and not just the one which was actually introduced (the well-known 'Hawthorne effect', called after the famous Harvard Business School experiments at the Hawthorne Works of the Western Electric Company in Chi- cago from 1926 to 1932,[2] in which any alteration of conditions of work will temporarily have an effect on workers' behaviour, irre- spective of what particular direction that change might take). The key analytic question in assessing public management arguments is to identify which premises have been concentrated upon and which have been suppressed.

Enthymeme often consists of a maxim followed by a chain of selected examples, with selective illustration being used for proof (Fischer (1971: 43) terms this approach the 'pseudo proof'). Fables and selective cases are typical sources of reasoning in manage- ment texts. David Osborne and Ted Gaebler's (1992) best-selling *Reinventing Government*, which influenced the administrative re- form plans of the early Clinton presidency in the USA and has been referred to on several occasions in earlier chapters, is a prime example of this approach. The book is rich in selective examples of inspirational public managers who 'turned round' poorly- performing bureaucracies, and of organizations 'turned round' or taken from rags to riches in some way. Mark Moore's (1995) more recent and more restrained *Creating Public Value* quite self-con- sciously uses a similar rhetorical technique to advance a new legit- imating philosophy of public managers as 'value-adders' rather than mere rule-following bureaucrats. Another example is what Rune Premfors (1996) calls the 'PUMA story' of contemporary public management development—that is, the idea of 'modernization' and convergence offered by the PUMA public management unit in

<hr/>

[2] See Roethlisberger, Dickson, and Wright (1939).

the OECD, which will be discussed in the next chapter. The 'PUMA story' takes the international popularity of a set of management catch-phrases as 'evidence' of convergence in behaviour and attitudes, but this claim is a 'pseudo-proof' because it could be argued with equal plausibility that the language has become popular precisely because it is so ambiguous that it can accommodate very different lines of action.

To make an argument seem plausible other than by 'hard data' or logical proof, four so-called 'master tropes' of rhetoric are commonly deployed: that is, metaphor or analogy (making one thing stand for another, as in likening human behaviour to a mathematical function), synecdoche (taking a part for the whole, as in probability of death per 1km travelled as an indicator of the safety of different forms of transport), metonymy (characterizing something in terms of an associated but not logically isomorphic property, like academic qualifications and intelligence), and irony (literally saying one thing and meaning the opposite, more generally focusing on paradox or reverse effects, for example in arguing policies or organizational designs will have the opposite of the intended result).

The general notion that argument about organization and management can be understood as a rhetorical process involving the components briefly described above is far from new (see Hood and Jackson 1991). For instance, Andrez Huczynski (1993: 1) begins his analysis of contemporary management gurus with the question, 'Why do certain management ideas achieve widespread popularity and bring fame and fortune to their writers, while others do not?' and sees the answer as lying in the familiar elements of rhetoric— the conjuncture of idea *content*, idea *context*, and idea *presentation*. What remains to be explored is the link between cultural biases and forms of rhetoric.

## 3. Rhetoric and Culture in Public Management

What cultural theory can add to the conventional analysis of rhetoric in public management is a way of sorting different elements of persuasion and modes of argument according to cultural bias. It starts from the presumption that instead of thinking in terms of 'universals' when it comes to personal credibility, 'mood music' or persuasive metaphors and stories, these components of rhetoric may vary according to cultural bias. The rhetorical key that will open one type of social lock is unlikely to serve as a master-key for all of the others. Cultural theory suggests that rhetoric has to mesh with culture and interact with it.

Huczynski's (1993) analysis of the rhetoric of management gurus deals only with variations on a dominant culture of hierarchism—in the sense of a belief that organization can only function effectively if human beings are divided into managers and managed, with the managers entitled to be paid more highly than those who do the 'real work'. Gurus, he suggests, essentially legitimate management as a morally justifiable calling based on arcane professional skills, present management in a positive rather than negative light, offer a means of out-foxing others and of re-legitimating drives for higher profits and productivity.

This portrait is recognizable enough for much of contemporary Western business management, but even there it does not capture the full variety of how-to-organize ideas. Arguably the weakest part of Huczynski's analysis lies in the *ad hoc* way in which he divides common management ideas into six 'idea-families', namely 'bureaucracy', 'scientific management', 'administrative management', 'human relations', 'neo-human relations', and 'guru theory'. The disadvantage of this approach is that it does not demonstrate that the categories chosen are 'of a kind', employing consistent building-blocks, or that they are mutually exclusive and jointly exhaustive. In contrast, applying a cultural-theory perspective to that material (another example of placing one cultural-theory 'lens' in front of another to bring out differences within a single type) gives us a rather different way of ordering those ideas into groups, as different variants of hierarchism. An ordering of that type is summarized in Table 8.1.

As Table 8.1 suggests, some of the management ideas Huczynski describes can be categorized as hierarchism tinged with fatalism, particularly the contemporary corporate craze for 'new ageist' mysticism which was commented on in the last chapter. Some of the other ideas he describes consist of hierarchism tinged with egalitarianism, particularly that element of human relations doctrine that naked competition within an organization should be heavily overlain by a more solidaristic 'family' approach, and later doctrines of 'employee empowerment' and 'organizational democ-

TABLE 8.1. *Huczynski's management-guru ideas arranged by cultural type*

| | |
|---|---|
| *Hierarchism tinged with fatalism*<br>  1990s New ageist and mysticist<br>  business fads | *Hierarchism 'on stilts'*<br>  1980s 'hero-manager' great<br>  leader literature |
| *Hierarchism tinged with*<br>*individualism*<br>  Intra-organization competition,<br>  'get ahead in the corporate<br>  jungle' literature | *Hierarchism tinged with*<br>*egalitarianism*<br>  Corporate 'family', democracy,<br>  employee empowerment<br>  literature |

racy'. Other doctrines amount to hierarchism tinged with individualism (such as Frederick Winslow Taylor's 'scientific management' doctrine of making every employee's pay depend on a measurement of their individual output; ideas of the corporation as an arena for internal competition; even the literature on how the individual can get ahead in the corporate jungle by methods that allegedly are not taught at business school). Others might be said to be hierarchism tinged with hierarchism, or 'hierarchism on stilts' (notably what might be dubbed the 'great leader' genre of management literature, which focuses on leadership, particularly in the form of extraordinary individuals who can heal sick organizations, cure corporate paralysis, and 'walk on water').

The analytic advantage of rearranging Huczynski's repertoire of business-management doctrines in this way—which cuts across the more conventional labels he employs—is that it clarifies the link between rhetoric and culture. Taken from the viewpoint of cultural theory, what the different management-guru rhetorics portrayed by Huczynski are doing is reaching out—at least limitedly—from hierarchism to other world-views and ways of life.

Nor does such an analysis apply only to business-management literature of the kind discussed by Huczynski. If anything, it is even more applicable to public management, with its broader political constituency. Each of the four polar ways of 'doing' public management discussed earlier in the book links to a particular type of rhetoric in terms of the fundamental components of persuasion identified by Aristotle and briefly outlined in the last section.

As noted there, one way of sustaining an argument is through the personal credibility of the advocate or guru. This element—*ethos*, in conventional rhetorical analysis—is likely to vary sharply with cultural context. The characteristic hierarchist ethos is that of 'authority figure', as conveyed by marks of high scientific or official status (the organizational equivalent of the white-coated government scientist, assiduously cultivated by the German cameralists, as discussed in Chapter 4). But an anti-authority ethos fits more closely with the world-view of egalitarians and individualists. The egalitarian ethos will be that of a member of a solidaristic group—the image epitomized by Greenpeace or dark green communitarians—facing threats from 'the power structure' represented by the upper ranks of business and government. The individualist ethos is that of the lonely figure fighting a heroic battle against forces of collectivism or organizational power. An example is Leslie Chapman's (1978) *Your Disobedient Servant* which portrayed the image of one man working single-handed in the British civil service to combat dramatic instances of waste which were condoned by the top leadership (the book is said to have been a major influence on Margaret Thatcher and Sir Keith Joseph in developing their approach to bureaucratic reform in the late 1970s). If there is a fatalist ethos, it is likely to be that of radical sceptic, distrustful of anything that passes for academic orthodoxy or received doctrine of any kind. But can there be an all-purpose *ethos*? Cultural theory suggests that what will create credibility in one social context is likely to undermine it in another.

The same goes for the second element in persuasion, achieving an appropriate emotional atmosphere for the argument being pursued. One of the most familiar approaches to *pathos*, as this element is called, in organizational argument is to cultivate an atmosphere of crisis in order to close debate. But 'mood music' may also vary to some extent with cultural bias. In an hierarchist context, the ideal pathos to be achieved is that of teacher and students or priest and flock. Many of Huczynski's (1993: 176 ff) business-management gurus seem to be trying to contrive a pathos of quasi-religious fervour about the importance of management, and even conduct their seminars in the style of US Christian revivalist meetings led by a strong prophetic figure, even to the extent of presenting 'converts' to their meetings to confess their past sins and testify to the power of the new faith. Religious imagery may also support a more egalitarian ethos, but the 'mood music' for the egalitarian message is more likely to include the development of an atmosphere of collective anger against abuse of power by those in high places. A collective feeling of distrust in authority may also be a *pathos* that fits individualist sensibilities, but individualist 'mood music' is likely to involve an atmosphere of self-help. If there is a fatalist *pathos*, on the other hand, it is likely to be one of 'what's the use?' scepticism about any cause or crusade.

Cultural variety is likely to be particularly important when it comes to the third element of persuasion, namely *logos*, or the argument itself, which needs to fit the social context and at least appear to 'prove' its case. Each of the four so-called 'master tropes' of rhetoric that were briefly noted in the last section can be used to make the public-management 'story' associated with each of the four cultural-theory world-views seem to be the most natural and plausible way to organize government and public services. Table 8.2 summarizes how the four polar world-views can connect to the master tropes for public management.

As noted earlier, *metaphor* means making one thing stand for another. It is a familiar and indispensable tool for thought as well as for explanation and the expression of wit: '. . . by what allegory will the narrator shape the data? In the hardest as in the softest science the choice of a metaphor reflects a worldview and the evidence to be examined' (McCloskey 1990: 63). In public management, as in political science more generally, cultural frames and preferred metaphors go together. We can, for instance, liken organizational life to a stock market in which individual reputations rise or fall; we can liken it to a ship where there needs to be an ordering of authority on the bridge to avoid chaos; we can liken it to a computer network like the internet, full of chance interconnections, discontinuities, and unexpected information; we can liken it to a weather system or any process of spontaneous self-regulation in which control is achieved without any overt 'controller'. All of those well-known metaphors have some prima-facie plausibility, but as presented above each resonates with a different implied world-view concerning what the world is like and how human organization should be ordered.

Moreover, most of the familiar metaphors for organization and government—like family, machine, dance, drama, body—can take a different shape according to the cultural bias to which they are being linked. There are different sorts of family relationships (from the 'absolutist' patriarchal structure to the egalitarian commune) and different aspects of biological or even mechanical processes which can be brought out according to the preferred picture of how to organize that the metaphor is intended to paint. To illustrate the point, consider the equally common use of the idea of a 'game' to characterize organization and management. The metaphor of 'game' is ubiquitous, from common-speech descriptions of 'the rules of the game' inside government to formal mathematicized 'game theory' accounts of strategic interaction in organizations (to the point where the underlying metaphor has become half-hidden).

However, the familiar metaphor of organizational life as a 'game' can be taken in rather different ways, and there are 'game' metaphors available to fit each of the polar ways of organizing identified by cultural theory. If we have a broadly hierarchist view of management and organization in mind, we will naturally tend to turn to the metaphor of a team game under a coach or a captain (that is, a game played in teams consisting of leaders and followers, with the needs of individual players secondary to that of the team as a collectivity, and much depending on how the team is organized). If we have a more individualist view of organizational design in mind, we are more likely to invoke the metaphor of individual games of skill like chess or squash (or perhaps the more vivid and common metaphor of the 'rat race'), where individual competition is paramount, subject only to arbitration or refereeing rules. If the preferred organizational recipe is more egalitarian in nature, we are more likely to select a game analogy from the sort of group sport that is non-competitive and non-captained, like some kinds of folk-dancing (the activity is necessarily 'groupy', success depends on the group working together, but there is no overt authority figure co-ordinating the players). From a fatalist viewpoint, we are more likely to draw on the metaphor of a game of chance, for example a gaming-machine or roulette wheel. Each of these different 'game' metaphors has some plausibility as a way of portraying at least some aspects of public management (and each is more or less capable of being formally modelled in game-theory terms), but the rhetorician's skill in public management lies in picking the metaphor that fits the argument and the audience being addressed, or in finding effective counter-metaphors to pit against those linked with rival doctrines.

*Synecdoche*, another of the master tropes of rhetoric, is less immediately familiar than metaphor but just as often invoked. As noted earlier, synecdoche means taking a part for the whole, as in the common case when one indicator is used as a 'proxy' for others (for instance, complaint rates for quality). As with metaphor, the skill of using synecdoche is to make it appear invisible, so the appropriateness of the chosen 'proxy' does not even enter debate. Accordingly for a hierarchist vision of public management, the appropriate synecdoche for public organizations may be the set of formal rules or machine-like procedures, so these elements need to be placed in the centre of the stage (as in the common portrayal of Max Weber's (1948) ideas of bureaucracy as a sort of slot-machine programmed by rules—though in fact Weber emphasized the role of bureaucratic culture and ethos). For an individualist vision of public management, on the other hand, analytic attention needs to be focused on those situations within organizations where rational players with differing interests try to get the better of one another (as William Niskanen (1971) did in his famous portrayal of bureaucracy as a two-person game between a budget allocator trying to get the biggest bang for a buck in public services and a bureaucrat aiming to get the largest possible budget for his or her bureau).

By contrast, the appropriate egalitarian synecdoche may be those instances of 'solidarity' in work groups or communities, cases where informal group behaviour consists of individuals forming common bonds, perhaps in defiance of official rules, authority or 'higher-ups' (as Shan Martin (1983) did in her account of the behaviour of informal work groups in public service provision at the 'coalface', to the point where managers were portrayed as unnecessary or dysfunctional). For a fatalist vision, on the other hand, it is the existence of 'snafus', or chance interactions that may be taken as the central feature of organizational life—as in Joseph Heller's great novel *Catch-22*, in which some individuals have extraordinary good fortune while others are repeatedly rebuffed, entirely as a result of unpredictable crossed wires, misunderstandings, or chance connections within the great military bureaucracy. Each of these four elements undeniably captures a part of public management, but again the skill of the public management rhetorician lies in finding the synecdoche that fits the audience and the what-to-do recipe being conveyed.

Third, each world-view can also be linked to a *metonym* of public management. Metonymy, another of the master tropes of rhetoric, comes somewhere in between metaphor and synecdoche, because it means letting something which is merely associated with the phenomenon in question stand for it (like green eyeshades for accountants and auditors, stopwatches for time and motion specialists, or bowler hats and rolled-up umbrellas to stand for the British senior civil service, to take a now-obsolete example). For instance, in a hierarchist vision of public management, the national coat of arms or royal crest might serve as the natural 'metonym' for the public service (linking state bureaucracy with traditional symbols of authority). A metonym more aligned with a fatalist vision, on the other hand, would be that of 'red tape'—easily the commonest metonym for public administration and one which conveys a suitably fatalist overtone of unpredictability and incomprehensible complexity. For an individualist view of public management, the 'contract' may be the metonym which conveys the appropriate notion of bargaining and exchange (as in those institutional economics theories of organization as a nexus of contracts). For egalitarians, however, the central metonym is likely to be that of the meeting, involving dialogue among a set of players each having their own say. These items are not exactly metaphors in a strict sense (though they may approach the status of metaphor), but nor are they necessarily part of any real-life public service organization. For instance, I have met public servants who have never encountered red tape in its literal sense (used to bind sheaves of documents together); there are organizations in which meetings are rare or non-existent; contracts in the sense of formal documents representing negotiated agreements are likewise often absent in organizational life. Such items are merely items which may or may not be associated with the phenomenon.

The fourth (and highest) 'master trope' of rhetoric is *irony*. As noted earlier, it strictly means saying one thing and meaning the opposite, but in a less pure form it is associated with paradox, and specifically with pointing out unanticipated consequences that are the reverse of those intended. Irony is a central element in effective argument, as in those economic analyses which amount to ironic stories about how different real tax incidence is from the legal assignation of liability or how counter-productive can be the effects of regulation, such as the fixing of maximum rents or minimum wages (cf. McCloskey 1990: 24–8). Other examples include John

Adams' (1985) 'risk compensation hypothesis', which argues that attempts to increase safety by regulation will only result in compensatory behaviour (for instance, by driving less carefully in response to safer automobiles) to maintain a given level of risk, or Alexis de Tocqueville's famous argument that the French Revolution only served to accentuate and perfect the 'statism' of the *ancien régime*.

All the social sciences, as well as the standard forms of political argument, feature ironic stories in that vein. But Albert Hirschman (1991: 165), in a well-known essay on reactionary rhetoric, argues that irony is peculiarly associated with reactionary positions: 'in the effective use of the potent weapon of irony [in the weaker sense used above], conservatives have had a clear edge over progressives', because it may be easier for them to give instances of 'perversity', 'jeopardy', or 'futility' brought about by social reform. Perversity means achieving the opposite of what you intend; jeopardy means sacrificing previous gains in order to achieve the current goal; futility means making no real impact on the problem.

Hirschman himself shows (ibid. 167) how the 'perversity', 'jeopardy', and 'futility' arguments of reactionaries can be exactly matched by parallel but not strictly ironic arguments (of impending peril, mutual reinforcement and historical inevitability) on the part of progressives. But even so, his basis for this claim about the special hold conservatives have on irony is debatable. A simple distinction between 'reaction' and 'progressivism' is not rich enough to capture the differences among the four different polar world-views of public management considered in this book. Each of those polar types incorporates a rather different view of what 'reaction' and 'progress' means, and hence each readily lends itself in principle to an ironic demonstration of unintended and reverse effects likely to be associated with the other recipes. In that sense, it would be surprising if only one of the polar world-views was particularly suited to the use of irony.

As we saw in the last chapter, fatalists have an ironic 'garbage-can' story to tell about how organizational processes work, debunking claims to strong rationality and stressing how easily any solution can produce effects very different from those intended through complex interactive processes only modellable through 'chaos theory'. The ironic story told by hierarchists to support their view of public management is more likely to be along the lines of Garrett Hardin's (1968) famous and rhetorically powerful parable of the 'tragedy of the commons', in which absence of binding regulation and oversight leads unintendedly to social disaster.[3] Egalitarians share hierarchists' distrust of 'government by the market', but the sort of irony expressed in Norman Dixon's (1976) famous *On the Psychology of Military Incompetence* (which was referred to in Chapter 2), together with many other accounts of the deep shortcomings of organizations which put exaggerated stress on top-level leadership, rank and 'bull', is more likely to appeal to egalitarians as part of their account of why top-down governance processes unintendedly lead to disaster. Individualists, on the other hand, can turn to ironic stories about how even the most apparently hierarchist or groupist structures can unwittingly turn into markets, even in the most unlikely settings, as in the case of Robert Radford's (1945) account of the development of unofficial markets within World War II prisoner-of-war camps. Rather than only a single vein of irony, each of these stories contains a potential paradox, in that each focuses on the unintended effects of basic forms of organization, their tendency to turn into their opposites or to produce reverse effects. In the next chapter we will return to the theme of 'reverse effect' mechanisms in public management.

What is being suggested here, in contrast to Huczynski's claims about business management, is that there is no single form of rhetoric about public management which is likely to be enduringly dominant. Rather, each of the polar ways of doing public management discussed in this book can be linked to a viable rhetorical mode, particularly in respect of *ethos* and *logos*, that is, the way that premises of argument can be selectively exposed and suppressed (enthymeme) and in the way that the 'master tropes' of rhetoric can be deployed. Further, the claim is that rhetoric and culture are

---

[3] In this story, one of the most-heavily cited parables in social science, shepherds graze their flocks on a piece of common land. If they graze too many sheep, the pasture will be ruined, so everyone is better off if the total number of animals is kept within limits that the common can support. But as individuals, each may reject individual self-restraint by reasoning thus: if I limit the size of my flock, others may expand theirs, and the common will be destroyed anyway, but if I expand and others hold back I will be able to get ahead. If everyone acts on that basis, the common turns into a dustbowl and everyone involved loses their livelihood. Of course, the hierarchist 'lesson' from the story is that oversight and regulation can help to avoid such unintentional disasters, while individualists will naturally argue for privatization of the commons, and egalitarians for collectivization of the sheep.

TABLE 8.2. *Rhetoric and culture: Possible rhetorical applications of four world-views*

| | Public management world-view | | | |
|---|---|---|---|---|
| | Hierarchist | Individualist | Egalitarian | Fatalist |
| Possible 'ethos' | Authority figure | Lonely figure battling collective pressures | Member of persecuted solidaristic group | Sceptic |
| Possible 'pathos' | Teacher and pupils or priest and flock | Self-help | Outrage against abuse of power at the top | 'What's the use?' scepticism |
| Possible 'logos' (master tropes) (i) Metaphor (= analogy, parallel) (Game metaphors used here) | Public management as a captained team game (e.g. hockey, football) | Public management as an individual game of skill (e.g. chess or squash) | Public management as a non-captained non-competitive group sport (e.g. folk dancing) | Public management as a game of chance (e.g. gaming-machine or roulette-wheel) |

TABLE 8.2. (*Continued*)

| | Public management world-view | | | |
|---|---|---|---|---|
| | Hierarchist | Individualist | Egalitarian | Fatalist |
| (ii) Synecdoche (= part taken for whole) | Formal rules and official machine (Weber 1948) | Strategic encounters between opposing players (Niskanen 1971) | Informal group behaviour (Martin 1983; Ferguson 1984) | 'Snafus', unexpected chance chaos-type connections (Heller 1964) |
| (iii) Metonymy (= associated property) | National coat of arms or royal crest | Set of contracts | Seminars or conferences | Red tape |
| (iv) Irony (= paradoxical effects or processes) | 'Tragedy of the commons' stories highlighting fragility of group solidarity and individualized competition | Tendency of groupism and hierarchism to produce corrupt or black markets | 'Social psychology of incompetence' accounts of disasters produced by top-down leadership | 'Garbage-can' stories; ease with any recipe produces reverse effects |

likely to be interactive in public management. Rhetoric is central to the way each world-view is sustained, defined and developed as part of a process of challenging other world-views.

Linking rhetoric to culture is a way of avoiding what is otherwise the tendency of rhetorical analysis to become simply an arid classification of techniques and figures of speech (as happened to the Aristotelian tradition). All the packaging in the world will not help if the basic content of an idea does not fit the cultural context at which it is being aimed. Some ideas will simply be 'unsellable' to particular audiences. After all, even management 'saints' like Frederick Winslow Taylor and Elton Mayo, who were in the first generation of modern business management gurus and whose presentational skills are heavily stressed by Huczynski, failed to stop their business clienteles from systematically filtering out even the mildly egalitarian aspects of their ideas (Huczynski 1993: 77). Culture interacts with persuasive skill in the process of rhetoric (in contrast to the naïve PR view of rhetoric as a clever box of tricks for manipulating gullible audiences, or 'selling ice-cubes to Eskimos').

## 4. Better *than* the Devil You Know? Reaction and Change in Public Management

'Better the devil you know than the devil you don't know,' says the proverb, meaning if in doubt, stay with your current system, with all its known failings. But a cultural theory perspective would suggest that the development of arguments in public management is more often a 'reactive' than a 'proactive' process, in that ideas about how to do better are typically not constructed on a blank slate but through a process of rejection of opponents' views, current institutional systems, or both.

Indeed, it is often observed that the faults of existing arrangements, which are relatively concrete and observable, tend to be more visible than the failings of alternative systems which are not currently in use. Following earlier writers like Henri Pirenne (1914), Albert Hirschman (1982) claims that the swing between 'collectivist' and 'individualist' methods of social organization follows a long-term cycle of euphoria and disillusion. The longer one method of social organization has been in good standing, the more obvious become its faults and the more it comes to be blamed for all the ills of society. The longer the alternative system has been out of favour, the rosier the light in which it appears to those disillusioned with the current orthodoxy, and the more its own faults tend to be forgotten. Over time, a head of steam builds up to such a point that the current orthodoxy is dethroned and its once-vanquished rival is restored to the position of received doctrine, in the expectation that it will cure all the problems associated with the former system. Slowly, however, the euphoria starts to wear off, the new heaven and new earth start to look all too much like the old ones, and the cycle of disappointment begins again. In relation to business management, too, Huczynski (1993) sees ideas as developing as a corrective to the perceived shortfalls of previous received ideas—as in the often-noted example of the 'human relations' approach developing in the 1930s as a reaction to what was portrayed as the purely technical approach of 'scientific management', and of the development of what Huczynski calls 'neo-human relations' (such as Organizational Development and Human Resource Management) in the 1950s and 1960s as a reaction to what by then was perceived as the 'authoritarianism' of human relations.

Thompson, Ellis, and Wildavsky (1990), in their account of how cultural shifts take place, go much further than Hirschman. Like Hirschman, but in a more elaborated model, they explain change by a theory of surprise: 'the cumulative impact of successive anomalies or surprises' (ibid. 69). What makes their theory of surprise more complex than Hirschman's, and more elaborated than Huczynski's, is that instead of one possible exit from each position, there are three possible exits (representing three different 'ways of life'), making twelve possible types of shift rather than only two. And those twelve routes are, they claim, constantly being traversed. Rather than the stereotype vision of culture as something which is passed on unquestioningly from one generation to the next, they argue that change is ubiquitous and endogenous: 'The relative strength of the rival ways of life . . . are constantly ebbing and flowing, but no one way of life ever wins' (ibid. 83). Their argument is that what moves people around the cultural configurations is surprise and disillusion at the behaviour of each institutionalized 'way of life' in the face of challenges from its environment. Because (as was suggested in Chapter 2) each way of

life has its built-in blind spots and weaknesses, along with its corresponding strengths, such surprise and disappointment is inevitable
and perpetual.

Such a picture would be consistent with the apparent tendency
for public-management systems in time to produce their polar opposites. Can it be an accident that the most 'egalitarian' approach
to public management developed in modern times—the 1960s Cultural Revolution against the bureaucracy and all established institutions in Mao's China—took place in the society which had
sustained perhaps the most developed form of 'hierarchist' public
administration the world has ever seen? Or that one of the most
centralized state traditions of modern Europe—that of Napoleonic
France—also produced the most radical recipes for decentralization, in the form of Proudhon's recipe for wholly contractual
relations among self-governing communes? Or that the radically
'managerial' public-management culture of Frederick the Great's
Prussia gave way to a system which carried 'juridification' to a
comparable level of excess? Or, to give a more recent case, that a
state commonly given as a textbook example of 'corporatist progressivism' in the 1970s—New Zealand—gave birth to the most
radically 'individualist' public-management design to emerge since
Bentham's plans of more than 150 years before? In many cases, at
least, a reactive pattern seems to fit developments in public management thought, though there are clearly periods of cumulative
change as well.

Likewise, the succession of public-management ideas often tends
to consist of a set of reactions to the excesses of yesterday's orthodoxy. Confucius' stress on the need for unitary authority and rule
by a scholarly élite was a reaction to an era of battles among feudal
warlords in pre-unification China; the cameralists' stress on managerial expertise was a reaction against the earlier stress on feudal
law as the proper field of expertise for state officials; Bentham's
stress on uniformity and rules was a reaction against the muddle
and pluriformity of British eighteenth-century administration; the
Progressives' stress on technical administration divorced from
politics was a reaction against the excesses of nineteenth-century
American machine politics; and today's 'New Public Management'
is likewise a reaction against the restrictions imposed by generalized process rules and a 'monastic culture' of public service. Each

of these movements drew its initial vigour and support as much from a perception of what *didn't* work as much as from a clear endorsement of its positive features.

## 5. Conclusion

In his introduction to the Penguin edition of Aristotle's *Art of Rhetoric* (1991: 2), Hugh Lawson-Tancred remarks that the two most striking characteristics of the social organization of classical Greece were competition and loquacity. Exactly the same could be said about the conditions under which public management is debated today. There has been an outpouring of ideas and arguments, many of a contradictory kind, and the traditional 'Whiggish' idea of 'the onward march of science' is less convincing as an account of what drives idea change in public management than a combination of rhetoric, reaction, and culture. Indeed, at the most basic level, the central activity of management, in so far as it consists of finding ways of communicating with others in a persuasive way (the 'power to persuade', in Harry Truman's well-known words (Neustadt 1961)) is the exercise of rhetorical power.

Those parts of the 'public-management problem' which are least connected to the advancement and justifications about what to do in specific circumstances in the here and now may be most amenable to scientific 'hardening'—but it is precisely those other elements which will always constitute the central problem in public management. It is commonly accepted today that deliberative rhetoric is unavoidable in reasoning about management (in spite of Herbert Simon's (1946) famous argument for a 'hard science' approach to the subject), though there is no clear view about how the deliberation should be conducted or precisely what has to be left to processes of persuasion as against hard science.

What a cultural-theory framework can add to the analysis of management rhetoric is a way of ordering and understanding the different varieties. Contrary to what authors like Huczynski say about business management, there is no single all-purpose form of rhetoric in public management. What this chapter has aimed to show is that each of the four polar organizational ways of life identified by cultural theory can generate its own rhetoric, in the form of a characteristic *ethos*, a predisposition to particular forms of *pathos*, and a distinctive *logos* in the sense of a set of stories and analogies for public management.

Accordingly, to make sense of argument in public management we need to combine the analysis of rhetoric with the analysis of cultural variety in how to organize. Such a framework may contribute not just to better understanding, but to better argument too. Typically the problem with management rhetoric is that there is too much loquacity and too little effective competition. If Huczynski is correct to see conventional management-guru rhetoric as an endless series of variations on an hierarchist theme, the insertion of arguments based on the other polar ways of organizing identified by cultural theory can add a different and richer perspective to that conversation (cf. Schwarz and Thompson 1990; Majone 1989: 2). Chapter 10 will return to the issue of how far a cultural theory perspective can 'add value' to theory and practice in public management. But before turning to that issue, the next chapter explores a cultural-theory perspective on the common contemporary idea that a new millenial paradigm is sweeping through public management worldwide.

# 9

# Contemporary Public Management:
# A New Global Paradigm?

Chairman, you may remember that at our last meeting I was asked to look at ways of empowering our staff, to give them ownership of their own projects . . . This is obviously going to be a learning loop for all of us. We must be proactive not reactive . . . What I am preparing is a number of seminars for everyone at manager level and over on activity versus process . . .

(Cartwright 1995: 42)

## 1. Modern, Global, Inevitable? The Claim of a New Paradigm in Public Management

One of the most powerful themes in the rhetoric of contemporary public management is the idea of 'modernization'. As noted earlier, 'modernization' is used extensively to explain and justify contemporary changes in the structure and operation of public services, with 'modernization' plans appearing for the public services in many European countries (see Müller and Wright 1994; Jones and Burnham 1995: 327). This chapter looks critically at that theme against the background of cultural theory. It argues that 'modernization' is a rhetorically successful idea because when the powerful but implicit metaphor of technological development that underlies it is carried over into human organization it is inherently ambiguous. So it lends itself to quite different and contradictory ideas about the wave of the future that fit with each of the world-views identified by cultural theory. Further, it argues that a vision of global transformation of public management into a convergent 'modern' style is likely to be exaggerated because it ignores powerful forces of path-dependency and self-disequilibration—that is, the capacity of management reform initiatives to produce the opposite of their intended result.

The idea of world-wide convergence on a single 'modern' form of organization is a beguiling and recurring one. Bernard Silberman (1993: p. ix) has examined early twentieth-century Weberian ideas that presaged convergence on a general model of modernity. He argues that those ideas turned out to be wrong, in that different states retained distinctive ways of running their public services, particularly in the way politics, law, and administration fitted together. Likewise, earlier Fabian and socialist ideas that the world would converge on what were then considered to be 'modern' collectivist modes of organization (because of their allegedly superior efficiency compared with the chaos and muddle of 'old-fashioned' individualist models), receive scant attention today. But in spite of the failure of earlier visions of convergent 'modernization' in public management, the idea remains central to current debate.

The idea of 'modernization' is appealing, because it can be linked metaphorically to universal themes in nature (Douglas 1987: 52)—changes in generations, the vigour of youth, the feebleness of age, the truism that in human affairs, 'nothing . . . is true but change, nothing abides' (Gibbon 1982: 252). More specifically, there is a half-hidden metaphor of organizational development as resembling the development of technology, such that 'novelty' and superiority are easy to establish.

However, 'modernization' is also an inherently ambiguous idea, and that may also account for some of its appeal. Distinguishing between what seems to be on its way out and what is coming in to replace it has often been the starting-point for thinking about organization and government in earlier times. It remains the source of many of the ideas about what is special to our own age, which appear as academic catch-phrases like 'Post-Fordism', 'New World Order', or 'New Public Management' (see Harvey 1989). But the idea of 'modernization' can be ambiguous when applied to public management. It has at least four possible meanings in that context, running from simple observation of adaptive change to a worship of 'newism'. The four senses are as follows:

(i) *Sense one*: a clear-cut movement can be identified away from outmoded traditional ways of organizing and conducting public business towards up-to-date, state-of-the-art methods and styles.

(ii) *Sense two*: such a shift is unavoidable and irreversible.

(iii) *Sense three*: such a shift will lead to convergence, with the same 'modern' styles appearing everywhere.

(iv) *Sense four*: the changes are broadly beneficent and to be welcomed.

To have any claim to a 'modernist' view at all, at least the first sense of the term needs to be endorsed. But it is far from unusual to find writing about contemporary public management which embraces each of the four different senses—seeing a pattern of change which is unambiguous, irreversible, convergent, and beneficent. Contrary to that view, this chapter argues that the idea of public management 'modernization' is problematic in each of these different senses.

You do not need to go very deep into current literature and debates on public management to encounter claims of 'modernization' in one or all of the four different senses distinguished above. The 'OECD story' of developments in public management in the wealthy democracies, which was referred to in the last chapter, tends to be modernist in all four senses (cf. Premfors 1996). Claims of modernization in the first sense are commonplace in practitioner and academic accounts of public-service changes. Claims of modernization in the second and stronger sense (unavoidability, inevitability) are implicit in the widespread claims that a long-term 'paradigm change'—that is, something more than a temporary change in fashion or nomenclature—is occurring in the governance of public services. For US public management, Michael Barzelay (1992: 115–33, especially 118) writes of a 'postbureaucratic paradigm' replacing an earlier 'bureaucratic paradigm' that was appropriate for most of the twentieth century but is now outdated (ibid. 133). Similarly, well-known textbooks on public management published over the last few years by Owen Hughes (1994) in Australia and the late Kieron Walsh (1995) in the UK discuss the past by means of a single chapter, in both cases titled 'the traditional paradigm'. Such claims, which rarely identify the threshold points for the transition to some 'post-' category, are commonplace in the burgeoning literature on 'New Public Management' and in the related literature on 'informatization' in public management (Margetts 1996).

Claims of modernization in the third sense (convergence, globalization) are also frequently encountered in contemporary writing about public management. That claim is made most famously by David Osborne and Ted Gaebler (1992: 325 and 328) in their assertion that a new 'entrepreneurial' paradigm of public management replacing outdated turn-of-the-century rule-bound designs is not just 'inevitable' but 'global'. Peter Aucoin (1990: 134) strikes the same note, arguing there is an inexorable 'internation-alization' of public management: 'What has been taking place in almost every government in developed political systems . . . is a new emphasis on the organizational designs for public management . . . This internationalization of public management parallels the internationalization of public and private sector economies.' Alan Jacobs (forthcoming) notes the prevalence of 'convergence' as a way of portraying changes in health care reforms across Europe, as for example in the OECD's (1994: 45) claim that 'The most remarkable feature of the health care system reforms across the 17 countries is the degree of emerging convergence'. In the same vein, President Clinton's 1993 US National Performance Review (Gore 1993: 6) asserted: 'Throughout the developed world, the needs of information-age societies were colliding with the limits of industrial-era government. Regardless of party, regardless of ideology, . . . governments were responding.' This view of the world implies that the same thing is happening everywhere, with any differences amounting more to variations in pace than content. Claims of public management modernization in the fourth (final and strongest) sense are implicit in the writings of the full-blown modernization gurus, such as the OECD, the World Bank, and Osborne and Gaebler; but convergence claims, associated with lengthy listings of the factors said to account for such development, also frequently appear in non-guru academic work.

The rhetoric of 'modernization' in contemporary public manage-ment tends to play on the ambiguities of the word 'modernization' such that its different meanings run imperceptibly together. Against the background of the cultural-theory framework, the next four sections aim to examine each of the four meanings identified earlier and identify what is contestable about them.

## 2. Public-Management Modernization as Deep Change

Sense one of 'modernization'—the notion of clear-cut change away from an old, outmoded order—is the minimum claim for modernists and the one that seems hardest to deny. Its appeal is heightened by the changes in technology that have so visibly reshaped the face of war and civil administration over the lifetime of the last generation. When Charles Dickens satirized the British Home Office as the 'Circumlocution Office' in his novel *Little Dorrit* in the 1850s, he portrayed an organization with an operating style (working with paper files produced by male clerks wielding quill pens, communicating by (royal) mail or personal callers) that would have been easily recognizable by a time-traveller from a century earlier. But a modern satirist, working on today's far more numerous equivalents of the Circumlocution Office, would be portraying a working environment dominated by totally different technologies for writing, communications, and record-keeping—the now familiar world of faxes, computers, mobile phones, the internet, and email rather than quill pens and the Pony Express. Even Max Weber's turn-of-the-century claim that control of telegraphs, mail, and railways were fundamental to the running of the modern Western state (Gerth and Mills 1948: 213), now seems prehistoric. Indeed, some observers, like Christine Bellamy and John Taylor (1994: 26), see 'New Public Management' changes as just a part of a broader 'attempt to deliver the transformational properties of informatization'. (The barbarous word 'informatization' denotes the linking of computers and telecommunications to produce new information networks.) Some of the informatization gurus see developments in information technology as heralding a quite new era of public management, taking us into the 'information polity' and even more dramatically, the 'virtualization' of public administration (Taylor 1992; Frissen 1994).

The claim that public management is 'modernizing', however, becomes problematic just at the point when it goes beyond the self-evident proposition that *physical* technologies are changing dramatically around us to suggest there are correspondingly inevitable changes in society and organizations. At a surface level, that claim is undeniable. At a deeper level—of *social* behaviour within organizations—it is more problematic, for two reasons. First, it is questionable whether fundamental social relationships will always change because technology changes (a premiss typically half-suppressed and amounting to another case of argument by enthymeme, as discussed in the last chapter), or whether common technology will lead to common organization. After all, the development of internationalized military hardware over the last century or so has not meant the adoption of a common structure of military organization. Some states have professional volunteer armies, others retain conscript citizen armies, others use foreign mercenaries for key tasks. Something similar may go for new communication systems: the ability of 'wired' citizens to send messages to their President or Prime Minister over the internet does not necessarily change their relationship with those high personages in any real sense. In such cases, the result is more likely to be a case of what Donald Schon (1971) calls 'dynamic conservatism', with power structures selecting and using new technologies to reinforce their pre-existing propensities. Some of the major studies on the relationship between informatization and organizations (cf. Kraemer and King 1986; Margetts 1991) suggest that organizations shape the way informatization is used just as much as informatization shapes the way organizations work—typically by reinforcing the existing management culture.

Moreover, a cultural theory analysis suggests that any given technological change can lend itself to very divergent visions of *social* 'modernization'. As noted in the first chapter, the development of computer networks can variously be viewed as leading to a 'modernity' involving more intense 'marketization' of social affairs (since computer links can be used to create internal and external marketplaces (or quasi-markets) in a form which could scarcely have existed before, for instance in spot pricing of electricity), or as heralding a 'modernity' which opens up access to power, dissolves old-style *arcanae imperii* and recaptures through lateral interaction the social solidarity of like-minded groups scattered around the world, whose culture, outlook, language, or beliefs might otherwise be lost in the workings of old-fashioned mass media. In a different vision, the 'modernization' that computer networks bring to society might be viewed as creating new opportunities for anarchic behaviour within organizations and leading to an utterly chaotic world of serendipity, random noise, and chance encounters. Or it might be seen as a new way of 'objectively' entrenching elaborate rules and social differentiation into the communication structure (for example in the form of complex passwords and differential levels of access to networks) and a tool for top-down management control within organizations (allowing more complete surveillance of workers and demanding more rapid responses to management questions for better co-ordination of organizational activity). Nothing about the technology as such tells us in which of those social directions it will or should be taken, and no one of those possible directions has an exclusive claim to be considered the most 'modern' one. Such observations suggest that the extent to which an unambiguous and coherent 'new paradigm' is emerging in contemporary public management, is a matter of interpretation, with the supporting arguments based more on the rhetorical device of selective example and implicit premisses than on systematic and unambiguous data.

### 3. Public-Management Modernization as Irreversible Change

Sense two of 'modernization'—as a once-for-all irreversible process, with 'no going back'—is equally beguiling, because again the 'read across' from technological change can be invoked as an implicit analogy. If the prospect of a return (say) to horse carriages or springwound clocks seems remote, an argument by analogy can be applied to social organization, to suggest there can be no reversion to earlier, outmoded styles.

The idea of contemporary change as irreversible adds rhetorical weight and grandeur to what is claimed to be current orthodoxy. But, like the notion of change as unambiguous, this claim is also based on something other than unanswerable logic or systematic case analysis. And that means it too is contestable. That is, instead of playing up the stability of the contemporary 'New Public Management' agenda, a contrary interpretation might portray a more haphazard picture, involving a succession of U-turns and policy shifts. After all, some aspects of management practice, as has often been remarked, seem to resemble the world of dieting, popular dance, or *haute couture*, with buzzwords and catch-phrases coming and going in a way that seems hard to reconcile with the idea of stable new systems or 'paradigms'. Far from a caravan proceeding purposefully in a consistent long-term direction, it can be portrayed from a 'Dilbert principle' perspective (Adams 1996) as a world of evanescent fads and fashions (Spann 1981)—Japanese company songs yesterday, New Ageist methods of releasing inner energy today (Huczynski 1993), some new, equally superficial and short-lived, panacea tomorrow.

The case of the UK, one of the alleged leaders of 'New Public Management', might be viewed in these terms as a story of successive shifts in approach over the last twenty years rather than steady reinforcement of a single trend. Christopher Pollitt (1993) has pointed to the shift from the 'neo-Taylorist' style developing in the late 1970s—a slash-and-burn emphasis on reducing public service employee numbers at any cost while buttressing the authority of 'macho managers' to cut then-powerful public-sector labour unions down to size—to the opposite stress on public-service 'quality' in the later 1980s. The mood began to swing away from a stress on 'manager power' ('free to manage') to greater stress on consumer power ('free to choose') allied with increasing ministerial attacks on the proliferation of managers, particularly in the National Health Service. Over the 1980s, the emphasis also shifted from efforts early in the decade to equip ministers to be effective managers of their departments—through devices like MINIS, a management information system for Ministers—to the effort to take management away from ministers at the end of the decade by creation of executive agencies at arm's length from departments. A related change was a move from the stress on 'results' or 'outputs' that were the constant catchwords of public management reformers in the early 1980s to the stress on 'governance' (a euphemism for 'process') as the hot topic of the mid-1990s, with rising concerns about sleaze and the 'proper conduct of public business' which emerged as part of a renewed debate about corruption and its diminutives within the OECD world in the early 1990s. Rather than irreversible change towards a clear 'modernist' destination, these different successive approaches might be depicted with equal prima-facie plausibility as ceaseless activity to grapple with the unacknowledged consequences of yesterday's mistakes.

## 4. Public-Management Modernization as Convergent Change

Sense three of 'modernization'—modernization as convergence—is also widespread, as noted earlier, and linked with ubiquitous notions of 'globalization'. As public-management systems 'modernize', they are said increasingly to resemble one another (and also, in many accounts, to resemble private-sector governance). And convergence might be seen as the logical way of arriving at the best of all worlds, combining the positive features of each of the polar ways of organizing discussed earlier into an institutional mixed salad.

Several pressures might be identified for 'internationalizing' public management, in Aucoin's phrase. In a well-known analysis, Paul DiMaggio and Walter Powell (1991) claim organizations in general are subject to 'isomorphic' processes which cause them increasingly to resemble one another. They say the commonest mechanisms by which such 'isomorphism' develops are 'coercive' (when legal or other power is used by one organization to shape others), 'mimetic' (when organizations imitate what they see as 'best practice' as a way of dealing with uncertainty), and 'normative' (when the growth of a common professional culture produces similarities across organizational boundaries). Each of those processes in principle applies to contemporary public management.

Notable among 'coercive' developments which might have an internationalizing effect on public management are those changes in international law affecting policy choice and administrative procedure. Half a century ago, at the end of World War II, there was much talk of the then newly established United Nations emerging into a form of world government to replace the era of warring states. Patently 'globalization' has not happened that way; instead, half-a-dozen empires have been replaced by over 170 separate states. But half a century of international law development has formally restricted those states' choices in public policy, for example through international trade law under the GATT agreements and international human rights law asserting entitlements that citizens can assert against governments (and their ability to complain to international monitoring bodies, for example under the Convention against Torture). For many of the former imperial powers which are now member-states of the European Union there are further much-debated restrictions on policy choice (notably on regulation, tax structures, agricultural support, and fiscal management). Member-states of the Council of Europe are even subject to monitoring of their degree of 'democracy'. In such circumstances, some claim that national politics in the wealthy democracy is becoming more like municipal politics, focused on service-delivery questions rather than issues of war and peace or class conflict (Hirst and Thompson 1996: 177), and thus increasingly putting the spotlight on public management.

DiMaggio and Powell themselves (ibid. 70) see public-management changes as heavily driven by 'mimetic' processes. Public organizations are notorious for the ambiguity of their goals, and that feature may make them especially liable to follow organizations perceived as 'similar' in some way but more successful or legitimate. At the same time, normative processes likely to promote homogenization include the development of an international network of multinational public-service providers and management consultants, including international bodies like the OECD PUMA, and the World Bank, purveying similar ideas about 'best practice' and 'benchmarks' for 'good governance'. Undoubtedly, the same managerial catch-words have acquired such a wide international currency that one can speak of a new global vocabulary— often satirized, for example by Justin Cartwright in the epigraph to this chapter. And many service functions in government, particularly in IT provision, are now provided by firms which cross national boundaries (just as happened in the armaments trade in the nineteenth century). Patrick Dunleavy (1994) sees a trend towards giant multinational corporations specializing in making a particular public service product part of their 'core competencies', along the lines of McDonalds or Coca-Cola, interacting with 'decentralized nets of implementing agencies' (ibid. 56).

Convergence is a powerful rhetorical theme, because by providing apparently convincing backing for the claim that the same thing is happening everywhere, it suggests (typically by suppressed premiss again) that running with the herd must be the best—or at least the only—thing to do. It is thus hardly suprising that both domestic reformers and international agencies like OECD and the World Bank tend to lay heavy stress on 'convergence'. Indeed, as was noted in the first chapter, the international organizations are almost by their *raison d'être* committed to a view of international convergence on some single 'best-practice' model which it is their role to 'benchmark' and foster, helping the 'laggards' to catch up with the best-practice techniques of the vanguard.

Public management convergence in vocabulary seems hard to

deny. More problematic is what may be happening 'underneath' the shared catch-phrases. On the face of it, we might expect uniformity and convergence in public management to belong more to the age of empires than of nation-states and local or regional democracy. After all, the most dramatic example of cross-national public service provision by world-wide multinationals is perhaps the case of colonial trading companies (like the British East India Company, a public services multinational to which key tax-collection duties were 'outsourced'—with dramatic and unexpected long-term effects—by the Mogul Emperor Shah Alam in 1765 (Narain 1971: 54) ). And the extent to which 'new managerial' talk is accompanied by new managerial *practice* may also be highly variable. It is, for instance, notable that the EU bureaucracy showed no discernible movement away from progressive principles of lifelong career service and highly legalistic operating procedures over the 'New Public Management' period (cf. Hay 1989), and indeed the OECD bureaucracy showed no signs of *itself* adopting the new management principles it has so earnestly preached to others as the wave of the future—instead remaining in a very traditional French bureaucratic mould.

As noted at the outset, Silberman (1993: p. ix) argues that early twentieth-century expectations of 'modernity' leading to convergence in organization turned out to be wrong because administrative systems are deeply 'path dependent'—that is, they are shaped by the way critical institutional-design dilemmas were handled at major historical turning-points, and the response to subsequent challenges varies according to those earlier decisions. For instance, some state structures responded to the political party systems that developed with the mass franchise by reserving top jobs in the public bureaucracy to nominees of the ruling party (as in the USA). Some responded by asserting a doctrine of 'political neutrality' for the civil service, which should be loyal to the government of the day, whatever party held office (as in the UK). Others adopted hybrid forms, such as the German doctrine of 'political retirement' adopted after the 1848 'Professors' parliament' (when the German Kaiser found the legislature dominated by elected representatives from 'his' public service who were opposed to the regime). Far from being irrelevant to the contemporary world, such historical experiences may well shape the way public service 'managerialism' develops today. A sweeping change in the structure of a public service based on the 'political appointment' style is likely to be reaching into a fundamental political settlement among political parties and/or ethnic and religious groups in a society in a way that may not arise for 'political neutrality' structures, and may well face more barriers in consequence.

Even where the same substantive changes are made, the motives, results or social consequences involved may be far from convergent. Hans Mueller (1984) claims that two states (Prussia and Britain) which historically adopted the same formal measures for civil service reform—recruitment on the basis of examinations rather than patronage—did so for quite different political reasons, and with different social consequences. The same may well apply to contemporary managerialization of public services. For instance, Alan Jacobs (forthcoming: 11) has shown that the same policy *instrument* (the move towards a more 'marketized' style in health-care reforms) can be used in quite different ways, for example to buttress cost containment by government rather than patient choice in the UK, but the opposite in Sweden: '. . . The British kept the government in the umpire's chair, allowing it to tilt the playing field in favor of its chief concerns: high output and cost-containment. But the Swedish let the patient decide, ceding control of the contest to critics of quality . . .'.

Moreover, there are striking differences within what is claimed to be an emerging 'global paradigm' of public management reform. For instance, in Japan more rather than less stress seems to have been put into 'legalistic' styles of administration by written documents (for example in business regulation), against a traditional style of informal and oral conduct of business. The contrary US emphasis on deregulation *within* government, as stressed by the 1993 National Performance Review, has not been strongly followed elsewhere, no doubt because the US separation of powers structure produces a pattern of Congressional micro-management of the bureaucracy that is not reproduced in other OECD states. In the key case of China, some of the key public management developments of the 1980s—like the return to a formal grading system in the bureaucracy, the resumption of examination rather than party patronage alone for public-service recruitment and greater emphasis on technical expertise—look more like a partial adoption of progressivism than a move away from it. To see these different reform themes as reflecting a single new 'global paradigm' requires creative interpretation of a high order, and the 'evidence' so far provided by the convergence gurus in public management reform consists more of selected example and reasoning at the everyday level of plausibility than of systematic examination of all available cases using clear-cut benchmarks and hard-logic demonstration.

## 5. Public-Management Modernization as Beneficent Change

The idea of modernity as beneficent is the fourth and most obviously problematic sense of 'modernization'. So it is not suprising that the benificence theme is often kept semi-implicit, reflecting once again the importance in successful rhetoric of which premises in an argument are to be exposed and which suppressed. Even if modernization in the first three senses were unproblematic, it does not follow that sense four also applies. The fact that something is new or inevitable does not necessarily mean it is desirable. Death and taxes, the saying goes, are inevitable; but not everyone would agree they are to be welcomed with enthusiasm as a result. Eliding novelty with desirability—the rhetorical strategy of 'newism' (or *argumentum ad novitum*, to use its old-fashioned title) has long been recognized as a 'fallacy of substantive distraction' in deliberative argument (Fischer 1971: 299–300). But it is still commonly encountered in contemporary public management as a means of conveying a sense of approval of what is claimed to be the wave of history (cf. Williams 1989; Margetts 1996).

To satisfy a logician, the desirability of any change has to be argued independently of its alleged inevitability or newness. But what is notable in contemporary public management debate is the absence of agreement on what is to be counted as beneficent or the reverse, or what counts as good 'modern' public management. And viewed from the cultural-theory framework used as the backdrop for this book, that is hardly a surprise.

As we have seen in Part II, for some beneficent change in public management means empowering managers so they can make a difference—by more upfront leadership, clearer strategy from the top, better understanding of who is responsible for what, and who is in charge. In part, that was the thrust of the late nineteenth century Progressive public administration movement and many of the same themes are shared (often without acknowledgement) by those strains of 'New Public Management' that stress the need for better corporate leadership and more professional management of public services. Osborne and Gaebler's (1992) much-quoted emphasis on the need for governments to 'steer' rather than 'row', for strong inspirational leadership 'from the front' and an organizational ethos heavily infused with 'public service' values, taps into hierarchist themes. So does the recurring 'agency' idea that politicians or legislatures should restrict their role to the establishment of broad policy frameworks, creating a legitimate space for the operations of professional managers working to 'deliver' the agreed targets. An image of 'steering', with its emphasis on broad strategic vision, offers an apparent alternative to features that are often seen as besetting sins of the policy process, such as inconsistency, 'tunnel vision', and 'random agenda selection' (Breyer 1993) as well as the commonly observable tendency for high-grade routine to drive out strategic thinking.

As we saw in Chapter 5, however, for others beneficent change in public management means changes that empower the consumer— the individualist theme of 'government by the market' (Self 1993) rather than by visionary leaders or expert regulators. From this worldview, good public management is less a matter of inspirational leadership telling people what to do than making public service producers responsive to consumers through market or quasi-market processes. For example, if consumers can be given an 'exit' option, there can be more stress on self-steering with little or no government hands on the tiller. Take this line of thinking to its limits, and 'good' accountability may come to look more like the ability to attract and retain customers against competitors than answerability to an hierarchical or constitutional superior.

For others again beneficent change means neither a 'great leader' obsession nor craven market-worship but the empowerment of 'front-line' groups to make decisions—if need be, overriding market signals—about their collective concerns (Goodsell 1993: 86). From this egalitarian viewpoint, communitarianism and managed self-help is the ideal of good public management. And (as was more tentatively explored in Chapter 7) still others are likely to be sceptical about *anyone's* ability to tell whether any proposed change in public management will be beneficent or not, because of all the intractable difficulties of foreseeing the consequences of any human action, so precarious and complex are the chains that link causes and effects and so common are the stories of grand visions or projects going awry because of some overlooked action or omission that seemed either obvious or trivial at the time. The best thing is to trust in no one's magic panacea and keep co-operation to the minimum.

There may be some sense in which these different views of what makes for beneficent change in public management might come together as different parts of the same elephant (so to speak). After all, it might take visionary leadership to get a marketized or communitarian structure of public services operating in the first place. But these different visions of beneficence only seem capable of being reconciled at the most general level, indicating some of the difficulties in moving from senses 1–3 of modernization to the fourth and strongest sense. Indeed, that modish word 'empowerment', much used by Osborne and Gaebler and so many other contemporary management gurus, itself indicates the range of different visions of what beneficent 'modernization' in public management amounts to. Since not everyone can be 'empowered' at the same time, who exactly is to be empowered against whom, and how, is a key test of cultural bias in visions of modernization.

### 6. Modernization—or 'Fatal Remedies'?

The preceding sections argued each of four different meanings of 'modernization' in public management contains propositions which are more contestable than modernization rhetoric suggests. The different world-views identified by cultural theory suggest contradictory visions of what 'modernization' might mean in each of the four senses discussed earlier.

A further problem with the beguiling idea of inexorable world-wide 'modernization' is that it plays up the stable trends in contemporary public-management change and plays down the self-disequilibrating processes. Self-disequilibration means the propensity of polar approaches to public management to turn into 'fatal remedies' (in Sam Sieber's (1981) graphic phrase) producing major unwanted by-products or even the very opposite of the intended effect. Such outcomes are commonplace in any organizational setting, and it seems hardly plausible that current public-management fashions can be exempt from this normal fate.

Each of the four basic approaches to control and regulation which were sketched out earlier in the book has a set of built-in strengths and weaknesses. But any 'balance' among the four basic types of control is likely to be problematic and precarious because each of the approaches involves an underlying logic which, if taken to its limits, will tend to destroy all the others.

The hierarchist recipe of oversight and review is good at concentrating the focus of control systems but is notoriously vulnerable to information asymmetry across organizational levels mixed with opportunism (cf. Dowding 1995). Pursue this approach to control single-mindedly, and a point will be reached at which any element of competition is at risk as the 'referees' continually handicap the players and move the goalposts. Likewise, processes of mutuality are liable to be 'trumped' by the exercise of top-down authority and elements of randomness to appear only by accident.

Competition, the individualists' sovereign remedy for the ills of public management, can be good at motivating people who would otherwise shirk or play safe. But at the same time it can impose heavy costs in terms of collective ethos by weakening trust and working against the pooling of information and other key resources among people or organizations. And the more competition is emphasized, the less it will be possible to deploy the other polar approaches to control. Any oversight will be problematic because no one can be above the fray to 'referee' the contest. Likewise, any element of mutuality will be hard to sustain in such conditions, because the time-consuming group processes it involves will be vulnerable to 'free riding' by opportunists trying to beat the system. Even the element of chance in who works with whom, and where inspection or audit will strike next—essential operating conditions for the gaming-machine model of organizational control described in Chapter 7—may come to be undermined, if competition undermines the sort of organizational framework (notably in size and geographical dispersion) which lends itself to conventional forms of randomized control.

The egalitarian formula of mutuality can be good at providing rich reciprocal surveillance in a culturally homogenous group but without expulsion cannot cope easily with more heterogeneous groups, leading either to endless feuds that cannot be resolved or over-comfortable accommodations that may result in disaster (as in the Birmingham cancer hospital case discussed in Chapter 2). The more mutuality is emphasized, the harder it will be to support control by oversight, because 'top-down' or 'outside' interference will tend to be rejected in favour of in-group decision-making. Likewise, individualized competition will not fit with the logic of subordinating the individual to group pressure, and the group bonds that mutuality puts into the centre of the stage are liable to undermine the operating conditions needed for contrived randomness as a method of organizational control.

The quasi-fatalist formula of contrived randomness built into organization can be good at discouraging conspiracy to commit fraud or some of the other sins of collaboration discussed in Chapter 2. But at the same time it may tend to damp down the sort of collaboration that can bring pay-offs to the collectivity in forms like joint initiatives or pooling of information. If all the stress goes on this approach, the co-operation on which the other three approaches to control have to rest will tend to be undermined. If you cannot foresee who you will be working with or what the rules of the game will be for any time into the future, the incentive to invest time and energy in individual efforts to compete or in group participation is weak. Even a hierarchist strategy of following the rules and taking cues from whoever is currently at the top may bring no effective payoff.

Each of the four basic types of control thus has its shortcomings as a possible approach to 'modernization' in public-management. And if each of these basic types, when pushed to the limit, tends to drive out all the others, a formula for 'modernity' which attempts to combine them to get the best of all worlds is likely to be hard to achieve. That is not to say hybrid forms are impossible or will never appear. On the contrary, six pairwise hybrids will be considered in the next chapter, and some are commonly observable in practice. But the elements of mutual repulsion among the basic types are likely to make combinations and hybrids precarious and self-disequilibrating. So instead of a vision of 'modernity' which involves the adoption of stable hybrid forms for a long period, public-management control systems seem just as likely to keep 'hunting around' among the various types, as surprise and disappointment over the capacity of any one approach to deliver satisfactory results leads to increasing support for one of the other options. Rather than the 'linear' metaphors conventionally associated with modernization (such as midwifery or design engineering), the essential skill of 'management' in such conditions might be more like that of the step-dancer—the ability to shift the balance among a set of ambitious positions no one of which can be sustained for long.

Why can we expect surprise and disappointment over the results that each approach to organization can deliver? Such an outcome seems likely because the more weight is put on any one of the polar approaches to organization in public management, the more the corresponding weaknesses can be expected to appear as side-effects and reverse effects. *Side-effects*, familiar from medication or dieting, denote the impact of interventions on targets other than those they are mainly intended to hit. Claims of unintended side-effects are universal in public policy (for instance, claims that welfare state programmes can weaken the work ethic or that 'green' policies can hit the poor hardest), and particularly in public management. An example is 'market-testing' obligations on public bodies requiring them to put specified services out to tender rather than automatically performing them by direct organization: intended to cut costs, such measures may cut across other policy goals, like the involvement of prisoners in the running and maintenance of prisons.[1] As was suggested above, each of the four polar ways of organizing will tend to produce side-effects that come with the package and may cast a cloud on their claim to be the wave of the future.

Different from side-effects, *reverse effects* occur when social interventions achieve the very opposite of the desired effect for some reason. It is the organizational equivalent of the slimming diet that turns out to make you fatter or the intended short cut that for some reason takes longer than the original route. Reverse effects are also commonplace in public management, but the potential reverse effects of contemporary changes in public management have been less discussed up to now than their side-effects. This lack of attention is curious, because any approach to public management is potentially vulnerable to all of the seven 'conversion mechanisms' identified by Sieber (1981) as ways in which social interventions can turn into 'fatal remedies'.

---

[1] See *Annual Report of HM Chief Inspectorate of Prisons for Scotland 1993–4*, Cm. 2649 1993–4. London: HMSO, iii.

Those seven reverse-effect mechanisms are shown in summary form in Table 9.1. *Functional disruption* means the unintentional destruction of some essential component of the system which it is intended to improve, like a child who makes a pet sicken or die by feeding it unsuitable food that is believed to be a treat. We saw a prime case of functional disruption in Chapter 2: the Chernobyl engineers who reduced the water supply to the plant during the ill-fated experiment to try to stabilize the reactor, and thereby unintentionally created exactly the opposite condition, with fatal consequences. *Exploitation* means the unintentional creation of opportunities for opponents to use to achieve the opposite of the intended purpose, like the creation of a corporate email network intended to facilitate 'tight management' which instead turns out to be a forum for subversive jokes against management, time-wasting gossip, flirtation, or worker grumbles. *Goal displacement* is the well-known process by which an instrumental value turns into a terminal value, for example when 'creative accounting' replaces a focus on substantive achievement in response to the introduction of quantitative performance targets, and thereby produces the opposite of the desired effect. Peter Blau's (1955) classic example is of US welfare agencies, intended to help disabled clients achieve independence, who instead held onto their clients and encouraged them to become dependent on the agencies, because their performance targets were couched in terms of caseload rather than 'discharges'. *Provocation* denotes the process by which attempts to secure compliance achieve the opposite effect, for example in the efforts by the Park and Chun regimes in South Korea in the 1970s and 1980s to focus trade union attention on 'economic' rather than 'political' matters by restrictions on trade union activity—which had exactly the opposite effect, of politicizing the labour movement (see Joo 1997). *Classification* refers to the way that labels intended to convey glory or shame can have the reverse effect, for instance in a culture where official reprimands or punishments simply add to the 'street credibility' of those reprimanded, as can happen in some school or prison environments. *Over-commitment* denotes the process by which interventions collapse because they over-extend the capacity of organizations or regimes in an attempt to achieve unrealizable objectives. A recurring theme in the collapse of imperial-type military expeditions, over-commitment is commonly observable in public management, as in the famous case of the blanket adoption of PPBS in the US federal budget in the 1960s, which caused the process to become discredited as a result of having been adopted 'top-down' without skill, experience, or discrimination. Finally, *placation* refers to the way that complacency over the apparent success of a measure can lead to the opposite outcome (like the ill-founded hubristic beliefs about the invincibility of the French Maginot line or Singapore's naval defences in World War II), or in which compromises that are successful in the short term cause situations to worsen in the longer term.

Reverse effects may also complicate the path to modernization through the surprise and disappointment they create, and some public management examples are given in the right-hand column of Table 9.1. All the four polar forms of organizing are prone to reverse effects through 'functional disruption', unintentionally destroying the foundations of important types of human behaviour. For instance, Michael Power (1994) suggests that the fashionable application of the 'audit' metaphor (originating in financial oversight) to scrutiny of activities like teaching or clinical practices in health care, can weaken rather than strengthen the regulation of such activities, because stepping up external 'audit' can unintentionally destroy collegial self-regulation and turn responsible professionals into cheating regulatees. Another example is Dunleavy and Hood's (1994: 13) argument that splitting up public bureaucracies into many different 'businesses' (a hallmark of many contemporary reforms) may have the unintentional effect of increasing the complexity of public-policy problems and thereby achieve the opposite of the intended effect of increasing the level of successful problem-solving.

Similarly, all of the polar ways of organizing can create reverse effects through 'exploitation', unintentionally helping rather than hindering their opponents. For instance, outsourcing services (like financial management) or processes (like information technology), ostensibly to use competition to cut costs or tighten control over 'agents', is often claimed to have the opposite effect as key strategic processes pass into the hands of players whose goals differ even more sharply from those of their political or administrative 'principals' than the bureaucrats they have replaced (cf. Margetts 1996). That is, after all, what happened to the Mogul empire when it 'outsourced' part of its tax-collection operation to the East India Company in the eighteenth century, as noted earlier. The US

TABLE 9.1. *Sieber's seven 'conversion mechanisms' and public-management reforms*

| Mechanism | Causal Process | Example |
|---|---|---|
| Functional disruption | The unintentional frustration of a 'system need' in public-service organization has the effect of worsening the condition which the reform is intended to improve | Power's (1994) argument that the 'audit explosion' weakens effective regulation by turning responsible (self-regulating) professionals into cheating regulatees |
| Exploitation | Public-management reforms can create opportunities for opponents or opportunists to use in ways that achieve the opposite of the desired effect | Dunleavy's (1991) argument that contracting out and hiving off leads to welfare-reducing over-outsourcing by high public servants for private benefit |
| Goal displacement | An instrumental value becomes a terminal value in a way that defeats the basic objective | Teubner's (1987) and others' claim that 'juridification' (emphasis on legal process) can reduce rather than enhance the ability of law to change society or organization |
| Provocation | Measures intended to increase compliance with authority have the opposite effect because of the antagonism they stir up, producing loss of co-operation | Bardach and Kagan's (1982) claim that strict rule enforcement can reduce compliance by producing principled dissidence |

| Classification | Labelling or categorization has reverse effects as intended stigmas are treated as badges of glory or intended prizes are treated as stigmas | Ingraham's (1993) claim that performance pay tends to demotivation in public services through a mix of grading inflation and capped funds |
|---|---|---|
| Over-commitment | Intervention is self-defeating because it exhausts resources in pursuit of objectives that cannot be achieved | Sieber's (1981: 162) claim that administrative reforms defeat themselves by initial hype that produces later disillusion |
| Placation | Intervention causes situations to deteriorate by compromises that come unstuck or illusions of success which produce complacency | Dunleavy and Hood's (1994) claim that over-emphasis on management can worsen policy-making quality by deflecting attention from large-scale substantive problems to endless reorganization |

community development programmes, discussed in Chapter 2, also unintentionally served to weaken the established political system rather than buttressing it. Likewise, 'goal displacement'—in which instrumental values turn into terminal values in a way that frustrates the original aims—is an ever-present problem for all of the polar forms of organizing. Many reform ideas in public management intended to be bold initiatives to transform behaviour are fated to end up as form-filling exercises pursued for their own sake.

'Provocation' and 'classification' are also familiar reverse-effect mechanisms in public management. For instance, it has often been argued that pay-on-performance systems, intended to increase public employees' motivation, frequently have the opposite effect (Ingraham 1993). The argument goes that 'grading inflation' (when everyone ends up being rated highly for merit pay), together with limited funding of performance pay budgets, disappoints the expectations of those who expect to receive big pay rises as a result of pay for performance systems (because they see their colleagues as less industrious and effective than themselves), and so reduces their motivation.

'Over-commitment', in which measures fail because they are pushed far beyond their natural limits, is also often argued to be a besetting sin of public-management reform, as practices which have apparently succeeded in one organization are foisted on every other organization in the public service without either adequate implementing capacity or general enthusiasm to sustain them. Finally, 'placation' may sometimes be the mechanism which causes public management measures to have the opposite of their intended effects. Those Chernobyl engineers who turned off all their plant's safety systems to pursue their ill-fated experiment (as described in Chapter 2) seem to have had a shared belief that nuclear-power plants were safe, forgiving, and resilient—because no accidents were ever reported in the Soviet nuclear-management system. Indeed, an excessive focus on 'management' in the conventional sense may itself produce a placation effect, if it unintentionally diverts the energies of politicians and top public servants away from major strategic policy issues into over-concentration on fiddling with organizations, thus producing major 'policy fiascos' (Dunleavy and Hood 1994; Bovens and 'tHart 1996).

The argument is not that contemporary public management

reforms are uniquely vulnerable to reverse-effect problems of the type shown in Table 9.1. Rather, it is claimed that such reforms are not uniquely exempt from such problems, and in consequence there may be more reversals on the road to 'modernization' of public management than the beguiling images carried over from technological development might lead us to expect. A cultural-theory framework would suggest that *any* approach to public management drawn from one of the polar 'ways of life' is likely to produce negative effects which reflect the weaknesses of that particular approach. Those negative effects can be expected to be more severe, the more weight is put on any one approach, for two main reasons.

First, the more reliance is placed on any one polar approach to public management, the more serious its 'blind spots' are likely to become, producing unexpected reverse effects through 'functional disruption' and 'placation'. For example, overextending mutuality as a principle of management where there is no inherent cultural homogeneity will tend to weaken control, not strengthen it (part of the story of 'maximum feasible participation' in the US Great Society programme of the 1960s, discussed in Chapter 2). Moreover, if each polar type of control comes to be presented as a general answer to public management, it will tend to create the conditions for reverse effects through 'over-commitment', as it moves from its natural heartlands (most favourable conditions, cultural congruence) to more problematic territory. Privatization as a key to lowering costs and simplifying the state's role may be headed for this fate as it moves from an original emphasis on the sale of government-owned stock in industrial firms to the 'East India Company' role in functions like tax collection.

Second, each polar approach as it comes into general currrency will tend to antagonize those who prefer alternative ways of organizing, creating the conditions for reverse effects through 'exploitation', 'provocation', and 'classification', and the more widely applied the approach, the greater the degree of antagonism it is likely to provoke. For example, putting more emphasis on formal review and oversight with the intention of tightening up control may in fact weaken it by provoking either open challenge or covert avoidance. Some have claimed that the application of formal 'natural justice' requirements to disciplinary hearings by prison governors and prison boards of visitors in the UK will tend to drive

prison discipline underground, 'such that formal disciplinary procedures become less important than informal and less open methods
of control' (Jabbari 1994: 194). Similarly, there are types of police
culture in which having a large number of formal complaints logged
against an officer becomes an essential asset in promoting the
image of a 'tough cop', and in such cases the development of
formal-complaints mechanisms intended to promote compliance
with formal codes may have the very opposite effect.

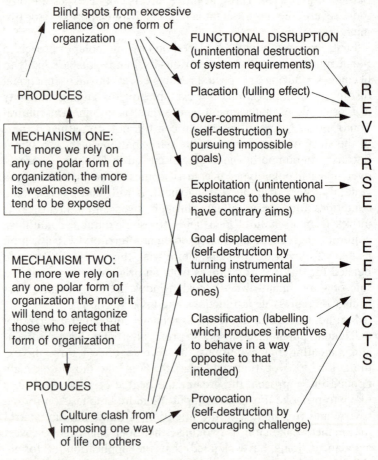

Fig. 9.1. How cultural form links to reverse effects: Two possible
mechanisms.

Figure 9.1 summarizes the argument. Two of Sieber's reverse-effect mechanisms, namely functional disruption and placation resulting from comfortable blind spot assumptions going unchallenged, seem more likely to be linked with heavy emphasis on any one polar type of control, fitting with what is known about the effects of 'groupthink' and the sources of military incompetence, as discussed in Chapter 2. Three of the other reverse-effect mechanisms in Sieber's set, on the other hand, seem more likely to be linked to control processes which involve cultural heterogeneity (exploitation, provocation, and classification resulting from processes which cross boundaries of trust and shared beliefs and thereby invite 'bending-back' responses).

## 7. Conclusion

Visions of once-for-all 'modernizing' change sweeping through public management everywhere are appealing. Perhaps they match a millenial need for a 'big vision' of the future that is not just more of the same. Certainly they match the needs of particular players, like OECD and the World Bank, for a legitimating role in what they do. But on closer examination those visionary 'modernizing' claims become more challengeable. They turn out to be ambiguous, since much depends on which meaning of 'modernization' is at issue. They tend to lack a strong historical perspective and to achieve persuasiveness by the choice of which assumptions to include and which to leave out, rather than by hard-data proofs.

Much of the case for 'modernization through the information revolution relies on a half-suppressed metaphor, reading across from technology-driven 'production engineering' aspects of modern organizations to their underlying social relationships. But when it comes to those relationships—structures of power and authority in the hands of different actors, who communicates with whom and how, basic ideas about justice and blame—the claim of the 'modernizers' that public-service organizations are or can be set on a single determinate track for the future is far from unanswerable. Indeed, it might be argued with at least equal plausibility that what we are seeing in contemporary public management is not so much a 'modernist' phase as a 'post-modern' one—that is, the conjuncture of several quite different styles simultaneously. For instance, some influential commentators see a shift away from 'process' and 'input' to an 'entrepreneurial' style of government (Osborne and Gaebler 1992) as the dominant trend. Others, on the contrary, see 'juridification'—ever-more-legalistic, process-obsessed, styles of operation—as the long-term trend (Teubner 1987); while still others (such as Moore 1995) see both, with 'entre-preneurship' expectations being laid (perhaps contradictorily) on top of all the traditional process controls over government in democratic societies.

The variety of these visions suggests it is far from certain that public management at the turn of the century is headed every-where towards the same 'modern' paradigm, unless 'paradigm' (admittedly a vague and elusive word) means no more than a set of ambiguous catchwords in common linguistic usage. A more plural future seems more plausible—and perhaps more desirable too, because every style of organization has its strengths and weak-nesses, and as was suggested in the last section, indiscriminate cloning of fashionable models into areas where they are deeply inappropriate is a cardinal recipe for the production of reverse effects through over-commitment.

Taking a cultural-theory 'angle', together with some historical perspective and alertness to the rhetorical dimensions of argument, helps to bring out multiple and contradictory perspectives on what organizational 'modernization' amounts to. Each major world-view implies a different vision not only of what a beneficent modernity would mean but also of major social applications of modern tech-nology. Moreover, such a framework helps to bring out some of the ways in which different approaches to organization can have a 'self-disequilibrating' character as much as a self-reinforcing one. If each of the polar ways of life has built-in weaknesses, the more weight is laid on each of them the more glaring those weaknesses are likely to become—a force which would tend to work against any single approach to organizational design becoming dominant for long. Moreover, each of those polar approaches to organizational design in public management may have a propensity to achieve exactly the opposite of the goals intended through the various reverse-effect mechanisms discussed in the last section. Such processes may also serve to make the path to public management 'modernization' more crooked and divergent than much of the modernists' rhetoric implies.

If this reasoning is correct, it suggests there can be no once-for-all solution to the different slants on 'good public management' introduced earlier in this book—no managerial 'judgement of Paris' to identify one clear and permanent winner in the contest. Tensions such as the conflict between 'career service' and 'spot hiring' approaches to organizing top public servants, legalist and managerial visions of organizational process, competition-centred and oversight-centred approaches to control over public services, are not likely to disappear through some ultimate 'modern' resolution. Like cooking without salt or sugar, it is probably quite feasible to do without some of the polar approaches to public management, at least for a time. Whether it is possible or desirable to do without them permanently is more doubtful, because, like salt or sugar, there are some effects that only some of the polar types of organization can easily produce. How far hybrid forms are feasible is a question to which we turn briefly in the next chapter.

# 10

# Taking Stock: The State of the Art of the State

... some master architect—not master builder—draws a rough sketch of a pyramid in the sand, and many laborers begin to hew their stones to fit. Before many are made ready, the fashion suddenly changes—pyramids are out; obelisks are in. Another master architect draws a sketch in the sand, and the hewing and chipping starts all over again. A few stones can be salvaged, but most have to be cut from scratch ...

(Fischer 1971: 5)

## 1. Public Management and Cultural Theory: Just Another Superficial Fad?

In most cities, motor traffic runs in the centre of the roads and cyclists ride at the edges (either in special cycle lanes or fending for themselves as best they can amidst the speeding juggernauts). Those who take that approach to organizing traffic as God-given and normal are in for a surprise when they come across cities like Havana, where the cyclists ride in special lanes in the middle of the roads and the motor traffic goes at the sides. Similarly in public management, what occupies central place and what belongs at the edges can be culturally variable. If we make that variety the central focus, as this book has aimed to do, we need to be wary of taken-for-granted assumptions about who is to count as a manager of public services, what management means, what 'best practice' amounts to and who or what to blame when things go wrong.

It will be recalled that Chapter 1 set out seven propositions about public management. First, it was claimed that grid/group cultural theory puts variety in doctrine and argument at the centre of the stage, and offers a framework that is compatible with much other work on organizational variety and 'contingency theory'. It directs attention to the variety of organizational forms and systems of regulation so often obscured by airy generalizations about '*the* modern Western state', 'contemporary business practice' or 'the market versus the state'. Cultural theory helps us to understand why there is no generally agreed answer to the question 'who should manage whom and how?' in government.

Second, it was argued that cultural theory can provide additional analytic 'purchase' on some of the central questions of public management. Cultural theory can contribute to the analysis of failure and collapse in public management, sharpening our understanding of the problem of 'no free lunches' in public organization (Jordan 1992: 31). It has a distinct approach to explaining why 'what works' in one context can be a recipe for disaster in others, as in the case of collegial professionalism in the Birmingham hospital case or polished routines in the Kobe earthquake case, as discussed in Chapter 2. It can give us a sense of the built-in limits of the main available organizational designs for public services—and even of management itself. By contrast, much of the popular literature about management (and even some of the cases taught in management schools) shares with religious evangelism and 'can do' military ethos the assumption that inspirational leadership can achieve feats that would be impossible for ordinary mortals, with improving tales of heroic achievement to raise financial and service performance against all the odds. Such a vision may well be effective for promoting the faith, for encouraging ingenuity, pertinacity, and lateral thinking by managers. But it hardly provides a basis for a general *theory* of public management.

As shown earlier in the book, cultural theory can provide a basis for analysing the variety of ways that control can work in, over and by public service organization. And it can help us to explore the variety of rhetorics—persuasive stories and analogies linked with 'recipes'—which are applicable to public management, by identifying the sorts of stories and metaphors that go with each organizational world-view. It can help us to understand why management-speak words like 'accountability' and 'empowerment' have the rhetorical power that they do, because they can be given a slant which supports each of the biases identified by cultural theory.

Third, it was argued that there are ideas and doctrines about public management which correspond to each of the major world-views identified by cultural theory, and that applies both to historical traditions of thought and contemporary doctrines. The different ways of thinking about organization that were discussed in Part II are historically deep-rooted and recurrent, and cultural theory offers a frame within which we can place the various competing traditions of thought in public management. That frame contrasts with the implicit picture of an undifferentiated 'traditional model' offered by many of the public management 'modernists'. Awareness of cultural variety linked to an historical perspective makes it less likely that we will be left high and dry when managerial fashions change from pyramids to obelisks, in the analogy used by David Fischer in the epigraph to this chapter, or that we will mistake every doctrine 'that has not been around for a while . . . for an original insight' (Hirschman 1991: 29).

Fourth, it was claimed that none of the polar recipes for good organization has any inherent claim to be considered more 'modern' than any of the others. Each, as was shown in Chapter 9, can lend itself to a vision of organization in a 'high-tech' information-society context. Even the fatalist view, which might be dismissed as belonging more to a world of peasants and serfs than of MBA graduates and mobile professionals, has a potential 'modern' variant through the randomness introduced into the world by computer networks and ramified multinational corporations.

Fifth, it was claimed that the inherent variety in approaches to organization identified by cultural theory is not likely to disappear. Unless the built-in weaknesses of each of the polar forms of organization suddenly disappear, the obstacles to any one of them becoming entrenched against all the others will remain. And though there are many signs of 'global' fashions in public management labels and phraseology, path dependency—the rock on which earlier prophecies of convergent organization have foundered—is not likely to disappear either, as was suggested in the last chapter.

The sixth proposition was that the cultural-theory framework was 'stretchable', in that it can be applied at a number of different levels. Chapter 1 referred to Mars' (1982) claim that the focus of cultural theory can be progressively increased by putting grid-group lenses in front of one another, and that approach has been used at several points in this book (for instance in Chapters 3, 7, and 8, and in three of the chapters of Part II to explore variants of the four main ways of life). Later in this chapter we will pursue the issue of hybrids among the polar types identified by cultural theory.

This chapter is addressed mainly to the seventh and most general proposition advanced in Chapter 1—namely that the understanding of cultural and organizational variety, within an historical perspective deserves a central place in the analysis of public management. It aims to take stock of the cultural-theory approach which has served as a backdrop for the book. How useful is that approach as an intellectual grounding for public management? Is it a frame that is capable of further development? Or is it like the books we read in the nursery—helpful enough for the early stages of exploration, to develop our awareness of the world, but to be put away with the toys of childhood when we come to a more grown-up stage later?

Claiming that cultural theory is a tool we can use in public management is not to say that it is necessarily a problem-free approach—one of those 'soft options' suitable for those who want to avoid the difficult algebra beloved of rational choice approaches. There are many potential pitfalls in using the approach, including the problem of how to obtain enough social 'distance' between the observer and the subject to gain a proper perspective. Cultural theory is by no means beyond all criticism as a frame for public-management analysis. Real-life ideas about public management, as we saw in Part II, are often hard to fit into any single one of the cultural-theory categories and often look like hybrids, in spite of the cultural theorists' claim that cosmologies characteristically tend to go out to the corners of the frame. And 'fatalists' are a particularly problematic category. The amount of research devoted to this way of life is suprisingly small,[1] given the cultural theorists' claim that it is the discovery of fatalism and egalitarianism, added to the already familiar categories of hierarchism and individualism which gives their account of society and organization its distinctive power (Thompson, Ellis, and Wildavsky 1990: 104). The cultural theory framework provides no obvious explanation of why some institutional forms have persisted over centuries or even millennia, such as the Chinese imperial system linked to the philosophy of

---

[1] Gerald Mars' (1982) work on occupational cheating is a notable exception.

Confucianism, while others have had a much more short-lived existence, such as some of the egalitarian political systems of the post-World War II era. And, as Barry Hindess (1991) has pointed out, the cultural theorists have yet to demonstrate to everyone's satisfaction that the two dimensions of 'grid' and 'group' are fully independent of one another, or why each dimension has to be considered as a dichotomy rather than a continuum.

To assess the cultural-theory approach, this concluding chapter will discuss three sorts of objections to this framework as a way of analysing public management. One possible line of criticism might be called the 'nursery toys' objection—that is, the claim that cultural theory is too simple for sophisticated analysis and is therefore better suited for the elementary stages of understanding than for advanced or professional analysis. A second possible line of criticism might be called the 'soft science' objection—that is, the claim that, whatever its level of sophistication or applicability to management, the 'theory' is, even on its own terms, limited, ambiguous, and perhaps even unfalsifiable. A third line of criticism might be called the 'wrong tool' objection—that is, the claim that cultural theory, however sophisticated, cannot be an adequate basis for a theory of *management*, because ultimately it has little to say about the central what-to-do questions of organization that management and managers need to be concerned with. So trying to apply cultural theory to public management is like trying to eat soup with a knife or cut grass with a spoon. It is, on this view, the wrong tool for the job.

It can be admitted that there is at least something in each of these objections. At a minimum, each represents an important challenge for further development of cultural theory-based analysis. But in each case the other side of the ledger also needs to be examined to get a balanced picture of the worth of this approach to public management; and the argument here will be that, for most of these objections, the analytic assets dwarf the liabilities.

## 2. The 'Nursery Toys' Objection: Too Simple for Sophisticated Analysis?

A first possible verdict on cultural theory applied to public management is that its main usefulness lies in the ability to serve as a broad

framing device and to draw fairly coarse-grained general distinctions about very basic types of organization (many of which, as has
been noted before, are in fact to be found elsewhere in social and
administrative science, albeit under confusingly different names).
But is there perhaps a point at which social scientists need to
discard a fixation with 2 × 2 analytic tables if their analysis is to be
taken beyond the 'first base' of opening up discussion? It might
be suggested that when it comes to that point, cultural theory may
begin to run out of intellectual 'horsepower', compared to some of
its rivals.

The 'nursery toys' charge cannot be lightly dismissed. Any
attempt to use cultural theory mechanically to explore the world of
public management undoubtedly rubs up against ambiguities and
hybrids that do not fit neatly into the conventional polar types. Nor
can every serious and complex thinker on the subject be pigeon-
holed unambiguously into any one of cultural theory's major analytic boxes, as was shown by the discussion in Part II. For example,
Jeremy Bentham and Frederick Winslow Taylor (the high priest of
'scientific management') were both 'authoritarian rationalists'
mixing up elements of individualism and hierarchism in their ideas.
As we noted in Chapter 6, Amitai Etzioni, currently the leading
guru of American 'communitarianism', mixes egalitarian and
hierarchist themes in his formula for better government. Similarly,
the Fabian luminaries Sidney and Beatrice Webb, whom we encountered in Chapter 4, were recognizably hierarchist in many of
their views of what good public management should be (in the
sense of management by the expert in the name of science), but
they also included an egalitarian streak in the recipe with their
mania for participation. And Confucian ideas of public management have some elements of all the cultural biases, particularly
when we consider alternatives to the 'mainstream' tradition. Indeed, it can be argued that political and organizational values tend
to defy any attempt at pre-set categorization because it is in their
very essence to be ambiguous and reactive.

There are at least three possible responses to the charge that a
cultural-theory approach is too simple to serve as an adequate basis
for analysis. First, the analytic capacity of the cultural theory does
not necessarily stop with the identification of four polar 'ways of
life'. As was noted in the first chapter, some cultural theorists argue
that grid-group 'lenses' can be put in front of one another *ad*

*infinitum* to increase the discriminatory approach of the approach—thus progressively increasing 'magnification' as it were.
That method has been used several times in this book, for example
in rearranging Huczynski's analysis of management gurus in
Chapter 8 and in exploring variants of the four main ways of life in
Part II. And, as will be argued later in this chapter (Section 4), the
basic approaches to control identified in Chapter 3 can be hybrid-
ized, to identify the strengths and weaknesses of a variety of mixed
approaches in public management.

A second counter-point is the late Aaron Wildavsky's response
to the charge of 'over-simplicity'. Wildavsky used to counter that
charge with the observation, 'there is no good deed without punishment' (note the use of irony here—the highest of the 'master
tropes' of rhetoric, as discussed in Chapter 8). What he meant by
that comment was that attacks on cultural theory for being 'too
simple' in the sense of not having enough classificatory boxes,
failed to take account of the fact that cultural theory had substantially increased the basic categories available to social science for
understanding forms of organization. That is, it had moved institutional analysis away from what were claimed to be stultifying conventional dichotomies like markets and hierarchies, or 'traditional'
and 'modern' societies (or at the most from trichotomies like
markets, hierarchy, and solidarity or exit, voice, and loyalty). Instead, it offered a more extended set of categories grounded in a
fundamental (i.e. jointly exhaustive and mutually exclusive) set of
co-ordinates. Wildavsky consequently saw it as ironic that an
approach which had effectively doubled the basic categorization
capacity of social science should be criticized as 'over-simple'.

Wildavsky's answer is, as suggested above, a rhetorical response,
not a systematic argument. To claim that one particular development has increased our capacity for analysis does not logically
preclude the possibility that further development and refinement
would be even more desirable. But even so, a cultural-theory approach helps us to notice and 'place' themes in public management
that would not be encountered using a different framework
(notably egalitarian and even fatalist currents in organization, both
of which tend to be almost invisible from mainstream management
science). It can bring more potential variety to light than conventional management theory.

Third, analysis based on cultural theory can offer a different slant on other ways of understanding and predicting the working of organization and bureaucracy. A case in point is rational choice analysis of public bureaucracy (including game theory and the 'bureau-shaping' theory[2] in particular), which, as was noted in Chapter 5, has become influential over the last decade or so. As we saw, such an approach starts from the assumption that organizations and institutions are shaped by calculating self-interest on the part of paticipants, for example in 'patrol avoidance' by police. A cultural-theory approach by no means denies the insights that can be gained from such approaches. But what it has to contribute is an account of how preferences are shaped which avoids the characteristic pitfalls of orthodox rational choice theory.[3] By offering an account of preferences which is varied but not infinitely so, cultural theory can help us to avoid those pitfalls. It therefore helps us to identify the main kinds of preference available to be 'rationally' pursued in the shaping of public organizations.

A second approach capable of being augmented by cultural theory is the tradition of rhetorical analysis, which has been argued to be central to the understanding of management. As noted earlier, the ideas of Andrez Huczynski (1993) and authors working in parallel fields like economics and sociology, have much to tell us in understanding why management doctrines persuade and how management gurus operate. But, while (as suggested in Chapter 8) Huczynski works within an exclusively hierarchist frame, cultural theory can extend the rhetorical approach by sharpening up our analysis of *multiple* forms of rhetoric, and thus produce a more differentiated account of the various strains of rhetoric and the cultural constituencies it appeals to in attributing blame for the things that inevitably go wrong and producing recipes for how to do it better. Without such a dimension, rhetorical analysis can become a rather directionless form of 'stamp-collecting', a cataloguing of

---

[2] That is, the idea that senior bureaucrats aim to 'shape' their organizations in ways that make their own jobs more interesting and rids them of grinding high-level routine (see Dunleavy 1991).

[3] The pitfalls include (a) dealing with the problem of who prefers what by simply assuming preferences to be 'given' (an unexceptionable but contentless approach); (b) by couching 'rational self-interest' in terms so narrow that a wide range of observable human behaviour (like fanaticism on the part of police rather than 'patrol avoidance') is excluded; or conversely (c) by factoring every conceivable type of preference into 'rational choice' (Douglas 1987: 9), such that the theory is unfalsifiable, but also vacuous.

forms of argument with no effective link to social science (which is what happened to it before and why it went into intellectual decline).

A third analytic field to which cultural theory can contribute in extending our understanding of public management is the study of the unintended consequences of social action. As noted in the previous chapter, such study is one of the central themes of all the social sciences. But for some reason it seems to have been somewhat neglected in the last decade or so as the sociology 'boom' of the 1960s went into decline, and it is only just coming back into prominence in public management, for example in the increasing analytic attention being paid to the paradoxes of regulation and institutional reform (cf. Sunstein 1990; Majone 1994). Building on the earlier analysis of types of failure and collapse, the previous chapter suggested that cultural theory can help to pinpoint the social mechanisms which produce those unintended and apparently paradoxical side-effects or reverse effects from institutional designs that may seem unassailably logical to the designers. The argument is that the seven ways of producing reverse effects that were identified by Sieber (1981) are not just banana-skins randomly distributed around the world of public management and waiting for unwary victims to step on them. Instead, some of those reverse-effect processes (like functional disruption) seem to be more likely to operate when one cultural way of life was relatively unchallenged, whereas others (like provocation) seem to be more likely when different ways of life rub up against one another. Exploring the link between cultural biases and reverse-effect mechanisms could help throw light on the pitfalls of policy implementation, a problem which received much attention in the 1970s and remains central to the analysis of public management.

### 3. The 'Soft Science' Objection: A Limited and Ambiguous Theory?

A second possible objection to cultural theory as a frame for understanding public management is that it is not altogether clear whether cultural theory is falsifiable or tautological or even quite what kind of 'theory' it is. Elinor Ostrom (1996) usefully distinguishes between 'frameworks', 'theories', and 'models' as

conceptual devices, though these words are often used interchange-
ably (and certainly each of them has been used to describe the
cultural theory). A framework is a general angle of vision, incorporating a view of what are the most crucial variables for explanation or
understanding, but gives no precise account of how those variables
work in any given situation. In that sense, it is pre-explanatory and
is not appropriately assessed by its predictive power. An example is
'rational choice' (institutions are shaped by people looking after
Number One) or 'historical institutionalism' (look at long-term
patterns of development to get an understanding of what drives
current institutions). By contrast, a theory is a body of more specific
assumptions about causal relationships, and it *is* appropriately assessed by its capacity to predict (relative to its conceptual parsimony), while a model is a still more detailed representation of
precise 'signed' relationships. Now cultural theorists use each of the
three terms to describe their approach. Does that mean cultural
theory fits uneasily into Ostrom's convenient categories—too
narrow for a 'framework', but too general for a 'theory' or 'model'?

In Ostrom's sense, most 'theory' in science does one or both of
two things. First, it can express ideas about *causal connections*, so
that if $x$ changes, $y$ can be predicted to change in a particular way—
for instance, that demand for yachts or limousines increases as the
number of millionaires in a society grows. Second, it can express
empirical generalizations without necessarily offering a causal account of a phenomenon—for example, claiming that the average
income above $x tends to be $3x or that suicide rates typically peak
in the spring. Although causality is much debated in political and
institutional science, much of history and even natural science is
more about *how* things happen than *why* they happen (see Fischer
1971). And cultural theory's main 'discovery' is most obviously a
claim of the second type identified above, in that it is an account of
how preferences tend to be arranged into bundles of related ideas
about justice, blame, and organization, and a claim about the sys-
temic linkages among those ideas. But, although it was originally
devised to solve an empirical problem—to reconcile the diverse
observations of a mass of studies in colonial anthropology—it does
not rest on a large base of empirical work in public management.
On the contrary, its empirical applications have for the most part
been relatively slender and impressionistic. Indeed, the theory
could even be claimed to be tautological or unfalsifiable, in the

sense that wherever empirical study reveals preferences or political positions not to be neatly arranged according to the cultural theorists' pre-set categories, cultural theorists can simply claim that if only the research instruments were more sensitively tuned, they would identify versions of the four polar positions or that any hybrids represent temporary but unstable ways of life.

This objection is probably the hardest to counter of the three lines of criticism considered here. Undeniably, cultural theory has had only patchy empirical application up to now. And parts of the cultural theory even seem to be poorly worked out conceptually. An example is Thompson, Ellis, and Wildavsky's (1990: 3, 86, 98) assertion of their 'impossibility principle'. That is the argument that there cannot be any major positions outside the four polar ways of life, because each type exists only as a reaction to all the others, and the process of mutual repulsion pushes organizations and individuals out to the far corners of the cultural 'map' rather than having them cluster messily in the middle. That claim is hard to reconcile with their assertion elewhere that there is in fact a viable 'hermit' position in the dead centre of the matrix. On their own logic, if a dead-centre position is viable after all, presumably so are hosts of intermediate points constituted by mutual repulsion between the hermit position and the polar types—which sits ill with the so-called impossibility principle.

Even against this more telling objection, however, some limited counter-points may be made. First, as suggested in the first chapter, it can be claimed that what distinguishes cultural theory from earlier and other versions of 'contingency theory' of organization is that the categories or basic variables it uses are grounded in a systematic conceptual frame built from co-ordinates that are mutually exclusive and jointly exhaustive. As was argued there, the same cannot be said of most other categorizations offered by the contingency theorists of the 1960s and 1970s, though the contingency approach contains many insights which are compatible with cultural theory. So on grounds of theoretical parsimony and comprehensiveness (though not of systematic testing), cultural theory might be argued to outperform most rival contingency theories of organization.

Second, cultural theory conceived as contingency theory of organization could be argued to contain a sharper and (in general) causally coherent view of how organizations collapse through their inherent weaknesses than most other forms of contingency theory. For at least thirty years (since Burns' and Stalker's (1966) land-mark study), it has been conventional in contingency theory to distinguish 'machine bureaucracies' from more organic forms of organization, and to argue that machine bureaucracies fit stable or simple environments (leading to breakdown when the environment becomes turbulent) while more organic forms are better adapted for turbulent or complex ones. Such arguments make it difficult to understand why all contemporary organizations are not 'organic' (what environment is not 'turbulent'?), and put all the stress on the environment as the crucial factor which shapes organizations. Cultural theory suggests a far less unidirectional link between organization and environment, and directs attention to sources of collapse that are part of an organization's internal dynamic rather than caused by changes in its habitat (cf. Hood 1994). It thus offers the prospect of revitalizing the contingency theory approach to organizations (which was highly fruitful and suggestive in the 1960s and 1970s but plateaued in the face of the 'New Right' onslaught on policy and institutional design thinking in the 1980s) and to provide the basis for a proper theory of institutional failure and collapse which public management currrently lacks.

## 4. The 'Wrong Tool' Objection: Is Cultural Theory Relevant for the What-To-Do Questions of Management?

The third possible charge against a cultural-theory perspective is that it is essentially an approach for *voyeurs* of management rather than practitioners. That is, it could be claimed cultural theory is better suited to interpretative analysis rather than to any kind of 'practical philosophy'. It may have a lot to tell us about how to understand the world (the argument might run), but it does not say much to hands-on people about how to change it. This reaction is a common first response by practitioners to a cultural theory per-spective, but again there are several points to be made on the opposite side of the argument.

First, such a criticism seems difficult to mount simultaneously with the 'too simple' or 'nursery toys' objection to using a cultural theory frame for the analysis of public management, as discussed in Section 2 above. In effect, such an objection is the opposite of the first one, because it could be interpreted to mean that cultural theory is, at least in some ways, *too* sophisticated to have what it takes for a successful approach to management (albeit perhaps too simple in other ways). That is, it could be argued (following Huczynski 1993) that management as a field of discourse is essentially about hierarchist organization, so that the other major cultural types are in effect redundant in this field and can only distract thought from the practical problems of how to make hierarchist forms of organization work better.

Second, it can be argued that a better understanding of organizational possibilities and preference structures *is* a tool—an indispensable tool for thinking systematically about organization. Indeed, as has been suggested earlier, a way of understanding cultural dynamics (linked to the analysis of rhetoric and with some historical perspective) is a far more robust point of departure for thinking about the essentials of management than the monocultural and ahistorical rational decision-making techniques which tend to dominate the curriculum in conventional management schools. Since management in general and public management in particular is unavoidably situated in the cross-fire of antagonistic cultural biases, those who practice or think about it need to have some means of identifying the rival positions and their strengths and weaknesses. At the least, there is potential 'survival value' in such capability.

Third, as was shown in Chapter 3, cultural theory can be applied in a very direct and practical way for identifying and thinking about the range of polar control processes available in public management. It helps us to chart that much-trodden but poorly-mapped territory, and at least to identify the major continents. As shown earlier, even the conventional four-part typology can be applied to identify control processes and styles operating (or capable of operating) between organizations and clients, within organizations or over organizations by state or society. Moreover (picking up the point made at the outset of Section 2 above), we can go beyond the conventional four-part typology to identify hybrid types of control. The four polar types of control which were identified in Chapter 3 can—up to a point, at least—be linked up with one another to produce a more complex architecture of control. Leaving aside more elaborate hybrids (three-way or four-way combinations),

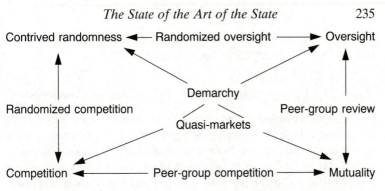

Fig. 10.1. Six hybrid types of control in public management.

there are six simple pairwise combinations of the four basic types, as shown in Figure 10.1.

### *Demarchy* (Contrived Randomness-Mutuality)

As was noted in Chapter 7, 'demarchy' is a term coined by John Burnheim (1985) for a system of control over public services which combines the elements of 'chancism' in combined randomness with the 'groupism' of the collegial or client-control processes which are found in mutuality, and thus constitutes a hybrid of two of the polar types of control identified in Chapter 3. In demarchy, all citizens are available for setting policy through a series of specialized 'administrative commissions', and selection of the members of these commissions is by lot.

An elegant design for a new hybrid way of organizing government and public services, Burnheim's idea has remained on the academic drawing board. But, as shown earlier, there are historical cases (notably classical Athenian government) which approximate to it. Probably the closest contemporary example of such a system is the American Grand Jury model, in which semi-randomized selection of the 'overseers' combines with a model of direct citizen control (Clark 1975). The model is occasionally used for oversight of public administration, as in the case of California water developments in the 1950s (Ostrom and Ostrom 1972). But the mutuality-randomness hybrid may also be approximated in a range of other ways, for example in James Fishkin's (1995) recent experiments with 'deliberative polling' of a randomly selected set of citizens on key social issues or even in those states, like Denmark, which use a lottery for selecting recruits for military service.[4]

### *Randomized Competition* (Contrived Randomness-Competition)

Introducing a random element into a competitive process (and thus producing a hybrid of combined randomness and competition) is rarely discussed but far from unknown. After all, randomness is commonly used for tie-breaking in electoral and other forms of competition, and often for other related purposes, such as determination of electoral candidates' running order, the numbering of examination candidates to conceal their identity from those who grade the written scripts and thus avoid bias in marking, or the US practice of adding a lottery to conventional competition for immigrant work permits. This hybrid does not seem to have been 'theorized' in the same way as the contrived randomness-mutuality 'demarchy' principle, but it can be seen as a relatively straightforward development of the 'gaming-machine' model of organizational design which was introduced in Chapter 7. For example, the introduction of a random element is potentially a powerful antidote to the classic 'goal displacement' reverse-effect mechanism associated with performance-indicator approaches to organizational control, as noted in the last chapter. It will be recalled that the reverse effects typically come about because the performance indicators tend to skew organizational behaviour towards looking good on the key quantitative measures on the performance rating system rather than pursuing the substantive goals in a more balanced way (like the tendency of police to 'cut corners'—by fabrication of evidence or intimidation of suspects—to increase crime clear-up rates, when such rates are taken as the be-all and end-all of police performance). Yet one factor which can, and commonly does, work against such an outcome is the inability of managers to predict which out of the many indicators that are recorded will be taken as the crucial ones, and when, by those appraising them, or what weight will be put when on which indicator. For example, if hospital managers or university managers can be potentially judged by their organizations' ranking on hundreds of different performance

---

[4] If a socially representative body of recruits is a way of checking military 'sectionalism' through processes of mutuality, random selection may be a way of achieving social representativeness.

indicators, which are the ones that will really count in the next round of review? Instead of deploring such uncertainty as somehow aberrant, we might see them as unrecognized forms of the 'randomized-competition' hybrid, with organizational performance being recorded on a range of indicators, but with a semi-random process being used to select the indicator(s) which will be given most weight in any one time period.

## *Randomized Oversight* (Contrived Randomness-Oversight)

A third hybrid, 'randomized-oversight' links an element of chance with the exercise of overseeing authority. At the level of control over clients in public management, this hybrid is far from uncommon. As has already been observed, there is widespread use of random terms in tax audit systems or customs examination (in contrast to the search-every-suitcase approach). But at the level of control over organizations it seems to be more exotic. As we noted in Chapter 7, the famous New Right guru economist William Niskanen (1971: 219–21) prescribed just such a system for oversight over public bureaucracies nearly thirty years ago. Niskanen's recipe was intended to counter what he saw as the inherent bias of representative democracy to overproduce public services as a result of a political alliance between expansionist bureaucrats intent on increasing their budgets and legislative oversight committees dominated by unrepresentative interests with unusually high demand for the public services under review. Niskanen proposed that oversight over each public bureaucracy or programme should contain a higher element of unpredictability, by randomly assigning members of the legislators to review committees, random assignment of review responsibilities among legislative committees and even random assignment of Cabinet members among portfolios (to avoid 'capture' through self-selection of committee members or through overseers 'going native').

Like Burnheim's demarchy, Niskanen's idea for a hybrid of contrived randomness and oversight has remained on the drawing-board (in sharp contrast to many of his other proposed remedies for bureaucratic overproduction, such as performance-related pay, competition among bureaucracies, business-type practices in public management, which have been enthusiastically—if selectively—adopted by the 'new right' in many OECD countries). Pure examples of random assignment of cases or people to bureaucratic oversight processes seem fairly rare, though Niskanen argued that parliamentary systems in practice approximate more closely to such a pattern than the US system of government (ibid. 220), and certainly some oversight systems use a random element in their operations (as in the unannounced 'snap inspection', military-style, that UK prisons are subjected to by the prisons inspectorate). Nevertheless, any oversight system which is *perceived* to contain a random element by those being regulated (such as Parliamentary questioning which is seen as unpredictable by ministers or civil servants, even if it is not in fact random in a scientific or statistical sense) approximates to this hybrid. And the traditional process of Treasury control in the UK and states with similar Treasury control traditions, in which requests for authority by departments to undertake some course of action (involving spending, salaries, pensions) elicited a process of questioning, the extent of which departments could not predict in advance, perhaps approximated to a variant of this hybrid too (cf. Parry, Hood and James 1997).

*Peer-group Competition* (Competition-Mutuality)

A fourth pairing joins the mutual assessment which is the central element of the mutuality approach to control with the striving among rival individuals or organizations that is at the heart of the competition approach. This hybrid, too, is far from unusual. Perhaps the clearest example, well-known in science and academia, is the use of a form of peer-group process to allocate competitive bids for scarce resources, notably in research funding, placement of journal articles, honours, prizes or ratings. Another example (which contains similar potential conflicts of interests) which will be familiar to some readers are those academic assessment schemes which combine competition by students for high grades, but include an element in which allocation of at least part of all students' grades is derived from an assessment of their performance by their peers. An analogous process also applies in those cases where ministers or other officials as a group have to decide on budgetary allocations in which as individuals they are rival bidders (the extended 'Treasury Board' model, as in the Canadian tradition or more generally in any system of cabinet government), and in effect such a mutuality-competition hybrid was the central part of the late Aaron Wildavsky's (1980) formula for keeping government spending in check.

## *Managed Peer Review* (Mutuality-Oversight)

In this fifth hybrid, the ladder of authority which underlies the oversight/review approach to control is linked to the peer-group dimension of the mutuality approach, to produce a structure of 'trial by peers'. Early forms of tax assessment in which determination of tax liability was laid on parish or village groups working in the shadow of an outside tax bureaucracy, can be seen as a hybrid of this type, and perhaps the closest modern equivalent of such processes is the widespread use of 'enforced self-regulation' (Ayres and Braithwaite 1991) in the form of business self-regulation schemes in which industry associations operate 'self-policing' arrangements under codes of conduct approved or guided by government (cf. Hague, Mackenzie, and Barker 1975). Traditionally this method of control has figured prominently in complaint-handling and discipline mechanisms, particularly in the professions like medicine and law, where disciplinary collegiate committees with powers to 'strike off' errant practitioners are steered by overall statutory or guidance frameworks. Other contemporary examples of managed peer review operating in the UK include clinical audits and university assessments, in which judgements about quality or performance are in some sense made by members of a common professional community, but 'authority' outside that group is significantly involved in the process in some way, in adjudicating disputes, selecting assessors and determining the use to which the 'peer-group' judgements are to be put.

## *Competition-Oversight*

In the final possible pairwise combination, the authority ladder of control by oversight is linked to the rivalry of the competitive approach to control. In this pairing, individuals or organizations compete, but within limits to be decided and adjusted by an overall authority structure which decides how and when to move the goalposts, how to handicap the rival teams, and what counts as a 'goal'. This hybrid is pervasive in public management. For instance, competition is commonly allied to oversight in budgetary management (see Heclo and Wildavsky 1974: 95). The same goes for managed league-tables applying a common metric to the various organizations within a provision system (like schools, hospitals, or prisons) and to the contemporary development of 'quasi-markets' as half-way houses between markets and hierarchical allocation (see LeGrand and Bartlett 1993) or what the late Kieron Walsh (1995: 46) termed 'quasi-organizations', such as regulated industries. But any rating system in which 'authority' puts potentially rival units into a league-table, is a hybrid of this kind.

Indeed, Andrew Dunsire (1978; 1990) has argued that public bureaucracies are typically kept under control by just such a hybrid control system, in which competition among rival pressures institutionalized into the structure of the bureaucracy is 'steered' by ministers or hierarchical overseers who can adjust the balance at will, by selectively inhibiting one or another of the rival forces in balance in a manner analogous to the fingertip adjustment of an 'Anglepoise' desk lamp. The stock example given by Dunsire is the contradiction between pressures for speedy handling of cases within bureaucracies and the contradictory pressure for accuracy or quality in their decisions, with the balance between the two rival forces being set by politicians or managers in the light of how many complaints of what kind are coming in at any one time. Although such systems are commonly observable as part of the process by which politicians steer public bureaucracies, the institutional requirements for setting up such a control system deliberately and systematically are surprisingly demanding (see Hood 1996c)—including the need to base organization on rival values rather than functions, which can go against the grain of ordinary politics, and the need to keep the 'losers' in business for another day.

## 5. Conclusion

The six simple pairings of types of control which were considered in the last section vary in the extent to which they have been explicitly 'theorized' and in the extent to which we can readily identify common real-life applications. The first three, all of which involve an element of contrived randomness linked to one of the other three polar approaches to control, seem either to consist of designs on the academic drawing-board with little real-world applications (notably demarchy) or processes which are common enough in practice but tend for some reason to be implicit and relatively 'untheorized' (notably randomized competition). Perhaps that reflects a widespread cultural discomfort with the contrived randomness approach to control in public management. But the last three approaches to control are commonplace and several have come into high managerial fashion in recent years (particularly the quasi-markets/managed league-table approach and the peer-group review approach).

Returning to the sixth and seventh proposition of Chapter 1, what this analysis shows is that the four-part account of institutional control systems introduced in Chapter 3 and used as the organizing principle for the chapters in Part II by no means exhausts the analytic power of cultural theory applied to public management. And much still remains to be explored. For example, can we identify more complex two-way and three-way combinations among the four polar types? To what exent are the simple pairwise hybrids identified there capable of operating on a permanent basis, or will they tend to be inherently unstable, dissolving into their component parts when they come under pressure? The idea that cultural theory is too simple for anything but the most elementary 'first-base' orientation in public management is hard to sustain when we consider the possible hybrids derivable from the four-part framework as well as the capacity, mentioned earlier, to increase analytic magnification by putting grid-group lenses in front of one another.

All the same, it cannot be denied that there is some force in each of the three objections to a cultural theory-centred view of public management that have been discussed in this chapter. No single analytic approach is without its weaknesss. What this book has tried to to show is that a cultural-theory approach has much to offer to the art of the state, as a framing approach for thinking creatively about available forms of organization and in exploring the variety of what-to-do ideas that will always surround public services and government.

# BIBLIOGRAPHY

Adams, J. G. U. (1985), *Risk and Freedom*. London: Transport Publishing Projects.

Adams, S. (1996), *The Dilbert Principle*. London: Boxtree.

Anechiarico, F. and Jacobs, J. B. (1996), *The Pursuit of Absolute Integrity*. Chicago: Chicago University Press.

Appleby, P. H. (1949), *Policy and Administration*. University, Ala.: University of Alabama Press.

Aristotle (1984), *The Complete Works of Aristotle*. Princeton: Princeton University Press.

——(1991), *The Art of Rhetoric* (trans. H. Lawson-Tancred). Harmondsworth: Penguin Books.

Aucoin, P. (1990), 'Administrative Reform in Public Management', *Governance*, 3/2: 115–37.

Austin, J. L. (1962*a*), *Sense and Sensibilia*. Oxford: Clarendon Press.

——(1962*b*), *How to Do Things with Words*. Oxford: Clarendon Press.

Ayres, I. and Braithwaite, J. (1992), *Responsive Regulation*. New York: Oxford University Press.

Bahmueller, C. F. (1981), *The National Charity Company*. Berkeley: University of California Press.

Baker, A. J. (1982), 'The Problem of Authority in Radical Movement Groups: A Case Study of Lesbian-Feminist Organization', *Journal of Applied Behavioral Science*, 18/3: 323–41.

Banfield, E. C. (1958), *The Moral Basis of a Backward Society*. Glencoe, Ill.: Free Press.

Bardach, E. and Kagan, R. A. (1982), *Going by the Book*. Philadelphia: Temple University Press.

Barker, R. (1984), 'The Fabian State', in B. Pimlott (ed.), *Fabian Essays in Socialist Thought*. London: Heinemann, 27–38.

Barker, S. E. (1948), *Traditions of Civility*. Cambridge: Cambridge University Press.

Barzelay, M. (with Armajani, B. J.) (1992), *Breaking Through Bureaucracy*. Berkeley: University of California Press.

Becker, B. (1989), *Öffentliche Verwaltung*. Percha am Starnburger See: Verlag R. S. Schulz.

Becker, G. (1968), 'Crime and Punishment: An Economic Approach', *Journal of Political Economy*, 76/2: 169–217.

Beer, S. (1966), *Decision and Control*. London: Wiley.

Beilharz, P. (1992), *Labour's Utopias*. London: Routledge.

Bellamy, C. and Taylor, J. (1994), 'Introduction: Exploiting IT in Public Administration: Towards the Information Polity', *Public Administration*, 72(Spring), 1–12.

Bent, A. E. (1974), *The Politics of Law Enforcement*. Toronto/London: D. C. Heath, Lexington Books.

Bentham, J. (1863), 'Panopticon vs. N. S. Wales', in J. Bowring (ed.), *The Works of Jeremy Bentham*. Edinburgh: William Tait.

—— (1931), *The Theory of Legislation* (trans. R. Hildreth, from the French of E. Dumont). London: Routledge and Kegan Paul.

—— (1962), *The Works of Jeremy Bentham*. New York: Russell and Russell.

—— (1983), *Constitutional Code*. Oxford: Clarendon Press.

Bielenstein, H. (1980), *The Bureaucracy of Han Times*. Cambridge: Cambridge University Press.

Bittner, E. (1963), 'Radicalism and the Organization of Social Movements', *American Sociological Review*, 28: 928–40.

Blainey, G. (1973), *The Causes of War*. London: Macmillan.

Blau, P. (1955), *The Dynamics of Bureaucracy*. Chicago: Chicago University Press.

Boston, J., Martin, J., Pallot, J., and Walsh, P. (1996), *Public Management*. Auckland: Oxford University Press.

Boulding, K. (1970), *Economics as a Science*. New York: McGraw-Hill.

Bovens, M. and 't Hart, P. (1996), *Understanding Policy Fiascoes*. New Brunswick, NJ: Transaction.

Brennan, H. G. and Buchanan, J. H. (1985), *The Reason of Rules*. Cambridge: Cambridge University Press.

Breton, A. (1995), *Competitive Government*. New York: Cambridge University Press.

Breyer, S. (1993), *Breaking the Vicious Cycle*. Cambridge, Mass.: Harvard University Press.

Brown, P. (1988), *The Body and Society*. New York: Columbia University Press.

Brownlow Committee on Administrative Management (1937), *Report of the Committee, with Studies of Administrative Management in the Federal Government*. Washington, DC: US Government Printing Office.

Bryson, J. and Crosby, B. (1992), *Leadership for the Common Good*. San Francisco: Jossey-Bass.

Bubeck, D. (1995*a*), *Care, Gender, and Justice*. Oxford: Clarendon Press.

—— (1995*b*), *A Feminist Approach to Citizenship*. Florence: European University Institute, EUF No. 95/1.

Buchanan, J. (1977), *Freedom in Constitutional Contract*. College Station: Texas A and M University Press.

Buchanan, J. (1983), The Achievement and the Limits of Public Choice in Diagnosing Government Failure and in Offering Bases for Constructive Reform, in H. Hanusch (ed.), *Anatomy of Government Deficiencies*. Berlin: Springer-Verlag, 15–25.

Burnheim, J. (1985), *Is Democracy Possible?*. Cambridge: Polity Press.

Burns, T. and Stalker, G. M. (1966), *The Management of Innovation* (2nd edn.). London: Social Science Paperbacks.

Capra, F. and Spretnak, C. (1984), *Green Politics*. London: Hutchinson.

Cartwright, J. (1995), *In Every Face I Meet*. London: Hodder and Stoughton.

Chadwick, E. (1854), *Memorandum*. London: HMSO.

Chandler, J. A. (1991), 'Public Administration: A Discipline in Decline', *Teaching Public Administration*, 11/2: 39–45.

Chapman, B. (1970), *Police State*. London: Pall Mall.

Chapman, L. (1978), *Your Disobedient Servant*. London: Chatto & Windus.

Cheung, A. (1995), *The Politics of Administrative Reform in Hong Kong: Corporatization of the Public Services During the 1980s*. Ph.D. thesis, London School of Economics.

Clark, L. (1975), *The Grand Jury*. New York: Quadrangle/The New York Times Book Co.

Coase, R. H. (1960), 'The Problem of Social Costs', *Journal of Law & Economics*, 3: 1–44.

Cohen, M. D., March, J. G., and Olsen, J. P. (1972), 'A Garbage Can Model of Organizational Choice', *Administrative Science Quarterly*, 17/1: 1–23.

Collingridge, D. (1992), *The Management of Scale*. London: Routledge.

Coram, B. T. (1996), 'Second Best Theories and the Implications for Institutional Design', in R. E. Goodin (ed.), *The Theory of Institutional Design*. Cambridge: Cambridge University Press, 90–102.

Corbett, D. (1965), *Politics and the Airlines*. London: Allen and Unwin.

Cornford, F. (1908), *Microcosmographia Academica, being a Guide for the Young Academic Politician*. Cambridge: Bowes and Bowes.

Craig, A. (1975), 'Functional and Dysfunctional Aspects of Government Bureaucracy', in E. Vogel (ed.), *Japanese Organization and Decision-Making*. Berkeley: University of California Press, 3–32.

Crain, W. M. and Ekelund, R. B. (1976), 'Chadwick and Demsetz on Competition and Regulation', *Journal of Law and Economics*, 19/1: 149–62.

Cranston, M. (1968), *Political Dialogues*. London: British Broadcasting Corporation.

Cranston, R. (1979), *Regulating Business*. London: Macmillan.

Creel, H. G. (1964), 'The Beginnings of Bureaucracy in China: The Origin of the Hsien', *Journal of Asian Studies*, 23/2: 155–83.

Davidson, L. (1983), 'Countercultural Organizations and Bureaucracy: Limits on the Revolution', in J. Freeman (ed.), *Social Movements of the Sixties and Seventies.* New York: Longman, 162–76.

de Tocqueville, A. (1946), *Democracy in America.* London: Oxford University Press.

——(1949), *L'Ancien Regime.* Oxford: Clarendon Press.

Deming, W. E. (1996), *Out of the Crisis.* Cambridge: Cambridge University Press.

Demsetz, H. (1968), 'Why Regulate Utilities?', *Journal of Law & Economics*, 11/1: 55–65.

Dickens, C. (1910), *Little Dorrit.* London: The Educational Book Co.

——(1985), *Hard Times.* Harmondsworth: Penguin English Classics.

DiMaggio, P. and Powell, W. (1991), 'The Iron Cage Revisited: Institutional Isomorphism and Collective Rationality in Organizational Fields', in P. DiMaggio and W. Powell (eds.), *The New Institutionalism in Organizational Analysis.* Chicago: Chicago University Press.

Dixon, N. (1976), *On the Psychology of Military Incompetence.* London: Jonathan Cape.

Dobson, A. (1990), *Green Political Thought: An Introduction.* London: Unwin Hyman.

Douglas, M. (1982), 'Cultural Bias', in M. Douglas, *In The Active Voice.* London: Routledge, 183–254.

——(1987), *How Institutions Think.* London: Routledge.

——(1991), 'The New Wave of Austerity: Effect of Culture on Environmental Issues', in *L'Association Descartes.* Paris: L'Association Descartes.

Dowding, K. (1985), *The Civil Service.* London: Routledge.

——and Dunleavy, P. J. (1996), 'Production, Disbursement and Consumption: The Modes and Modalities of Goods and Services', in S. Edgell, K. Hetherington, and A. Warde (eds.), *Consumption Matters.* Oxford: Blackwell, 36–65.

Downs, A. (1957), *Inside Bureaucracy.* New York: Wiley.

Downs, G. W. and Larkey, P. D. (1986), *The Search for Government Efficiency.* Philadelphia: Temple University Press.

Drucker, P. F. (1981), *Toward the Next Economics: and Other Essays.* New York: Harper and Row.

Dunleavy, P. J. (1991), *Democracy, Bureaucracy and Public Choice.* Hemel Hempstead: Harvester Wheatsheaf.

——(1994), 'The Globalization of Public Services Production: Can Government be "Best in the World"?', *Public Policy and Administration*, 9/2.

Dunleavy, P. J. (1995), 'Policy Disasters: Explaining the UK's Record', *Public Policy and Administration*, 10/2: 52–70.

—— and Hood, C. (1994), 'From Old Public Administration to New Public Management', *Public Money and Management*, 14/3: 9–16.

Dunsire, A. (1973*a*), *Administration*. Oxford: Martin Roberston.

——(1973*b*), 'Administrative Doctrine and Administrative Change', *Public Administration Bulletin* (15 Dec.), 39–56.

——(1978), *The Execution Process*, ii. *Control in a Bureaucracy*. Oxford: Martin Robertson.

——(1990), 'Holistic Governance', *Public Policy and Administration*, 5/1: 4–19.

Edmonson, R. (1984), *Rhetoric in Sociology*. London: Macmillan.

Eilstein, H. (1995), 'The Virus of Fatalism', in K. Gavrogulu, J. Stachel, and M. Wartofsky (eds.), *Science, Mind and Art*. Dordrecht: Kluwer, 71–88.

Enwright, D. J. (1969), *Memoirs of a Mendicant Professor*. London: Chatto and Windus.

Etzioni, A. (1993), *The Spirit of Community*. New York: Crown Publishers.

Everitt, C. W. (1931), *The Education of Jeremy Bentham*. New York: Columbia University Press.

Farrell, J. G. (1979), *The Singapore Grip*. London: Fontana/Collins.

Ferguson, K. (1984), *The Feminist Case Against Bureaucracy*. Philadelphia: Temple University Press.

Feyerabend, P. (1975), *Against Method*. London: Humanities Press.

Finer, S. E. (1952), *The Life and Times of Sir Edwin Chadwick*. London: Methuen.

Finley, M. (1985), *Democracy, Ancient and Modern* (2nd edn.). London: Hogarth Press.

Fiorentini, G. and Peltzman, S. (1995) (eds.), *The Economics of Organized Crime*. London: Cambridge University Press.

Fischer, D. H. (1971), *Historians' Fallacies*. London: Routledge and Kegan Paul.

Fishkin, J. (1995), *The Voice of the People*. New Haven: Yale University Press.

Foster, C. D. (1992), *Privatization, Public Ownership and the Regulation of Natural Monopoly*. Oxford: Blackwell.

Foucault, M. (1977), *Discipline and Punish* (trans. A. Sheridan). Harmondsworth: Penguin.

Frissen, P. (1994), 'The Virtual Reality of Informatization in Public Administration', *Informatization and the Public Sector*, 3.

Fukuyama, F. (1995), *Trust*. London: Hamish Hamilton.

Gerth, H. H. and Mills, C. W. (1948) (eds.), *From Max Weber*. London: Routledge.

Gibbon, L. G. (1992), *Sunset Song*. London: Pantheon.

Goodin, R. (1992), 'The Green Theory of Agency', in R. Goodin, *Green Political Theory*. Cambridge: Polity Press, 113–68.

Goodsell, C. T. (1993), 'Reinvent Government or Rediscover It?' (review of Osborne and Gaebler, *Reinventing Government*), *Public Administration Review*, 53/1: 85–7.

Gore, A. (1993), *From Red Tape to Results*. Washington, DC: US Government Printing Office.

Grabosky, P. and Braithwaite, J. (1986), *Of Manners Gentle*. Melbourne: Melbourne University Press.

Gray, P. (1996), 'Disastrous Explanations—Explanations of Disaster?—A Reply to Patrick Dunleavy', *Public Policy and Administration*, 11/1: 74–82.

Hague, D. C., Mackenzie, W. J. M., and Barker, A. (1975), *Public Policy and Private Interests*. London: Macmillan.

Halberstam, D. (1972), *The Best and The Brightest*. New York: Fawcett Crest.

Hall, P. and Taylor, R. C. R. (1997), 'Political Science and the Three New Institutionalisms', *Political Studies*, 44/5: 936–57.

Hammond, T. H. (1990), 'In Defence of Luther Gulick's "Notes on the Theory of Organization"', *Public Administration*, 68/1: 147–73.

Harden, R. (1996), 'Institutional Morality', in R. E. Goodin (ed.), *The Theory of Institutional Design*. Cambridge: Cambridge University Press, ch. 5.

Hardin, G. (1968), 'The Tragedy of the Commons', *Science* (Dec.), 1243–8.

Harvey, D. (1989), *The Condition of Postmodernity*. Oxford: Blackwell.

Hawkes, N., Lean, G., Leigh, D., McKie, R., Pringle, P., and Wilson, A. (1986), *The Worst Accident in the World*. London: Pan Books/Heinemann.

Hay, R. (1989), *The European Commission and the Administration of the Community*. Luxembourg: Office for Official Publications of the European Community.

Haynes, V. and Bocjun, M. (1988), *The Chernobyl Disaster*. London: Hogarth Press.

Heclo, H. and Wildavsky, A. (1974), *The Private Government of Public Money*. London: Macmillan.

Hegel, G. W. F. (1896), *Philosophy of Right* (trans. S. W. Dyde). London: Bell.

Heller, J. (1964), *Catch-22*. London: Transworld.

Hennestad, B. W. (1990), 'The Symbolic Impact of Double Bind Leadership: Double Bind and the Dynamics of Organizational Culture', *Journal of Management Studies*, 27/3: 265–80.

Hindess, B. (1991), 'Review of Thompson, Ellis, and Wildavsky, *Cultural Theory*', *Australian Journal of Political Science*, 26/2: 390–1.

Hirschman, A. O. (1970), *Exit, Voice and Loyalty*. Cambridge, Mass.: Harvard University Press.

——(1982), *Shifting Involvements*. Oxford: Blackwell.

——(1991), *The Rhetoric of Reaction*. Cambridge, Mass.: Belknap Press.

Hirst, P. and Thompson, G. (1996), *Globalization in Question*. Cambridge: Polity.

Hobsbawm, E. J. (1968), 'The Fabians Reconsidered', in E. J. Hobsbawm, *Labouring Men*. London: Weidenfeld and Nicholson, 250–71.

Hockenos, P. (1993), *Free to Hate*. New York: Routledge.

Hood, C. (1976), *The Limits of Administration*. London: Wiley.

——(1986), *Administrative Analysis*. Sussex: Wheatsheaf Books.

——(1991*a*), 'A Public Management for All Seasons?', *Public Administration*, 69/1: 3–19.

——(1991*b*), 'Privatisation Good, Sale of Office Bad?', *Contemporary Record*, 4/3: 32–5.

——(1994), 'Policies and Institutions as Their Own Worst Enemies', in C. Hood, *Explaining Economic Policy Reversals*. Buckingham: Open University Press, 13–17.

——(1996*a*), 'Beyond "Progressivism": A New "Global Paradigm" in Public Management', *International Journal of Public Administration*, 19/2: 151–77.

——(1996*b*), 'Control over Bureaucracy: Cultural Theory and Institutional Variety', *Journal of Public Policy*, 15/3: 207–30.

——(1996*c*), 'Where Extremes Meet: "SPRAT" versus "SHARK" in Public Risk Management', in C. Hood and D. K. C. Jones (eds.), *Accident and Design*. London: UCL Press, 208–27.

——and Jackson, M. W. (1991), *Administrative Argument*. Aldershot: Dartmouth.

——and James, O. (1997), 'The Central Executive', in P. J. Dunleavy *et al.* (eds.), *Developments in British Politics, 5*. London: Macmillan, 177–204.

Horn, M. (1995), *The Political Economy of Public Administration*. Cambridge: Cambridge University Press.

Horváth, A. and Szakolczai, A. (1992), *The Dissolution of Communist Power*. London: Routledge.

Hsieh, P. C. (1925), *The Government of China (1644–1911)*. Baltimore: Johns Hopkins University Press.

Huczynski, A. A. (1993), *Management Gurus*. London: Routledge.

Hughes, O. E. (1994), *Public Management and Administration*. London: Macmillan.

Hume, L. J. (1981), *Bentham on Bureaucracy*. Cambridge: Cambridge University Press.

Hunt, R. N. (1984), *The Political Ideas of Marx and Engels*. London: Macmillan.

Ingraham, P. W. (1991), *A Summary of the Experiment in Pay for Performance in the US*. Paris: OECD.

——(1993), 'Of Pigs in Pokes and Policy Diffusion: Another Look at Pay for Performance', *Public Administration Review*, 53: 348–56.

Jabbari, D. (1994), 'Critical Theory in Administrative Law', *Oxford Journal of Legal Studies*, 14/2: 189–215.

Jacobs, A. M. (forthcoming), 'The Divergence behind Convergence: Market Health Reform in Europe', *Journal of Health Politics, Policy and Law*.

Jacobs, J. B. and Anechiarico, F. (1992), 'Blacklisting Public Contractors as an Anti-Corruption and Racketeering Strategy', *Criminal Justice Ethics* (Summer/Fall), 64–76.

Jacobson, H. (1987), *Redback*. London: Black Swan.

Janis, I. (1972), *Victims of Groupthink*. Boston: Houghton Mifflin.

Johnson, H. C. (1975), *Frederick the Great and his Officials*. New Haven: Yale University Press.

Jones, A. H. M. (1957), *Athenian Democracy*. Oxford: Blackwell.

Jones, G. W. and Burnham, J. (1995), 'Modernizing the British Civil Service', in J. J. Hesse and T. A. J. Toonen (eds.), *The European Yearbook of Comparative Government and Public Administration*. Baden-Baden: Nomos, i. 323–45.

Jones, J. M. (1980), *Organizational Aspects of Police Behaviour*. Farnborough: Gower.

Joo, J. (1997), 'Policy Dynamics in South Korea: State Responses to Low Wage Levels and Compensation for Pollution Victims (1961–1978)', Ph.D. thesis, London School of Economics.

Jordan, G. (1992), *Next Steps Agencies: From Managing by Command to Managing by Contract?* Aberdeen: Aberdeen University, Department of Accountancy.

Jørgensen, T. B. and Larsen, B. (1987), 'Control: An Attempt at Forming a Theory', *Scandinavian Political Studies*, 10/4: 279–99.

Kamenka, E. (1989), *Bureaucracy*. Oxford: Blackwell.

Kanter, R. M. (1972), *Commitment and Continuity*. Cambridge, Mass.: Harvard University Press.

Karl, B. D. (1963), *Executive Reorganization and Reform in the New Deal*. Cambridge, Mass.: Harvard University Press.

Kaufman, H. (1967), *The Forest Ranger*. Baltimore: Johns Hopkins Press for Resources for the Future.

Kaufmann, F.-X. and Krüsselberg, H. (1984) (eds.), *Markt, Staat und Solidarität bei Adam Smith*. Frankfurt am Main: Campus Verlag.

Kaufmann, F.-X. Majone, G.-D., and Ostrom, E. (1986), *Guidance, Control, and Evaluation in the Public Sector*. Berlin: W. de Gruyter.

Kay, J. (1996), 'A Quest for Truth', *Financial Times*, 27 Sept., p. 18.

Kennedy, C. (1993), *Guide to the Management Gurus*. London: Century Business.

Kiel, D. (1994), *Managing Chaos and Complexity in Government*. San Francisco: Jossey-Bass.

King, D. S. (1997), 'Creating a Funding Regime for Social Research in Britain', *Minerva*, 35: 1–26.

Kingdon, J. W. (1984), *Agendas, Alternatives and Public Policies*. Boston: Little, Brown.

Kosko, B. (1993), *Fuzzy Thinking*. New York: Hyperion.

Kraemer, K. and King, J. L. (1986), 'Computing and Public Organizations', *Public Administration Review*, 46(Special).

Kuhn, T. (1970), *The Structure of Scientific Revolutions* (2nd edn.). Chicago: University of Chicago Press.

Landau, M. (1969), 'Redundancy, Rationality and the Problem of Duplication and Overlap', *Public Administration Review*, 29/4: 346–58.

Lane, J.-E. (1993), *The Public Sector*. London: Sage.

Le Grand, J. and Bartlett, W. (1993), *Quasi-markets and Social Policy*. Basingstoke: Macmillan.

Leibenstein, H. (1976), *Beyond Economic Man*. Cambridge, Mass.: Harvard University Press.

Lenin, V. I. (1919), *State and Revolution*. London: British Socialist Party/ Socialist Labour Press.

——(1963), *What is to be done?* (originally pub. in 1917) (trans. S. V. Utechin and P. Utechin). Oxford: Clarendon Press.

Leonardi, R. (1995), 'Regional Development in Italy: Social Capital and the Mezzogiorno', *Oxford Review of Economic Policy*, 11/2: 165–79.

Letwin, S. R. (1965), *The Pursuit of Certainty*. Cambridge: Cambridge University Press.

Lynn, J. and Jay, A. (1981), *Yes Minister*. London: British Broadcasting Corporation.

Lynn, J. and Wildavsky, A. (1990) (eds.), *Public Administration: The State of the Discipline*. Chatham, NJ: Chatham House.

Mackenzie, B. (1975), *Explorations in Government: Collected Papers (1951–1968)*. London: Macmillan.

McCloskey, D. N. (1985), *The Rhetoric of Economics*. Madison, Wisc.: Wisconsin University Press.

——(1990), *If You're So Smart*. Chicago: Chicago University Press.

McGregor, D. (1966), *Leadership and Motivation*. Cambridge, Mass.: MIT Press.

McLean, I. and London, J. (1990), 'The Borda and Condorcet Principles: Three Medieval Applications', *Social Choice and Welfare*, 7: 99–108.

Maier, H. (1980), *Die ältere deutsche Staats–und Verwaltungslehre*. Munich: C. H. Beck'sche Verlagsbuchhandling.

Majone, G. (1989), *Evidence, Argument and Persuasion in the Policy Process*. New Haven: Yale University Press.

——(1994), 'Paradoxes of Privatization and Deregulation', *Journal of European Public Policy*, 1/1: 53–69.

March, J. and Olsen, J. (1989), *Rediscovering Institutions*. New York: Free Press.

Marenin, O. (1985), 'Police Performance and State Rule: Control and Autonomy in the Exercise of Coercion', review article, *Comparative Politics*, 18/1: 101–22.

Margetts, H. Z. (1991), 'The Computerization of Social Security: The Way Forward or a Step Backwards?', *Public Administration*, 69/3: 325–43.

——(1996), *Computerization in American and British Central Government 1975–1995: Policy-making, Internal Regulation and Contracting in Information Technology*. Ph.D. thesis, London School of Economics.

Mars, G. (1982), *Cheats at Work*. London: Allen and Unwin.

——and Frosdick, S. (forthcoming), 'Operationalising the Theory of Cultural Complexity: A Practical Approach to Risk Perceptions and Behaviours, *International Journal of Risk, Security and Crime Prevention* (special edn. on 'Risk' ed. E. Borodwicz).

Martin, S. (1983), *Managing Without Managers*. Beverly Hills: Sage.

Marx, K. (1871), *The Civil War in France* (3rd edn.). London: International Working-Men's Association, General Council.

——and Engels, F. (1948), *The Communist Manifesto*. London: Communist Party.

Medvedev, G. (1991), *The Truth About Chernobyl* (trans. E. Rossiter). London: I. B. Tauris.

Merkle, J. A. (1980), *Management and Ideology*. Berkeley: California University Press.

Merton, R. K. (1965), *On The Shoulders Of Giants*. New York: Harcourt, Brace & World, Inc.

——(1968), *Social Theory and Social Structure* (enlarged edn.). New York: Free Press.

Meyer, M. and Zucker, L. (1989), *Permanently Failing Organizations*. Newbury Park: Sage.

Mintzberg, H. (1993), *Structure in Fives*. Englewood Cliffs, NJ: Prentice-Hall.

Miyasaki, I. (1976), *China's Examination Hell* (trans. C. Shirokauer). New York: Weatherhill.

Moore, M. H. (1995), *Creating Public Value*. Cambridge, Mass.: Harvard University Press.

Morçol, M. (1996), 'Fuzz and Chaos: Implications for Public

Administration Theory and Research', *Journal of Public Administration Research and Theory*, 6/2: 315–25.

Mould, R. F. (1988), *Chernobyl: The Real Story*. Oxford: Pergamon.

Moynihan, D. P. (1969), *Maximum Feasible Misunderstanding*. New York: Free Press.

Mueller, H. E. (1984), *Bureaucracy, Education and Monopoly*. Berkeley: University of California Press.

Mulgan, G. (1988), 'New Times: The Power of the Weak', *Marxism Today* (Dec.), 24–31.

——and Leadbeater, C. (1995), 'Ideas for Our Times', *Independent* 29 Nov. (Section 2), p. 2–7.

Müller, W. and Wright, V. (1994) (eds.), *The State in Western Europe: Retreat or Redefinition?*, special issue of *West European Politics* (17/5). London: Frank Cass.

Narain, V. A. (1971), 'Experiments in Land Revenue Administration in Bengal', in R. S. Sharma (ed.), *Land Revenue in India*. Motilal: Banarsidass, 54–70.

Nethercote, J. F. (1989*a*), 'Public Service Reform: Commonwealth Experience' (paper presented), in *Academy of Social Sciences of Australia—25 February 1989*. Canberra: Australian National University.

——(1989*b*), 'Revitalising Public Service Personnel Management', *Canberra Times*, 11 June.

Neustadt, R. E. (1961), *Presidential Power*. New York: Wiley.

New Zealand Treasury (1987), *Brief to the Incoming Government* 1987. Wellington: Government Printing Office.

Nicholson, T. (1986*a*), 'I Killed 5,000, boasts Argentine General', *Sydney Morning Herald*, 30 Sept.

——(1986*b*), 'The Man with 5,000 "Disappearances" to his Credit', *Sydney Morning Herald*, 4 Oct.

Niskanen, W. (1971), *Bureaucracy and Representative Government*. Chicago: Aldine.

OECD (1994), *The Reform of Health Care Systems*. Paris: OECD.

Olson, M. (1971), *The Logic of Collective Action* (rev edn.). New York: Schocker Books.

Osborne, D. and Gaebler, E. (1992), *Reinventing Government*. Reading, Mass.: Addison-Wesley.

Ostrom, E. (1965), *Public Entrepreneurs: A Case Study in Ground Water Basin Management*. Ph.D. thesis, University of California, Los Angeles.

——(1990), *Governing the Commons*. Cambridge: Cambridge University Press.

——(1996), 'Institutional Rational Choice: An Assessment Paper', from Theoretical Developments in Public Policy Panel, *American Political Science Association—92nd Annual Meeting* 28 Aug.–1 Sept. San Francisco: American Political Science Association.

Ostrom, V. (1974), *The Intellectual Crisis in American Public Administration* (2nd edn.). University, Ala.: University of Alabama Press.

——and Ostrom, E. (1972), 'Legal and Political Conditions of Water Resource Development', *Land Economics*, 48/1: 1–12.

Ouchi, W. (1980), 'Markets, Bureaucracies and Clans', *Administrative Science Quarterly*, 25 (Mar.), 129–41.

——(1993), *Theory Z*. New York: Avon Books.

Overman, E. S. (1984), 'Public Managment', *Public Administration Review*, 44: 275–9.

Painter, M. (1990), 'Values in the History of Public Administration', in J. Power (ed.), *Public Administration in Australia: A Watershed*. Sydney: RAIPA/Hale and Iremonger, 75–93.

Parkinson, C. N. (1965), *Parkinson's Law*. Harmondsworth: Penguin Books.

Parry, C. (1963), Enlightened Government and its Critics in Eighteenth-Century Germany. *Historical Journal*, 6/2: 178–92.

——, Hood, C., and James, O. (1997), 'Reinventing the Treasury: Economic Rationalism or an Econocrat's Fallacy of Control?', *Public Administration*, 75/3: 395–415.

Perri, G. and Sheridan, M. (1995), 'A World Order of Scandal and Graft', *Independent*, 11 May, p. 15.

Perrow, C. (1984), *Normal Accidents* New York: Basic Books.

Peters, T. (1989), *Thriving on Chaos*. London: Pan Books/Macmillan.

Peters, T. and Waterman, R. (1982), *In Search of Excellence*. New York: Harper and Row.

Pirenne, H. (1914), *Les périodes de l'histoire sociale du capitalisme*. Bruxelles: Hayez.

Pollitt, C. (1993), *Managerialism and the Public Services* (2nd edn.). Oxford: Blackwell.

Popham, P. (1994), 'Shock Treatment', *Independent Magazine*, 4 Feb., pp. 22–9.

Posner, R. (1972), *Economic Analysis of Law*. Boston: Little, Brown.

Power, M. (1994), *The Audit Explosion*. London: DEMOS.

——and Loughlin, R. (1992), 'Critical Theory and Accounting', in N. Alverson and H. Wilmott (eds.), *Critical Management Studies*. London: Sage, 113–35.

Premfors, R. (1996), 'Reshaping the Democratic State: Swedish Experience in a Comparative Perspective', in *American Political Science Association—92nd Annual Meeting (Aug.29–Sept.1)*. San Francisco: American Political Science Association.

Priesmeyer, H. R. (1992), *Organizations and Chaos*. Westport, Conn.: Quorum Books.

Prigogine, I. (1979), *Order Out of Chaos*. London: Heinemann.

Pye, L. W. (1988), *The Mandarin and the Cadre*. Ann Arbor, Mich.: Center for Chinese Studies, University of Michigan.

Raadschelders, J. C. N. (1994), 'Administrative History: Contents, Meaning and Usefulness', *International Review of Administrative Sciences*, 60/1: 117–29.

——and Rutgers, M. R. (1996), 'The Evolution of Civil Service Systems', in H. A. G. M. Bekke, J. L. Perry, and T. A. J. Toonen (eds.), *Civil Service Systems in Comparative Perspective*. Bloomington: Indiana University Press, 67–99.

Radford, R. (1945), 'The Economic Organization of a POW Camp', *Economica*, 12/48: 189–201.

Raeff, M. (1983), *The Well-Ordered Police State*. New Haven: Yale University Press.

Randall, V. (1987), *Women and Politics*. London: Macmillan.

Read, P. P. (1993), *Ablaze*. London: Secker and Warburg.

Rhodes, R. A. W. (1997), *Understanding Governance*. Buckingham: Open University Press.

Rihs, C. (1973), *La Commune de Paris 1871*. Paris: Seuil.

Roach, J. (1985), 'The French Police', in J. R. and J. Thomaneck (eds.), *Police and Public Order in Europe*. London: Croom Helm, 107–14.

Robson, W. A. (1948), *Public Administration Today*. London: Stevens and Stevens.

Roethlisberger, F. J., Dickson, W. J., and Wright, H. A. (1939), *Management and the Worker*. Cambridge, Mass.: Harvard University Press.

Rose, R. and Peters, B. G. (1978), *Can Government Go Bankrupt?* New York: Basic Books.

Rose-Ackerman, S. (1978), 'Bureaucratic Structure and Corruption', in S. Rose-Ackerman, *Corruption: A Study in Political Economy*. New York: Academic Press, 167–88.

Rosenberg, N. (1960), 'Some Institutional Aspects of the Wealth of Nations', *Journal of Political Economy*, 68/6: 557–70.

Sagan, S. D. (1993), *The Limits of Safety*. Princeton: Princeton University Press.

Sako, M. (1992), *Prices, Quality and Trust*. Cambridge: Cambridge University Press.

Sawer, M. (1990), *Sisters in Suits*. Sydney: Allen & Unwin.

Schachter, H. L. (1989), *Frederick Taylor and the Public Administration Community*. Albany: State University of New York Press.

Schon, D. (1971), *Beyond the Stable State*. London: Maurice Temple Smith.

Schwarz, M. and Thompson, N. (1990), *Divided We Stand*. Hemel Hempstead: Harvester Wheatsheaf.

Seibel, W. (1992), *Funktionaler Dilattentismus*. Baden-Baden: Nomos.

Self, P. (1993), *Government by the Market*. London: Macmillan.

Sieber, S. (1981), *Fatal Remedies*. New York: Plenum.

Silberman, B. S. (1993), *Cages of Reason*. Chicago: Chicago University Press.

Simon, H. (1946), 'The Proverbs of Administration', *Public Administration Review*, 6/1: 53–67.

Sisson, C. H. (1976), 'The Civil Service After Fulton', in W. J. Stankiewicz (ed.), *British Government in an Era of Reform*. London: Collier MacMillan, 252–62.

Small, A. (1909), *The Cameralists*. Chicago: Chicago University Press.

Smith, A. (1937), *The Wealth of Nations*. New York: Random House.

——(1978), *Lectures on Jurisprudence*, ed. R. L. Meek *et al.* Oxford: Clarendon Press.

Spann, R. N. (1981), 'Fashions and Fantasies in Public Administration', *Australian Journal of Public Administration*, 40/1: 12–25.

Spender, J.-C. (1989), *Industry Recipes*. Oxford: Blackwell.

Speth, J. G. (1994), *Initiatives for Change: The Future of the United Nations Development Programme*, report of the Administrator, 2 May 1994, Executive Board of the United Nations Development Programme and the United Nations Population Fund DP/1994/39.

Sproule-Jones, M. (1982), 'Public Choice Theory and Natural Resources', *American Political Science Review*, 76/4: 790–804.

Srinivas, M. N. (1952), 'A Note on Sanscritization and Westernization', *Far Eastern Quarterly*, 15/4: 481.

Stewart, J. (1995), 'Is Public Management Possible?', *Canberra Bulletin of Public Administration* (June), 78.

Stigler, G. (1971), 'The Theory of Economic Regulation', *Bell Journal of Economics & Management Science*, 2/1: 1–21.

Stockwell, J. (1978), *In Search of Enemies: A CIA Story*. New York: W.W. Norton.

Stove, D. (1982), *Popper and After*. Oxford: Pergamon.

Sunstein, C. R. (1990), 'Paradoxes of the Regulatory State', *University of Chicago Law Review*, 57/1: 407–41.

Syvantek, D. J. and De Schon, R. P. (1993), 'Organizational Attractors: A Chaos Theory Explanation of Why Cultural Change Efforts Often Fail', *Public Administration Quarterly*, 17/3: 339–55.

Sztompka, P. (1986), *Robert K. Merton: An Intellectual Profile*. London: Macmillan.

Taylor, F. W. (1911), *The Principles of Scientific Management*. New York: Harper.

Taylor, J. A. (1992), 'Information Networking in Government', *International Review of Administrative Sciences*, 69: 375–89.

Tenner, E. (1996), *Why Things Bite Back*. London: Fourth Estate.

Teubner, G. (1987), 'Juridification: Concepts, Aspects, Limits and Solutions', in G. Teubner, *Juridification of Social Spheres*. Berlin: W. de Gruyter.

Thompson, H. (1994), *Joining the ERM: Core Executive Decision-Making in the UK 1979–1990*, Ph.D. thesis, London School of Economics.

Thompson, M., Ellis, R., and Wildavsky, A. (1990), *Cultural Theory*. Boulder, Colo.: Westview.

Tiebout, C. (1956), 'A Pure Theory of Local Expenditure', *Journal of Political Economy*, 64/5: 416–24.

Tuchman, B. W. (1984), *The March of Folly*. London: Michael Joseph.

Tullock, G. (1965), *The Politics of Bureaucracy*. Washington, DC: Public Affairs Press.

Turner, B. A. (1978), *Man-made Disasters*. London: Wykeham Press.

Unger, R. M. (1986), *The Critical Legal Studies Movement*. Cambridge, Mass.: Harvard University Press.

——(1996), *What Should Legal Analysis Become?*. London: Verso.

Vaughan, D. (1996), *The Challenger Launch Decision*. Chicago: Chicago University Press.

Volensky, M. (1984), *Nomenklatura*. London: Bodley Head.

Waddington, P. A. J. (1974), 'The Coup d'État: An Application of a Systems Framework'. *Political Studies*, 22/3: 299–310.

Waldo, D. (1968), Scope of the Theory of Public Administration, in J. C. Charlesworth (ed.), *Theory and Practice of Public Administration*. Philadelphia: American Academy of Political and Social Science/American Society for Public Administration, ch. 1.

Walsh, K. (1995), *Public Services and Market Mechanisms*. London: Macmillan.

Wanna, J., O'Faircheallaigh, C., and Weller, P. (1992), *Public Sector Management in Australia*. Melbourne: Macmillan.

Webb, S. and Webb, B. (1920), *A Constitution for the Socialist Commonwealth of Great Britain*. London: Longman.

Weber, M. (1948), *Aus den Schriften zur Religionssoziologie*. Frankfurt am Main: Georg Kurt Schauer.

Weinberg, A. (1972), 'Science and Trans-Science', *Minerva*, 10/2: 209–22.

Wells, H. G. (n.d.), *The New Macchiavelli*. London: Collins.

Wildavsky, A. (1980), *How to Limit Government Spending*. Berkeley: University of California Press.

——(1988), *Searching for Safety*. New Brunswick, NJ: Transaction.

——and Swedlow, B. (1991), 'Is Egalitarianism really on the Rise?' in A. Wildavsky (ed.), *The Rise of Radical Egalitarianism*. Washington, DC: American University Press, 63–98.

Williams, R. (1980), *The Nuclear Power Decisions*. London: Croom Helm.

Williams, R. (1989), *The Politics of Modernism*. London: Verso.

Williamson, O. (1994), 'Transaction Cost Economics and Organization Theory', in R. Swedberg and N. J. Smelser (eds.), *The Handbook of Economic Sociology*. Princeton: Princeton University Press.

Wilson, J. Q. (1963), 'The Police and Their Problems', *Public Policy*, 12: 189–216.

——(1968), *Varieties of Police Behavior*. Cambridge, Mass.: Harvard University Press.

——(1989), *Bureaucracy*. New York: Basic.

Wilson, W. (1887), 'The Study of Administration', *Political Science Quarterly*, 2/2: 197–222.

Wran, N. (1986), 'The Wran Government and the Whitlam Heritage', in *NSW Fabian Society 1986 Whitlam Lecture (11 November 1986)*. Sydney: NSW Fabian Society.

Yates, J. (1989), *Control Through Communication*. Baltimore: Johns Hopkins University Press.

Zimmerman, B. J. and Hurst, D. K. (1993), 'Breaking the Boundaries: The Fractal Organization', *Journal of Management Inquiry*, 2/4: 334–55.

# INDEX